D1196718

Rich Nations – Poor Nations

Rich Nations – Poor Nations

The Long-Run Perspective

Edited by

Derek H. Aldcroft

Research Professor in Economic History
Manchester Metropolitan University

and

Ross E. Catterall

Director of the Financial Markets Research Centre
Anglia Polytechnic University

Edward Elgar
Cheltenham, UK • Brookfield, US

338.9009
R499

Published by
Edward Elgar Publishing Limited
8 Lansdown Place
Cheltenham
Glos GL50 2HU
UK

Edward Elgar Publishing Company
Old Post Road
Brookfield
Vermont 05036
US

British Library Cataloguing in Publication Data
Rich Nations – Poor Nations: Long Run
Perspective
  I. Aldcroft, Derek H. II. Catterall, Ross
  330.9

Library of Congress Cataloguing in Publication Data
Rich nations, poor nations : the long run perspective / edited by
  Derek H. Aldcroft and Ross Catterall.
      p.   cm.
      'The original versions of the papers in this volume were presented
  in Session C42: Why the West grew rich and the Third World
  stagnated, of the Eleventh International Economic History Congress
  held at the University of Bocconi, Milan in September 1994' — Pref.
      Includes bibliographical references and index.
      1. Developing countries — Dependency on foreign countries.
  2. Developing countries — Economic conditions. 3. Economic history.
  I. Aldcroft, Derek Howard.   II. Catterall, Ross. 1948 –
  III. International Economic History Congress (11th : 1994 : Milan)
  HC59.7.R487 1996
  338.9'009—dc20   95–19498
                                                                    CIP

ISBN 1 85898 059 3

Typeset by Manton Typesetters, 5–7 Eastfield Road, Louth, Lincolnshire LN11 7AJ, UK.
Printed and bound in Great Britain by
Hartnolls Limited, Bodmin, Cornwall

MIC

Contents

Figures

Tables

NA

Notes on contributors

Derek H. Aldcroft is Research Professor in Economic History at the Manchester Metropolitan University and Visiting Professor at Anglia Polytechnic University. Formerly Professor and Head of Department in the Universities of Sydney and Leicester, he has published widely on British and European economic history in the nineteenth and twentieth centuries. Recent publications include *Education, Training and Economic Performance, 1944–1990* (Manchester University Press, 1992), *The European Economy, 1914–1990* (3rd ed. Routledge, 1993), and with Steven Morewood, *Economic Change in Eastern Europe since 1918* (Edward Elgar, 1995).

Werner Baer is Professor of Economics at the University of Illinois at Urbana-Champaign. He specializes in Latin American economies, with special emphasis on Brazil. He is author of many books and articles on industrialization, inflation, state enterprise and privatization, including *The Brazilian Economy* (4th ed. Praeger, 1995), *United States Policies and the Latin American Economies*, co-edited with D. Coes (Praeger, 1990), and *Privatization in Latin America*, co-edited with M. Birch (Praeger, 1994).

Ross E. Catterall is Director of the Financial Markets Research Centre at Anglia Polytechnic University and is Senior Lecturer in the Department of European Business Economics. He is author of numerous articles, conference papers and consultancy reports on international financial markets and issues in financial and monetary economics and history. He is currently working on a study of technological change in relation to the British electricity supply industry with Steven Morewood, based on data collected from a recent study financed by the UK Economic and Social Research Council.

Subrata Ghatak is Reader and Director of Graduate Studies in Economics at Leicester University. He has taught in universities in the United States, Canada and India and acted as a consultant to many international agencies including the United Nations and the World Bank. He has written eight books on money and international economic development problems and contributed numerous articles to leading international economic journals.

David F. Good is Professor of History and Director of the Center for Austrian Studies at the University of Minnesota where he also serves as executive editor of the *Austrian History Yearbook*. He is author of numerous articles and several books on the economic development of Central and Eastern

Europe, including *The Economic Rise of the Habsburg Empire 1750–1914* (Berkeley, 1984) and most recently *Economic Transformations in East and Central Europe: Legacies from the Past and Policies for the Future* (Routledge, 1994).

Stuart Jones is Professor in the Economics Department of the University of South Africa. He has taught in South African universities for over a quarter of a century and was editor of the *South Africa Journal of Economic History* from 1986 to 1994. He is co-editor, with André Müller, of *The South African Economy 1910–1990*, and edited *Financial Enterprise in South Africa since 1950*. He has completed a study of the business of the imperial banks in South Africa and is currently working on two special issues of the *South African Journal of Economic History*, one analysing the South African economy in the 1980s and the other devoted to business imperialism in South Africa.

A.J.H. Latham is Senior Lecturer in International Economic History at University College, Swansea. He is the author and editor of six books on Asian and African economic history, one of which (1978) has been translated into Japanese (1987). He is currently working on the history of the international rice trade.

Joseph L. Love is Director of Latin American Studies and Professor of History at the University of Illinois at Urbana-Champaign. His special interests include the economic and political history of Brazil and the history of Latin American economic thought. He is author of *Rio Grande do Sol and Brazilian Regionalism* (1971), *São Paulo in the Brazil Federation* (1980), and *Crafting the Third World: Theorizing Underdevelopment in Rumania and Brazil* (1995), all published by Stanford University Press.

J.R. McNeill learned his trade at Swarthmore College in Pennsylvania and Duke University in Durham, NC. He is currently Professor of History at Georgetown University in Washington, DC. His books include *The Atlantic Empires of France and Spain* (Chapel Hill, NC: University of North Carolina Press, 1985), *Atlantic American Societies: From Columbus through Abolition, 1492–1888*, co-edited with A. Karras (London: Routledge, 1992) and *The Mountains of the Mediterranean: An Environmental History* (New York: Cambridge University Press, 1992). His next notable indiscretion will be an environmental and demographic history of the world in the twentieth century.

Erik S. Reinert is Senior Research Scientist at STEP (Studies in Technology, Innovation and Economic Policy) in Oslo, Norway, and is responsible for the teaching of economics of the ESST Programme (European Studies in Society, Science and Technology) at the University of Oslo. He holds an MBA from Harvard University and a PhD in economics from Cornell University. He has taught at universities in the United States, worked in strategy consulting internationally, and has been managing director of a multinational firm based in Italy. His research and publications are focused on areas of uneven economic growth and the history of economic policy – at the intersection of economic theory, business theory and history.

Utku Utkulu is a PhD graduate of Leicester University and Assistant Professor in the Department of Economics at the University of Dokuz Eylul, Izmir, Turkey. He has co-authored (with Subrata Ghatak) papers on trade liberalization and economic growth in Turkey.

NA

Preface

The original versions of the papers in this volume were presented in Session C42: 'Why the West Grew Rich and the Third World Stagnated', of the Eleventh International Economic History Congress, held at the University of Bocconi, Milan, in September 1994.

As editors we would like to thank the authors for their collaboration and for preparing their final versions of their papers for publication. In doing this they have had the advantage of valuable and relevant comments made by the participants in Session C42.

We would also like to express a special vote of thanks to the Anglia Business School of Anglia Polytechnic University for their generosity in funding the costs of our attendance in Milan, and in particular to David Kinnear (Head of the Department of European Business Economics) and John Davies (Pro-Vice-Chancellor [Research] and Dean of the Faculty of Business, Management Development and Law), for their support and encouragement throughout the project.

DHA
REC

Introduction

Today the gap between rich and poor nations is larger than it has ever been in recorded history. A small number of nations account for the bulk of the world's income, while the majority of countries are very poor and struggling even to maintain their relative position in the world economy. This has not always been the case, however. The farther one goes back in time the greater the equality in income between nations. Recent critics of the 'European miracle' thesis have argued that until about the sixteenth century 'Africa, Asia, and Europe shared equally in the rise of capitalism', after which Europe took the lead (Blaut 1993, 206). Even by the eighteenth century some would argue that the development differential between nations was still small and may even have been tilted in favour of the East (Bairoch 1981).

One of the most ferocious critics of the 'European miracle' has refuted many of the previous notions of the long-term unique superiority of Europe (Blaut 1993, 206). Modern economic growth, he argues, could have happened anywhere, at least before 1492, since the Europeans were in no way more modern, more advanced or intellectually brighter than the inhabitants of other civilizations. In the light of modern research on Eastern civilizations no one would probably take great exception to this contention (Abu-Lughod 1989; Smith 1991: Landes 1994; Hodgson 1993). However, the idea that the rise of European hegemony was a matter of almost pure accident, namely that Europe's convenient location in respect of America enabled her to be the first to exploit the wealth of the New World and subsequently that of Asia and Africa, thus providing the underpinning for the development of modern capitalism, may strain the credulity of some readers.

On the other hand, there may be good reason to reduce the Eurocentric emphasis on modern development which has permeated the literature and the textbooks for so long. Nevertheless, the fact remains that, critics or no critics, Europe, along with its overseas appendages, has been the dominant force in economic development since the sixteenth century, and it is inevitable therefore that one should look to that experience to see if there are lessons to be gleaned for today's aspiring developers.

The papers in the present volume have a wide geographical coverage and they are not anchored solely in the European past. Nevertheless, from time to time the European mirror is consulted to see what is reflected therein. It would be a precocious student, whether of European or non-European origin, who could afford to neglect the historical experience of the world's first industrialized continent. What went yesterday may not of course always serve for the benefit of today's LDCs, but a negative conclusion can be as useful as a positive one.

In any case, as some of the essays show, there may be more positive things to glean from the European past than some latter-day critics would acknowledge. After all, even Marx appreciated that would-be developers had to follow the European capitalist paradigm on the road to the socialist millennium (Brenner 1977, 26).

References

Abu-Lughod, J. (1989), *Before European Hegemony: the World System A.D. 1250–1350*, New York: Oxford University Press.

Bairoch, P. (1981), 'The main trends in national income disparities since the industrial revolution', in P. Bairoch and M. Lévy-Leboyer (eds), *Disparities in Economic Development since the Industrial Revolution*, London: Macmillan.

Blaut, J.M. (1993), *The Colonizer's Model of the World*, New York: The Guilford Press.

Brenner, R. (1977), 'The origins of capitalist development: a critique of neo-Smithian Marxism', *New Left Review*, 104.

Hodgson, M.G.S. (1993), *Rethinking World History: Essays on Europe, Islam, and World History*, Cambridge: Cambridge University Press.

Landes, D.S. (1994), 'What room for accident in history?: explaining big changes by small events', *Economic History Review*, 47.

Smith, A.K. (1991), *Creating a World Economy: Merchant Capital, Colonialism and World Trade, 1400–1825*. Boulder, Co: Westview Press.

1 Rich nations – poor nations: the penalty of lateness

Derek H. Aldcroft

The European connection

It was once thought that there were advantages in being a latecomer to economic development since late developers could learn from the mistakes of the early starters, adopt the latest technology and skills, and, hey presto! before very long they would overtake the latter who tended to develop inertia and slow down. Such might roughly describe the paradigm of Britain's position and its eventual loss of pre-eminence to Germany and the US. Rostow (1980) believed that there was a time in history when rich nations slowed down and the laggards began to catch up, though he was primarily concerned with the shifts in relative positions among countries with relatively high incomes. Nearly a century ago Cunningham (1904) perhaps had a similar notion when he predicted that the march of industrial progress would eventually encircle the globe.

But history hasn't quite worked out like that. As Landes (1991) points out, the gap between rich and poor nations is now so large that it seems almost unbridgeable. Even using the most generous corrections to take account of differences in local purchasing power, the gap in per capita incomes between the very rich and very poor nations is now enormous, at least in the region of 30:1 (World Bank 1990: Landes 1993, 165). This was not always the case, however. In Europe's dark ages the great Eastern civilizations of Islam, China and the Arab world may well have attained a higher level of development than anything to be found in Europe (Kiesewetter 1994, 9; Smith 1991, 27). Even at the dawn of modern economic growth, circa 1750, what we now term the Third World could still lay claim to absolute superiority in the production of manufactures, while by all accounts differences in income levels between nations or regions were quite modest. There was no sharp division between rich and poor nations that we have today, and income differentials within countries were probably much larger than those between nations. According to Bairoch (1981, 1991), the non-European world possibly had a slight advantage.

During the course of the next two centuries the position changed dramatically. Income inequality within some nations declined, while that between nations steadily grew more pronounced (Whynes 1988, 68). By 1850 income

1

per capita levels in the Third World were only just over half those of the developed world, by 1913 they were less than one-third (29 per cent) and by 1990 they were down to a mere 12 per cent (Bairoch 1993, 95).

Today the vast majority of the world's population has a smaller share of global income than at any previous stage in history. The high-income countries (those with a per capita income of more than US $6 000 in 1988) account for over 80 per cent of the world's income, yet they contain only 16.6 per cent of its population. At the other end of the spectrum nearly 61 per cent of the world's population (with incomes averaging $545 or less) has to make do with a mere 5.6 per cent of global income (World Bank 1990; Aldcroft 1991).

Such a large gap between rich and poor nations poses a daunting prospect for many Third World countries and implies that there may well be a penalty for being late in the development stakes. On the other hand, the most significant development since the Second World War is not the growing gap between the Third World and Western nations but the sharp divergence in growth rates within the Third World itself (Reynolds 1986, 45). The experience of the East Asian economies – Hong Kong, Singapore, Korea, Taiwan, Indonesia, Malaysia and Thailand – suggests that the penalty for lateness can sometimes be overcome. After all, most of them had experienced little growth in the first half of the twentieth century and by the early 1960s economic conditions and income levels in these countries were not far removed from those in African countries today (World Bank 1994, 37; Maddison 1989, 15). A description of the Republic of Korea in 1960 could easily be that of an African country in the 1980s and early 1990s:

> The trade regime was characterised by import substitution, including the familiar set of complex multiple exchange rates, import licensing, and overvaluation. The economy was heavily reliant on foreign aid, with exports accounting for 3 percent of output, while imports amounted to over 10 percent. While inflation had been brought under control, output growth rates were stagnant. Furthermore, manufacturing accounted for just 11 percent of GNP, with over 45 percent of output concentrated in the primary sector (World Bank 1994, 219).

Such exemplary performance by once backward countries would imply that there is little to prevent entry into the growth circle as long as the right conditions are present. But what are these conditions? In the vast literature on growth and development a multitude of causal or conditioning factors have been identified, from the purely economic through to the sociological and cultural (Colman and Nixson 1994). Some writers of course see the original breakthrough in the West as purely accidental, the assumption being that it could have happened anywhere, again presumably if the conditions had been right (Jones 1981; Blaut 1993; cf. Landes 1994).

There was a time when economists and economic historians tried to derive lessons from past development, only to become disillusioned when it appeared that many less developed countries (LDCs) failed to conform to the 'rules' of the past. However, it was not so much that there was nothing to be gleaned from past experience, but that the postwar development planners read the wrong signals. They therefore sought to impose capital-intensive programmes on the labour-surplus LDCs; they neglected agriculture, and transplanted metropolitan educational systems and other infrastructures which were often inappropriate to indigenous conditions. When former dependent territories were freed from the colonial yoke they had a legitimate grievance that Western control and influence had stultified their development.

This was particularly unfortunate since it meant that the LDCs were now impatient to catch up and to do so quickly. They therefore tried to telescope the development process by policies which could not succeed in the prevailing conditions. They too misread the historical experience of the early developers, namely that Rome was not built in a day, and more specifically that the Western breakthrough to intensive growth was preceded by centuries of preparation. They failed also to observe that the past is littered with examples of premature or abortive attempts at modernization, for example Turkey and Egypt, largely because the initial conditions were not ripe for development (Landes 1991, 15).

But what special attributes did Europe possess that enabled her to monopolize world development? By all accounts, a millennium or less before the breakthrough Europe was little more than a backwater and it was 'The wider world ... [that] seemed braced for the take-off into modernity' (Smith 1991, 27; Hodgson 1993, 26–7; Abu-Lughod 1989). The prospects that Europe would eventually exercise world dominion were, according to Landes (1994, 638), close to zero. That Eastern civilizations failed to capitalize on their initial lead is a major theme in itself and not one that we can enter into here. Suffice it to say that by the sixteenth century at least it was becoming clear that Europe was laying claim to increasing pre-eminence while the East was in a state of terminal decline (Landes 1994, 638; Cipolla 1981, 300; Lewis 1970, 144–5, 162–5).

There is an awkward corner to negotiate at this point, however. If we follow Bairoch (1981, 1991, 1993) then we have to acknowledge that income differences between regions and countries were very modest at the dawn of modern economic growth and that Europe may still have been trailing slightly. On this matter we have reservations. First, we should note that the global income estimates for this period are very tenuous. Second, it is doubtful whether the data for broad regional groupings are really indicative of the widening gap in income levels between East and West, especially Western

Europe. Moreover, as Pedreira (1991, 349) has reminded us, GNP figures do not always adequately reflect ongoing structural changes in an economy and may therefore underestimate the extent of any progress.

As far as Western Europe is concerned there is growing evidence to suggest that it was far more advanced than any other part of the civilized world by the eighteenth century. Landes (1969, 13–14, 63) argued that it was already rich before the industrial revolution in comparison with most other parts of the world, with the implication that it was ready for the breakthrough into modern economic growth. McNeill (1963, 653) notes the superior wealth and power at Europe's disposal, circa 1700, which 'clearly surpassed anything that other civilised communities could muster', while Jones (1981, 41, 182) believes that a decisive gap between Europe and Asia was emerging before industrialization (cf. Ashworth 1974, 298).

It is important to stress that this position was not achieved by any revolutionary change but by the slow accretion of incomes over a lengthy period of time. Economic growth is not the exclusive preserve of modern society; it has been going on for centuries in one form or another (often extensive but sometimes intensive), though sometimes so imperceptibly and subject to periodic setbacks that it has not always been easy to detect (Caldwell 1977). This slow evolutionary process is confirmed by recent research findings and also by more circumstantial evidence relating to structural changes and accumulation. It now seems likely, for instance, that there was a slow upward trend in income levels from as far back as Domesday, especially in England, and quite possibly in other parts of Western Europe. Certainly in England income per capita growth was far more robust than once thought possible, not dramatic by modern standards perhaps, but at least sufficient to allow steady accumulation by the sixteenth and seventeenth centuries (Persson 1988; Snooks 1993, 1994; Anderson 1991). Snooks (1994, 44) maintains that growth has been a persistent feature of English society during the past millennium, occurring in periodic waves of which the industrial revolution was the beginning of the last great wave.

Other Western economies may well have shared a similar experience. Landes (1969, 14) conjectures that income per head in Western Europe probably tripled in the 800 years to the eighteenth century. Snooks (1994, 47–8) also infers from his case study of England that Europe was experiencing 'relatively rapid, sustained and systematic growth', though admittedly on rather slender evidence. However, country studies of Austria and the Netherlands (Komlos 1983, 1989a; van Houtte 1977; van Zanden 1992, 1993) would lend some support to this assertion. Even the more cautious students of the subject acknowledge that incomes were more than keeping pace with population growth (intensive growth), barely perceptible though the changes may have sometimes been to contemporaries (Maddison 1982, 6–7).

The grim Malthusian picture painted by some of the more pessimistic continental historians and the stagnationist Anglo-Saxon scholars is certainly not consistent with what we know about changes in trade patterns, factor markets, technology, agrarian systems, and the accommodation of population changes (Matowist 1966). These changes were taking place well before modern industrialization and were widely spread throughout the Low Countries, parts of France, the Germanies, Scandinavia, Switzerland and northern Italy, as well as in England (Goodman and Honeyman 1988, 9–11). As Chirot (1985, 192–3) argues: 'Later industrialisation could not have occurred had markets of all sorts not achieved such a high state of development in preindustrial Europe: capital markets; land markets; labour markets; commodity markets; and, even by analogy, a kind of intellectual market for new ideas, important thinkers and artists, and technological innovations.' Many of these developments originated in the urban and mercantile centres of Western Europe.

One of the most notable manifestations of progress was undoubtedly the vast expansion of mercantile activities associated with the opening up of trading opportunities by Western traders in both the East and the New World from the sixteenth century onwards, though Europe's initial trade expansion can be dated much earlier (Solow 1987, 711; Phillips 1988, 254; Rothermund 1981). By the early eighteenth century Europe had become the dominant force in international trade, accounting for 69 per cent of world trade in 1720 and 77 per cent by 1800; the respective shares of Western Europe were 42 and 66 per cent, with Britain, Germany, France and the Low Countries the main participants (Chisholm 1982, 60). However, the fact that intra-European trade constituted the dominant element in this intercourse should not obscure the important contribution of the periphery, and especially the New World, to the development of the metropolitan core, notwithstanding O'Brien's (1982) attempt to downgrade its role. The New World in particular was not only an important source of mercantile accumulation and a market for industrial products, but it also had the advantage of providing Western Europe with an additional resource base and an outlet for surplus population. This eventually ensured that Western progress would not be swamped by pressure on resources as was the case in the East (Goldstone 1991, 405). These 'ghost acreages' in newly discovered lands served to enhance man–land ratios and helped to stabilize population densities at the European core (Jones 1981, 83; Reynolds 1985, 29). By contrast, population densities in India, China and the Ottoman Empire, already higher than those in Europe in 1500, deteriorated steadily in the succeeding centuries (Jones 1981, 232).

It may be argued therefore that Western Europe, together with her overseas appendages, was in a much better position than either the rest of Europe or Eastern civilizations to accumulate capital, since expanding mercantile activities, a favourable resource base and a slow rise in incomes meant that there was an increasing margin above subsistence to allow this to take place. Moreover, apart from higher incomes and savings, income distribution was more favourable than in the East, the overheads of state were lower, and there was less conspicuous waste in the utilization of income either for consumption or investment purposes, for example in ostentatious lifestyles or in unproductive investment in the form of 'pyramid' building or the construction of places of worship. Some of the latter characteristics can be found in today's low-income countries.

According to Batou (1990, 464), there was no social class in Asia, the Middle East or China, or for that matter in Eastern Europe, comparable to the European bourgeoisie who accumulated so much moveable wealth over such a long period of time. This process of accumulation was to prove vital for the later exploitation of new technologies and for the development of manufacturing, as well as for the modernization of agriculture. It also provided the means with which to improve infrastructure and social overhead capital. The European instinct to accumulate, albeit often very slowly, over many centuries, in contrast to the more destructive phases of many Eastern civilizations, provides a key pointer to the long-run origins of the development process, emphasizing the essential continuity of that process as opposed to the concept of a dramatic structural break (Komlos 1989b, 203–5). Of even greater significance, it placed Western Europe in a strong position to spring the Malthusian population trap.

There are several pointers of relevance here for the LDCs. For one thing it seems more than likely that per capita income levels in Western Europe before industrialization were somewhat higher than those in the LDCs of the third quarter of the twentieth century (Kuznets 1974, 179; Maddison 1983, 28). Second, these higher income levels were the product of a long process of accumulation stretching back over several centuries. Third, they allowed a steady accumulation of capital and infrastructures in productive activities. It is the absence, for one reason or another, of this long-run build-up which places many LDCs in a difficult position given the imperative to make up for lost time. Unfortunately too, impatience with lateness has often led to bad government and bad policies resulting in 'the poisoning of development efforts in the direction of haste, waste, and corruption' (Landes 1991, 19).

Malthusian ghosts
Today's Third World countries might envy the early developers. However, the latter did have their problems. Periodic population pressure was a common feature of both Europe and Eastern civilizations in the centuries before 1800, and more often than not it tended to be relieved by Malthusian checks rather than by upward shifts in the productive ceiling. It could at times prove fatal

for regimes as Goldstone (1991, 476) explains: 'Population growth in the context of inflexible economic and social institutions is fully capable on its own of producing income polarization, élite conflict, and state breakdowns, as the cases of Ming China and Ottoman Turkey demonstrate.'

Western Europe's position was somewhat more favourable. Western civilization was never suffocated by the same sort of population pressure which confronts Third World countries today or which faced some Eastern civilizations in the past (Ohlin 1965, 36). Although in pre-industrial Europe population did outstrip food supply from time to time, population pressure was never so acute as to upset the balance of the environment. This is partly explained by Europe's unique family life cycle whereby abstinence from marriage and the late age of marriage served to keep the situation under control (Laslett 1988, 235–8). Significantly, Japan was the only other country to experience this unique life cycle.

Europe's main population breakthrough did not occur until the resource constraint had been lifted, or to put it another way, Europe's population revolution took place as and when it could be accommodated (van der Woude 1992, 247–8). By the eighteenth century West Europeans were able to emancipate themselves from the spectre of a Malthusian crisis largely because the supply capability of their economies had improved to a point where it was possible to cope with increased population pressure (Komlos 1989a, 220–21). The English and Dutch responses are well documented (van Houtte 1977; de Vries 1974); less well so, until recently, was the Austrian case, where an enterprising government reacted favourably to population pressures in the latter half of the eighteenth century by instituting reforms which encouraged both industry and agriculture. It was in a position to do this because of the enhanced financial, military and bureaucratic power of the state and the improved social infrastructure (Komlos 1989a, 161).

Komlos (1989b, 204–5) sees these developments as part of a long continuum of change involving a build-up of the supply capability of Western nations to a point where they were able to respond successfully to population-driven expansion. The important point to note is that both the agrarian and non-agrarian sectors of Western Europe were improving simultaneously. Agricultural productivity was increasing, albeit slowly and irregularly, well before the industrial revolution, so that domestic food supplies, supplemented from time to time with imports from the Baltic and elsewhere, were at least able to keep pace with population growth (Mokyr 1976, 23–4; Grigg 1992, 2, 33; Brenner 1982; Clark 1991). Bairoch's study (1989) of the delivery potential of agrarian systems suggests that those of Western Europe were capable, by the eighteenth century, of meeting population pressure when it came, not necessarily by raising overall living standards initially, but by preventing them from falling away as had happened under earlier, less vigorous population expansions. It was this ability to match food and population that turned one of the keys in the development door. Equally important in the light of later experience in the Third World, non-agricultural employment was also expanding, thereby enabling intersectoral labour shifts to take place, which meant that the agrarian sector was never swamped with manpower to the point where diminishing returns, or zero labour productivity, took hold.

In other words, the real significance of the industrial revolution 'is not the rates of growth that were achieved but the fact that for the first time many European societies escaped the Malthusian trap' (Komlos 1989a, 205). Viewed in this light the critical role of earlier long-run developments becomes readily apparent. The favourable changes were most pronounced in Western Europe, but even some of the more backward and traditional societies in Europe managed to respond to population pressure. In Russia, for example, per capita food supplies expanded quite markedly in the later nineteenth century, thereby providing sustenance for the enlarged population as well as a much needed surplus for export. However, in much of Eastern and Southern Europe the long-run dynamic changes in agriculture were generally weaker and more attenuated than in the West, which helps to explain why they lagged behind in the development process (Tortella 1994; Warriner 1965, 1–19; Berend and Ranki 1982, 12–18).

The population scenario in many Third World countries is quite different from that of the earlier developers. From the mid-twentieth century onwards rates of population growth in Africa, Asia and Latin America have averaged 2–3 per cent a year, very much higher than the rates recorded earlier by European countries which rarely exceeded 1 per cent per annum (Livi-Bacci 1992, 31, 147). Although there is no unique relationship between population growth and economic change and poverty (Colman and Nixson 1994, Ch. 4; Simon 1986), it is worth noting that with one or two exceptions, for example China, no large country has made the breakthrough to intensive growth with a population growth rate of more than 1.1 per cent per annum (Bairoch 1975, 204). Even the Asian 'tigers' managed to grind down their population growth rates to approximately those of the nineteenth-century developers of around 0.8 per cent a year (World Bank 1993b, 263).

In this regard Third World countries have been trapped by late entry into the development race since the forces which have worked to bring down death rates, while birth rates still remain high, have meant that populations exploded before these countries were in a position to accommodate them. Population pressure has not by and large led to a pure Malthusian situation, whereby income gains are swamped out by population growth so that per capita incomes stagnate or even fall, as occurred from time to time in the centuries before 1700. In the majority of LDCs output growth exceeded that of population so that income per capita changes were positive, at least in most countries until the 1980s. However, the important point to note is that in order to overcome the population handicap the LDCs have to grow that much faster in absolute terms even to maintain their already lowly position in the world economy. For most of them even this has not been possible. Except in one or two cases, notably the high-performance economies of East Asia (Hong Kong, South Korea, Singapore, Taiwan, Indonesia, Malaysia and Thailand), per capita income growth has not kept pace with that of the West because of the markedly differing population experience. For the period 1965–88 low-income countries, excluding China, grew on average by only 1.5 per cent a year in per capita terms, as against 2.3 per cent in the case of OECD countries (World Bank 1990). Even more disturbing is the increasing number of countries which eventually became Malthusian victims as rates of growth slowed down and turned negative. Most of these are in Sub-Saharan Africa and Latin America where growth has been falling on average since the 1960s and in some cases it turned negative in the 1980s (Holman 1994a, 1994b; World Bank 1989, 16–18). Real per capita incomes in Latin America are now some way below those of 1975, while in Africa they are back to the levels of 1960 (Wolf 1994). McCarthy (1990, 35) states that 'For many Africans, conditions of life are scarcely better, and possible worse, than they were when their colonial rulers departed.'

In many Third World countries therefore the pressure of population has led to a widening of the income gap *vis-à-vis* the high-income countries. Some countries in Africa and Latin America are not especially densely populated, but that is scarcely a relevant consideration at a time when population growth is putting intense pressure on the immediate economic potential of the countries in question. Not only is there the problem of actually finding employment for the growing numbers, but the accompanying rise in dependency ratios means that more investment is required to improve infrastructures and social overhead capital for such things as health, education, housing, transport and communications, at a time when investment resources are severely stretched. Even more critical for some countries in the immediate term is the question of food supply. It is here that many underdeveloped countries have encountered serious difficulties in the face of unyielding agrarian systems.

Since agriculture is the dominant sector in the economic life of pre-industrial economies, it is not surprising that it should be regarded as having a critical role to play in the process of modernization (Reynolds 1985, 406; World Bank 1993b, 109–10). In the past it has fulfilled several functions including that of a source of labour and capital accumulation, providing food for an expanding population and foreign exchange for the purchase of imports. Western experience suggests that agriculture responded to the needs of modernization in these respects. But in today's Third World countries agriculture has not always lived up to these expectations. For much of the twentieth century agricultural productivity has either been falling or at best static in many parts of the underdeveloped world, with the result that food output has struggled to keep pace with population growth (Bairoch 1975, 38). In some of the low income countries, especially in Africa, per capita food output was actually falling in the 1980s (Kelley 1988, 1711). Again the chief problem has been population pressure on the land which, coupled with land shortages, poor fertility, primitive techniques, lack of resources, unyielding agrarian structures, and in some cases hostile climatic conditions, has led to diminishing yields. Neglect of agriculture by policymakers has also exacted its toll, as East European statesmen learned to their cost only too well (Aldcroft and Morewood 1995).

Bairoch (1975, 40–41) reckons that by the 1960s agricultural productivity in Africa and Asia was only about half that in the developed countries at the start of their industrialization. Moreover, the other big difference is that the latter achieved the breakthrough with relatively stable agrarian populations, since the expansion of non-agrarian activities was able to siphon off the excess labour on the land. This in turn was made possible by the prior or accompanying improvements in agricultural productivity which raised purchasing power and savings for use elsewhere.

For many of the impoverished countries this route to success has been closed because of the continuation of severe population pressure coupled with poor agricultural performance. To relieve the pressure on the land would require impossible rates of expansion of industrial employment. In any case, for many countries it is as much as they can do to maintain levels of food output and, over time, dependence on food imports has increased. Before the war the developing countries had a grain surplus for export equivalent to 7 per cent of output, whereas by the 1970s this had been transformed into a deficit of 8 per cent. Agriculture is therefore not fulfilling its role as an exchange earner. Moreover, dependence on food imports is not a long-term solution despite the food surpluses elsewhere in the world. It tends to have negative effects on domestic output; it leads to increasing dependence on aid and the accumulation of debt which is something most countries wish to avoid, while it does little to tackle the fundamental problems of the underdeveloped world.

Human resources
Rapid population growth exerts pressure on emerging economies in another direction in so far as it leads to increasing dependency ratios of young people who need to be catered for through the provision of social and infrastructure facilities. In Africa, for example, around half the population is aged fifteen or under, and one of the most urgent tasks is that of educating and training this large potential workforce.

Though the relationships between education and economic development are complex, it has been increasingly recognized that human resource formation plays an important role. The World Bank (1993b, 349; 1994, 25) sees it as probably the most important single contributor to growth. 'Of all endowments, human capital probably does most to fuel long-term economic growth. Simply put, countries with skilled people grow faster. The fact that Sub-Saharan Africa trails other regions in social indicators can thus help to explain its slow growth.' Initially the crucial factor seems to be the early attainment of universal, high-quality primary education since this has a higher pay-off in terms of growth and equity than other forms of education which are more expensive; it also encourages the reduction in fertility (assuming equal educational opportunities for girls) which leads to a moderation in numbers; while more generally it encourages changes in attitudes and behaviour which are helpful to economic development (Colclough 1982; World Bank 1993b, 349; Abramovitz 1989, 45–6; Núñez 1990, 135).

Past experience suggests that one common feature of early developers is their high level of literacy and educational provision. Western countries had a marked advantage in this respect over all other nations. On the basis of primary school enrolments covering a wide selection of countries Easterlin (1981, 10–14) presented a persuasive case for the importance of education as a modernizing force. The spread of mass education of a secular and rationalistic type not only helped to foster attitudes and attributes conducive to the acquisition of new skills, new technology and new ways of doing things, but it also heralded a shift in political power which allowed greater scope for the ambitions of a wider segment of the population. The build-up in human capital stock was a fairly lengthy process. As early as the mid-seventeenth century more than half the adult population of the major Western cities were deemed to be literate (Cipolla 1981, 93). Two centuries later many citizens in Northwest Europe and North America had had exposure to some type of education. Literacy rates were already quite high (50 per cent or more), formal schooling was quite extensive, and in some cases, for example Germany and North America, it had preceded modern economic growth.

A similar picture is presented by Sandberg (1982, 687–97) in his study of the relationship between education and income levels for a wide range of European countries. Literacy levels achieved by 1850 are, he argues, 'an amazingly good predictor of *per capita* income in the 1970s.' Using adult literacy rates as a proxy for human resource stocks, he found that countries which were highly literate at the start of the period, even though sometimes poor, were generally the ones that eventually attained high levels of per capita income. Conversely, the lower the initial per capita stock of human resources, the slower the rate of modernization, as was the case in Southern and Eastern Europe. The reasoning is close to Easterlin's, namely that to exploit new opportunities, countries require a highly articulate and mobile labour force, an elastic supply of financial services, the ability to develop and utilize new technology, in addition to 'a more rational and receptive approach to life on the part of the population' (Cipolla 1969, 102) . Without improvements in the educational stock these attributes are unlikely to emerge.

Apart from North America and Western Europe, most parts of the world lacked even rudimentary education systems in the nineteenth century and literacy levels were very low. Even in much of Southern and Eastern Europe the spread of education was very limited and the resulting low levels of human capital formation have been seen as one of the main barriers to economic advancement (Tortella 1994; Berend and Ranki 1985, 46). The major exception was Japan which had a much higher literacy capability in the mid-nineteenth century than once supposed, and her subsequent development trajectory serves to confirm the point.

A century or so later the position had not changed very much. Most of Africa, large parts of Asia and certain areas of Latin America lacked even basic educational facilities. In Asia and Africa over three-quarters of the population was illiterate and in Latin America around one half. After the Second World War there was some improvement as massive educational programmes were implemented. Rates of illiteracy fell quite dramatically in many countries. Africa however continued to remain the most underschooled continent: primary education touched barely two-fifths of the relevant age group, secondary and tertiary education reached a mere one or two percentage points (Colclough 1982, 167). Even by the mid-1980s there were still many low income countries in Africa and also in Asia including India (the main exceptions being China and Sri Lanka), where illiteracy rates exceeded 50 per cent, that is well above the levels recorded in Western Europe in the previous century.

Moreover, notwithstanding the greater quantitative provision of education, doubts remain as to its quality and utility. It has been alleged that the great educational drives of the postwar years were 'expensive, inefficient and inadequate', and that they failed to promote the well-being of the majority of the world's population. This was not because of any inherent defect in education *per se*, but largely because the educational strategies were ill conceived in terms of the specific needs of the countries in question and were frequently frustrated by political and social opposition and subversion. And, as with much capital investment, the characteristics of the educational changes were all too often modelled along Western lines by planners incapable of appreciating local requirements. Hence the content of the curricula was often unsuitable, the quality of teaching poor, and the equipment and textbooks tended to reflect the interests and aptitudes of pupils in the metropolitan economies of the West. Consequently, attendance rates were often poor, and failure and drop-out rates high. Some of these problems could no doubt have been obviated had slavish imitation of Western practice not occurred, but politicians and policymakers were all too eager to adopt the styles of the West in the belief that they held the key to modernization. But, as Simmons (1979) aptly remarked: 'Education may be the key to change, but it sometimes appears to be locked on the other side of the development door.'

There is a marked contrast however in the case of the high-performance economies of East Asia where public investment in education was not only larger than elsewhere in absolute terms, but also better adapted to the needs of emerging economies. The main emphasis here was on universal high-quality primary education and basic secondary education including the development of cognitive skills of the labour force, with the demand for higher education being left largely to the private sector. This was socially both more efficient and equitable since the returns on basic education are higher, while subsidies for tertiary education tend to go disproportionately to better-off families. In African countries, on the other hand, the unit costs of education are relatively high and there has been some serious resource misallocation. Spending on higher education has accounted for some 20 per cent of total educational expenditure as against 9–15 per cent in Korea, Malaysia, Thailand and Indonesia. Moreover, salaries have consumed a large part of recurrent educational budgets at the primary level, leaving little to spend on textbooks, materials and other consumables. Subsidies and scholarships for higher education have tended to go largely to families with means (World Bank 1993b, 203, 1994, 27–8, 173; Colman and Nixson 1994, 114).

It is ironic, as well as a sad reflection on the institutional structure and society of many developing countries, that many of those fortunate enough to be educated to a reasonably high standard (often with the help of subsidies) have sought jobs in the tertiary sector of the economy, especially in the public sector, partly because the pay and prestige are better than for employment in industry or agriculture, and partly because their education and training has conditioned them for jobs in non-productive activities. This means a drain of talent away from industry which has failed to attract a satisfactory number of skilled workers and where skill formation remains poor compared with that in some parts of the service sector.

The specification of the relationships between human resource formation and economic growth and development may require further refining before we can be fully certain of the precise causal links, but the evidence so far does suggest that education matters. And as Núñez (1990, 135) has recently demonstrated using the Spanish case as her model, the ramifications of educational change may be very wide-ranging, and one of the important and overlooked contributions could well be 'a better disposition towards change and social mobility in a very general sense'. In which case there are strong grounds for arguing that the head-start achieved by Western societies in this field was an important factor in their rise to economic dominance. The uneven development in Europe itself can in turn be explained partly by the disparities in human capital formation, especially as the diffusion of techniques and modern methods of production depended so much on the transfer of skills and knowledge originating in the West (Inkster 1990). Later successful developers in East Asia also had the advantage of a good stream of human capital. By contrast, many of the low-income countries of the Third World were still deficient in both the quantity and quality of educational provision which did not match the attainments of Western countries in the nineteenth century.

The institutional setting
It can be argued that the development of Western civilization would not have been possible had states and institutions not been adapted to the needs of a modernizing society. Following the work of North and Thomas (1970, 1973; North 1981) there is now much greater recognition among economic historians and development economists that these can have a significant bearing on the rate at which a society progresses. States and institutions can act as a barrier to the exploitation of new opportunities if they fail to adapt to the needs of an acquisitive society. They will remain restrictive and repressive, corruption and graft will be rife, and they will fail to provide an institutional and legal framework which guarantees individual property rights and respects economic transactions. Under these conditions there is little incentive for individuals to show initiative and enterprise if property assets of whatever kind are constantly in danger of violation by plundering or expropriation by the state or by individuals, as was the case in medieval Europe, or where there is no proper authority to uphold the legal basis of economic transactions. In the words of Batou (1990, 465) 'Who would have taken the risk of investing his assets in commerce and industry without being protected from the exactions of the authorities?'

In much of Eurasia state structures changed little and they remained essentially feudal and repressive. The great dynasties of India, China and the Ottoman Empire were essentially military despots bent on preserving their power by exacting tribute from impoverished subjects which left them with little more than subsistence. The overhead costs of state were high as a result of the demands of the military, the large bureaucracy and parasitical élite groups, which sapped the strength of these empires in much the same way as had happened in the later Roman Empire (Kahn 1979, 30–31). Little encouragement was given to individual initiative and enterprise since this would have undermined the basis of feudal power.

Such features were not uncommon in the more backward parts of Europe in the nineteenth century and even beyond. In Turkey and the Balkans, for example, corrupt and despotic rulers were the order of the day. They imposed heavy taxes on their subjects to finance the army, an overblown bureaucracy and ostentatious public works. The state drew more human and fiscal resources away from productive investment than it itself contributed, except for those wasted on forms of 'symbolic modernisation' (Berend and Ranki 1982, 69–71) .

A similar situation existed in medieval Europe under the fragmented control of individual rulers. Pillage, plunder and exaction were part of everyday life and the legal framework for commercial transactions was at best still rudimentary. Fortunately, when Europe emerged from this situation it escaped falling into the hands of monolithic dynastic rulers and so avoided many of the pernicious features of the great empires of the East. Instead, in the West at least, a system of nation states with fairly clearly defined boundaries gradually evolved out of the multiplicity of political units of the late medieval period. Thus the political structures which had once been the basis for the conquest and subjugation of territories and peoples now became the means to subjugate nature for the benefit of mankind (Dobbin 1994, 19). Further to the east conditions were less propitious for such developments since the ethnic fragmentation of populations, the periodic threat of invasion, and the absence of clearly defined geographical boundaries made the concept of the nation state something of an anachronism (Newman 1970, 37–50).

What was particularly important about the new states was that they were both more competitive and in time more liberal than the administrations of the East. This gave rise to greater economic security and a corresponding increase in the rights to property (Anderson 1974, 420, 429). In time they removed or modified some of the more inhibiting features of feudal society which reduced market transaction costs and strengthened the links between effort and reward. Sometimes the state itself became a positive force in economic development by promoting or encouraging the formation of economic enterprises. More often than not, however, the state was a passive agent and its costs rarely absorbed as much as 10 per cent of national income. Finally, modernization and industrialization tended to be accompanied by increasing democratization of societies, so that government became more open and pluralistic.

However, the most striking difference between West and East was in the differing legal frameworks with respect to market transactions and the protection of property rights. The emergence of the nation state in Europe was accompanied by the revival of Roman law which many commentators see as being the most effective instrument for encouraging capitalist transactions. The chief advantages of Roman law are that it facilitates titles to property, provides a means of defining and enforcing contracts, and more generally it establishes a systematic and coherent legal framework for the purchase, sale, lease, hire, loan and transfer of goods and chattels. This legal basis laid the foundations for the security of property rights and the conduct of economic transactions without which modern capitalism could not have flourished as it did in the West. Eastern Europe lagged well behind and in many respects had not progressed far from the pillage, plunder and corruption stage of earlier centuries. Likewise, the legal systems of the East gave little support to economic agents. Islamic law was extremely vague on real-estate matters, Chinese law was repressive and concerned itself relatively little with civil and economic issues, while Japanese law was rudimentary in the extreme.

The effect of differing institutional forms may be seen in the contrasting responses of agriculture to the market opportunities for capitalist farming. In the West the commercialization of agriculture, the increased use of wage labour and technical innovation were encouraged, whereas in Eurasia, Eastern Europe and parts of Southern Europe the sector was seen simply as a covenient source of revenue.

All the changes in legal forms, civil administrations and institutions that took place in the West did not occur overnight. It is important to stress that they evolved gradually and erratically over the course of several centuries and this is partly the key to their success and the lesson for others. There was no dramatic revolution but a slow process of adapting state structures and institutions to the needs of societies in the process of modernization. Attempts to speed up the process by drastic changes in political regimes, structures and institutions, as for example in Eastern Europe in the later nineteenth century and again more recently, and in many less developed countries in the present century, have not always been successful.

The situation today in many parts of the Third World is varied and complex, but it would not be a distortion of the facts to say that political structures and institutions are far less conducive to economic progress than they were in nineteenth-century Western Europe. In many countries in Africa, Asia and Latin America the attempt to copy Western institutions has not generally met with success. There are serious internal political and social tensions and conflicts, exacerbated by strong tribal or sectional interest groups, which give rise to unstable and corrupt governments and in some cases to the suppression of democratic rights. The classic case of political disintegration has occurred in Africa where, despite good intentions following independence, two-thirds of the states had fallen under military control by the mid-1980s (Tilly 1992, 209–13). The World Bank (1993a, 22) described the situation as follows: 'In many African countries the administrations, judiciaries, and educational institutions are now mere shadows of their former selves. ... Equally worrying is the widespread impression of political decline. Corruption, oppression, and nepotism are increasingly evident.'

Such characteristics should occasion no surprise since they have been a common feature of poor and stagnant societies throughout history. They may even be the symptoms of development and change. After all, it took many centuries before coherent states were forged from the political fragmentation and diversity in Europe and even by the nineteenth century Eastern and Southern European countries retained many of the vestiges of traditional society (Bean 1973; Kennedy 1988, 17–20). It may therefore take some time before Third World countries can adapt their state structures and institutions to those approaching Western Europe in the nineteenth century. The task of state building today is in any case far more difficult since there is often no real concept of statehood or citizenship, and the notion of sacrifice for the good of the country is alien to many people (Reynolds 1986, 103). This is not surprising, of course, since many new states have been forged in haste, incorporating unnatural boundaries along with a host of tribal and ethnic hostilities (Landes 1990, 9). In this context it is worth noting that the successful developers in Western Europe, North America and Japan, and latterly East Asia, had much more homogeneous societies than most of today's Third World countries.

In turn, many emerging nations have tried to do too much, too quickly and with too few resources (Reynolds 1986, 129). The strategy of accelerated development has been conditioned by the quest for quick results to make up for lost time, and in this respect lateness is 'the parent of bad government' and bad policies, many of which have ended in failure (Landes 1990, 9). Reynolds (1986, 107) stresses the importance of good government. The most successful countries, he noted, tended to be those with high scores on political stability, administrative staffing and effective economic policies (cf. World Bank 1994, 37).

Unfortunately two few Third World countries can lay claim to good government and institutions. The drift to political and constitutional disintegration is all too frequent and is reflected in the fact that the majority of underdeveloped countries are governed by either a military group, a civilian oligarchy or even a personal monarch. Free and open leadership elections are the exception rather than the rule. The result has been a system of government and administration which runs counter to best Western practice in several respects, for example in the role of the state and the power and conduct of administrations, the position of élite groups, the distribution of income and wealth, the extent of land concentration, and the security of property rights. Compared with European nations in the previous century, many low-income countries have a high state presence in economic matters. Public expenditures account for between a fifth and a quarter of national income. This of course may be no bad thing were the expenditures dispensed wisely and fruitfully, but this does not appear to be generally the case. Up to two-thirds of budgetary outlays on average go on defence, spending on which is high by most past Western standards, and 'other sources'. The latter consist mainly of expenditure on general administration, including employee compensation. Budgetary outlays on social services tend to be very modest, while the remaining expenditure of around a quarter is devoted to economic services, the benefits of which are far from apparent.

Many Third World countries have expenditure and tax regimes that are highly regressive and tend to benefit a small minority at the expense of the majority of the population (Maddison 1971). This is a common feature of underdeveloped countries in the past, yet oddly enough not one from which lessons are readily drawn, except in the case of the high-performance East Asian economies where income is much more equitably distributed. Even the limited social security systems are loaded in favour of the well-paid professional classes (often government employees) and there is little real protection afforded to the bulk of the population. Hence state policies tend to strengthen the already unequal distribution of income and wealth, compounded in some cases by excessive concentration of land ownership due to the absence of land reform. In short, government is by and for the élite groups. The majority of the population, including the small-scale entrepreneurial class, is marginalized by the political process.

Perhaps even worse is the fact that the exacting and unpredictable nature of state policies has effectively weakened the security of property rights and incentives for the individual. The proliferation of administrative controls and licences, the imposition of various exactions and the distortion of market forces by regulatory decrees, have inevitably encouraged corruption, bribery and nepotism throughout society and set the individual against the system (World Bank 1993a, 22; McCarthy 1990, 26; Reynolds 1986, 129). This in turn has stifled the enterprise and investment of small-scale producers in both industry and agriculture. The climate has not therefore favoured the growth of a strong, acquisitive and market-oriented bourgeoisie, which was the essence of nineteenth-century European development. After all, why should it when the risk and reward patterns so blatantly favour the politically astute and those with connections at the expense of individuals with enterprise and initiative? (Landes 1990, 10.)

Conclusion
It would be wrong to believe that the lessons of the past are set in tablets of stone to serve as a blueprint for aspiring developing countries. History does not, and cannot, repeat itself exactly, and in any case the ubiquitous nature of nations would not permit parallel trajectories to those of the West (Singer and Ansari 1982, 43). Nevertheless, it would also be capricious to reject out-of-hand the general pointers of historical experience. The most obvious is that

the origins of modern development have long historical roots. Modern economic growth is not there for the asking. Several centuries elapsed before Europe was in a position to make the vital breakthrough, and even in the case of Japan the lead-time was a lengthy one. By contrast, when attempts were made to force the pace of development prematurely, as in the case of Egypt, Turkey, Eastern Europe and some Latin America countries, the results were often very mixed, sometimes abortive, and at best produced lopsided development at high social cost.

More specifically, the LDCs in the latter half of the present century are in a much weaker position than the Western nations at the dawn of modern economic growth. They are considerably poorer, their populations are growing much faster, their agrarian systems are less responsive, while their institutions and political frameworks are markedly inferior. Some of these problems can no doubt be rectified if the will is there, but many LDCs feel that time is not on their side. They want jam today, not tomorrow; and they blame, rightly or wrongly, the West for their predicament, a convenient scapegoat when things go wrong. And they frequently do, because to overcome the 'backlog of backwardness', they adopt policies designed to achieve the impossible, that is to bridge the gap in development within the space of decades even though their economic and political systems are not in a position to deliver the goods. Consequently, many of the efforts end in disaster. Unfortunately, corrupt regimes and bureaucratic institutions remain in being on the pretext that the West is to blame for the abortive attempts at modernization.

In other words, LDCs are trying to accomplish in a much shorter time and with more limited resources and inferior institutions what in the West took many centuries. But while they may incur penalties by being late, the situation is not beyond redemption. The high-performance economies of East Asia have shown the way forward and there seems no reason why others should not follow in their footsteps. If not, the consequences could be serious for mankind as a whole if, as Landes (1990, 12) suggests, the Third World resorts to exporting violence and people rather than goods and services.

References

Abramovitz, M. (1989), *Thinking About Growth*, Cambridge: Cambridge University Press.

Abu-Lughod, J. (1989), *Before European Hegemony: the World System A.D. 1250–1350*, New York: Oxford University Press.

Aldcroft, D.H. (1991), 'World income distribution', *The Economic Review*, 9.

Aldcroft, D.H. and Morewood, S. (1995) *Economic Change in Eastern Europe since 1918*, Aldershot: Edward Elgar.

Anderson, J.L. (1991), *Explaining Long-term Economic Change*, Basingstoke: Macmillan.

Anderson, P. (1974), *Lineages of the Absolutist State*, London: New Left Books.

Ashworth, W. (1974), 'Industrialisation and the economic integration of nineteenth-century Europe', *European Studies Review*, 4.

Bairoch, P. (1975), *The Economic Development of the Third World since 1900*, London: Methuen.

Bairoch, P. (1981), 'The main trends in national income disparities since the industrial revolution', in P. Bairoch and M. Lévy-Leboyer (eds), *Disparities in Economic Development since the Industrial Revolution*, London: Macmillan.

Bairoch, P. (1989), 'Les trois révolutions agricoles du monde développé: rendements et productivité de 1800 à 1985', *Annales*, 44.

Bairoch, P. (1991), 'How and not why: economic inequalities between 1800 and 1913: some background figures', in J. Batou (ed.), *Between Development and Underdevelopment: the Precocious Attempts at Industrialisation of the Periphery, 1800–70*, Geneva: Droz.

Bairoch, P. (1993), *Economics and World History: Myths and Paradoxes*, Hemel Hempstead: Harvester Wheatsheaf.

Batou, J. (1990), *Cent ans de résistance au sous-développement: l'industrialisation de l'Amérique latine et du Moyen-orient au défi européen, 1700–1870*, Geneva: Droz.

Bean R. (1973), 'War and the birth of the nation state', *Journal of Economic History*, 33.

Berend, I.T. and Ranki, G. (1982), *The European Periphery and Industrialisation, 1780–1914*, Cambridge: Cambridge University Press.

Berend, I.T. and Ranki, G. (1985), 'The East Central European variant of the industrial revolution', in B.K. Kiraly and N.F. Dreisziger (eds), *War and Society in East Central Europe: Vol. XIX, East Central European Society in World War I*, Boulder, Co.: Atlantic Research and Publications.

Blaut, J.M. (1993), *The Colonizer's Model of the World: Geographical Diffusionism and Eurocentric History*, New York: The Guilford Press.

Brenner, R. (1982), 'The agrarian roots of European capitalism', *Past and Present*, 97.

Caldwell, M. (1977), *The Wealth of some Nations*, London: Zed Press.

Chirot, D. (1985), 'The rise of the west', *American Sociological Review*, 50.

Chisholm, M. (1982), *Modern World Development*, London: Hutchinson.

Cipolla, C. (1969), *Literacy and Development in the West*, Harmondsworth: Penguin.

Cipolla, C. (1981), *Before the Industrial Revolution: European Society and Economy, 1000–1700*, London: Methuen.

Clark, G. (1991), 'Yields per acre in English agriculture, 1250–1860: evidence from labour inputs', *Economic History Review*, 4

Colclough, C. (1982), 'The impact of primary schooling on economic development: a review of the evidence', *World Development*, 10.

Colman, D. and Nixson, F. (1994), *Economics of Change in Less Developed Countries*, 3rd edn, Hemel Hempstead: Harvester Wheatsheaf.

Cunningham, W. (1904), *An Essay on Western Civilisation in its Economic Aspects*, Cambridge: Cambridge University Press.

de Vries, J. (1974), *The Dutch Rural Economy in the Golden Age*, New Haven: Yale University Press.

Dobbin, F. (1994), *Forging Industrial Policy: the United States, Britain and France in the Railway Age*, Cambridge: Cambridge University Press.

Easterlin, R.A. (1981), 'Why isn't the whole world developed?', *Journal of Economic History*, 41.

Goldstone, J.A. (1991), *Revolution and Rebellion in the Early Modern World*, Berkeley, Ca.: University of California Press.

Goodman, J. and Honeyman, K. (1988), *Gainful Pursuits: the Making of Industrial Europe*, London: Edward Arnold.

Grigg, D. (1992), *The Transformation of Agriculture in the West*, Oxford: Blackwell.

Hodgson, M.G.S. (1993), *Rethinking World History: Essays on Europe, Islam, and World History*, Cambridge: Cambridge University Press.

Holman, M. (1994a), 'In 40 years' time black Africa might reach the level of wealth it had 20 years ago', *Financial Times*, 13 April.

Holman, M. (1994b), 'The sounds of a continent cracking', *Financial Times*, 23 July.

Inkster, I. (1990), 'Mental capital, transfers of knowledge and techniques in eighteenth-century Europe', *Journal of European Economic History*, 19.

Johnson, D.G. and Lee, R.D. (eds), (1987) *Population Growth and Economic Development*, Madison: University of Wisconsin Press.

Jones, E. (1981), *The European Miracle*, Cambridge: Cambridge University Press.

Kahn, H. (1979), *World Economic Development, 1979 and beyond*, London: Croom Helm.

Kelley, A.C. (1988), 'Economic consequences of population change in the Third World', *Journal of Economic Literature*, 26.

Kennedy, P. (1988), *The Rise and Fall of the Great Powers: Economic Change and Military Conflict from 1500 to 2000*, London: Unwin Hyman.

Kiesewetter, H. (1994), 'Europe's industrialisation – coincidence or necessity?', *German Yearbook on Business History*.

Komlos, J. (1983), *The Habsburg Monarch as a Customs Union: Economic Development in Austria–Hungary in the Nineteenth Century*, Chicago: University of Chicago Press.

Komlos, J . (1989a), *Nutrition and Economic Development in the Eighteenth Century Habsburg Monarchy: an Anthropometric Study*, Princeton, NJ: Princeton University Press.

Komlos, J. (1989b), 'Thinking about the industrial revolution', *Journal of European Economic History*, 18.

Kuznets, S. (1974), *Population, Capital and Growth: Selected Essays*, London: Heinemann Educational Books.

Landes, D.S. (1969), *The Unbound Prometheus: Technological Change and Industrial Development in Western Europe from 1750 to the Present*, Cambridge: Cambridge University Press.

Landes, D.S. (1990), 'Why are we so rich and they so poor?', *American Economic Review, Papers and Proceedings*, 80.

Landes, D.S. (1991), 'Does it pay to be late?', in C. Holmes and A. Booth, (eds), *Economy and Society: European Industrialisation and its Social Consequences: Essays Presented to Sidney Pollard*, Leicester: Leicester University Press.

Landes, D.S. (1993), 'The fable of the dead horse; or, the industrial revolution revisited', in J. Mokyr (ed.), *The British Industrial Revolution: an Economic Perspective*, Boulder, Co: Westview Press.

Landes, D.S. (1994), 'What room for accident in history?: explaining big changes by small events', *Economic History Review*, 47.

Laslett, P. (1988), 'The European family and early industrialisation', in J. Baechler, J. A. Hall and M. Mann, (eds), *Europe and the Rise of Capitalism*, Oxford: Blackwell.

Lewis, B. (1970), *The Arabs in History*, 5th edn, London: Hutchinson.

Livi-Bacci, M. (1992), *A Concise History of World Population*, Oxford: Blackwell.

Maddison, A. (1971), *Class Structure and Economic Growth: India and Pakistan since the Moghuls*, London: Allen & Unwin.

Maddison, A. (1982), *Phases of Capitalist Development*, Oxford: Oxford University Press.

Maddison, A. (1983), 'A comparison of levels of GDP per capita in developed and developing countries 1700–1980', *Journal of Economic History*, 43.

Maddison, A. (1989), *The World Economy in the 20th century*, Paris: OECD.

Matowist, M. (1966), 'The problem of the inequality of economic development in Europe in the later middle ages', *Economic History Review*, 19.

McCarthy, S. (1990), 'Development stalled: the crisis in Africa: a personal view', *European Investment Bank Papers*, no. 15.

McNeill, W.H. (1963), *The Rise of the West*, Chicago: University of Chicago Press.

Mokyr, J. (1976), *Industrialisation in the Low Countries, 1795–1850*, New Haven, Conn.: Yale University Press.

Newman, K.J . (1970), *European Democracy between the Wars*, London: Allen & Unwin.

North, D.C. (1981), *Structure and Change in Economic History*, New York: Norton.

North, D.C. and Thomas, R.P. (1970), 'An economic theory of the growth of the western world', *Economic History Review*, 23.

North, D.C. and Thomas, R.P. (1973) *The Rise of the Western World: a New Economic History*, Cambridge: Cambridge University Press.

Núñez, C.F. (1990), 'Literacy and economic growth in Spain 1860–1977', in G. Tortella (ed.), *Education and Economic Development since the Industrial Revolution*, Valencia: Generalitat Valenciana.

O'Brien, P. (1982), 'European economic development: the contribution of the periphery', *Economic History Review*, 35.

Ohlin, G. (1965), 'Remarks on the relevance of western experience in economic growth to former colonial areas', *Journal of World History*, 9.

Pedreira, J.M. (1991), 'The obstacles to early industrialisation in Portugal, 1800–70: a comparative perspective', in J. Batou (ed.), *Between Development and Underdevelopment, 1800–70*, Geneva, Droz.

Persson, K.G. (1988), *Pre-industrial Economic Growth: Social Organisation and Technological Progress in Europe*, Oxford: Blackwell.

Phillips, J.R.S. (1988), *The Medieval Expansion of Europe*, Oxford: Oxford University Press.

Reynolds, L.G. (1985), *Economic Growth in the Third World, 1850–1950*, New Haven, Conn.: Yale University Press.

Reynolds, L.G. (1986), *Economic Growth in the Third World: an Introduction*, New Haven, Conn.: Yale University Press.

Rostow, W.W. (1980), *Why the Poor Get Rich and the Rich Slow Down: Essays in the Marshallian Long Period*, London, Macmillan.

Rothermund, D. (1981), *Asian Trade and European Expansion in the Age of Mercantilism*, New Delhi: Manohar Publications.

Sandberg, L.G . (1982), 'Ignorance, poverty and economic backwardness in the early stages of European industrialisation: variations on Alexander Gerschenkron's grand theme', *Journal of European Economic History*, 11.

Simmons, J. (1979), 'Education for development reconsidered?' *World Development*, 7.

Simon, J.L. (1986) *Theory of Population and Economic Growth*, London: Blackwell.

Singer, A. and Ansari, J. (1982), *Rich and Poor Countries*, 3rd edn, London: Allen & Unwin.

Smith, A.K. (1991), *Creating a World Economy: Merchant Capital, Colonialism and World Trade, 1400–1825*, Boulder, Co.: Westview Press.

Snooks, G.D. (1993), *Economics without Time: a Science Blind to the Forces of Historical Change*, London: Macmillan.

Snooks, G.D. (ed.) (1994), *Was the Industrial Revolution Necessary?* London: Routledge.

Solow, B.L. (1987), 'Capitalism and slavery in the exceedingly long run', *Journal of Interdisciplinary History*, 4.

Tilly, C. (1992), *Coercion, Capital and European States, AD990–1990*, Oxford, Blackwell.

Tortella, G. (1994), 'Patterns of economic retardation and recovery in south-western Europe in the nineteenth and twentieth centuries', *Economic History Review*, 47.

van der Woude, A.M . (1992), 'The future of west European agriculture: an exercise in applied theory', *Review, Fernand Braudel Centre*, 15.

van Houtte, J.A. (1977), *An Economic History of the Low Countries, 800–1800*, London: Weidenfeld and Nicolson.

van Zanden, J.L. (1992), 'Dutch economic history of the period 1500–1940: a review of the present state of affairs', *Research Notes from the Netherlands*, 2.

van Zanden, J.L. (1993), *The Rise and Decline of Holland's Economy*, Manchester: Manchester University Press.

Warriner, D. (ed.) (1965), *Contrasts in Emerging Societies: Readings in the Social and Economic History of South-east Europe in the Nineteenth Century*, London: Athlone Press.

Whynes, D.K. (1988), *Comparative Economic Development*, London: Butterworths.

Wolf, M. (1994), 'If you go down to the woods today', *Financial Times*, 26 July.

World Bank (1989), *Sub-Saharan Africa: from Crisis to Sustainable Growth*, Washington, DC: World Bank.

World Bank (1990), *World Development Report 1990*, Washington, DC: World Bank.

World Bank (1993a), *Annual Report*, Washington, DC: World Bank.

World Bank (1993b), *The East Asian Miracle: Economic Growth and Public Policy*, Oxford: Oxford University Press.

World Bank (1994), *Adjustment in Africa: Reforms, Results, and the Road Ahead*, Oxford: Oxford University Press.

2 The reserve army of the unmarried in world economic history: flexible fertility regimes and the wealth of nations*

J.R. McNeill

The problems of population, that is to say the question what it is that determines the size of human societies and what the consequences are that attend the increase or decrease in the number of a country's inhabitants, might well be the first to occur to a perfectly detached observer as soon as he looks at these societies in a spirit of scientific curiosity. The view that the key to the historical process is to be found in the variations of populations, though one-sided, is at least as reasonable as is any other theory of history that proceeds from the prejudice that there must be a single prime mover of social or economic evolution – such as technology, race, class struggle, capital formation, and what not.

Joseph Schumpeter (1954)

Framing the question

Why are some societies much richer than others? This is one of the most interesting and consequential questions of modern world history. It has been answered many times, and often well, by reference to the experience of Western Europe.[1] But that approach, fruitful as it has been, looks increasingly incomplete in the 1990s. By now surely Japan's long-term economic history is central too. An updated inquiry into the causes of the wealth of nations must take into account both the cases of Western Europe and Japan. What might they have had in common – and other societies did not have – that helped them get rich?

Geographically, Japan and Western Europe share one feature which may help to account for their economic histories. They lie at the extremes of Eurasia, and so located have felt the effects of the interaction and intersocietal competition that have characterized most of Eurasia and North Africa – the intercommunicating zone of world history – on and off for 2,000 years. At the same time, their position has shielded them from the ravages of steppe warriors. The Mongols never consummated an intended invasion of Japan, and to the West ventured no further than the Hungarian plain. Until the twentieth century, most – not all – of the military damage felt in these

*For their critical readings of this paper or their answers to my questions I thank J. Collins, P. Dunkley, B. Dunne, T. Geiger, D. Goldfrank, S. Hanley, B. Hill, D. Kaiser, A. Kaminski, J.A. Moran, W. McNeill, N. Melcher, R. Schofield, H. Spendelow, C. Totman and A. Yamamoto.

societies was self-inflicted and (comparatively) mild. Hence Japan and Western Europe have enjoyed the benefits of participation in the intercommunicating zone with fewer of the costs.

In cultural matters another parallel deserves a moment's notice. In explaining twentieth-century economic success in Japan, South Korea, Taiwan, Singapore, Hong Kong, and perhaps now some of the coastal provinces of mainland China, some observers point to Confucianism. Its emphases on harmony, discipline, deference, and so forth are held to promote social relations conducive to (capitalist) economic success. This cultural explanation is an analogue to other arguments, such as those of Max Weber, about the role of Protestant values in promoting Western European capitalism and prosperity (Rozman 1991; Vogel 1992; Tai 1989).[2]

Countless other parallels between the situations, conditions and circumstances of Japan and Western Europe are no doubt possible. Japan, like Western Europe, has an imperialist history, replete with attempts to profit from the resources and labour of others (although not much of one until the 1890s). In Japan, as in Western Europe, local magnates diluted the power of the state, checking its confiscatory urges (but this was true in countless other settings). These parallel circumstances and experiences probably contributed something to the peculiar economic histories of Western Europe and Japan.

Less obvious but perhaps more important was the presence in both Japan and Western Europe of a marriage pattern that permitted societal adjustments in fertility: the strangest feature of this unusual situation was the reserve army of the unmarried, the shock troops of economic growth. (By economic growth I mean not mere expansion of scale, but continuous investment, growing productivity of labour, and rising standards of living that last for successive generations.)

In what follows I shall point out similarities in the marriage patterns and demographic regimes that underlay Japanese and Western European societies in early modern times, and argue that these regimes, in slightly different ways, provided each society with a means to tailor population to existing resources, encouraging slightly stabler and more predictable economic conditions than those that obtained in other parts of the world. Western Europe and Japan also achieved more favourable age distributions – more people in the prime of life per capita – than those found elsewhere. Through custom and social regulation they unconsciously created uncommonly favourable (economically speaking) ratios between production and reproduction (at a considerable social cost). In the eccentric but parallel marriage patterns and demographic regimes of Japan and Western Europe, I suggest, lies one key to their unusual economic histories. (I readily admit that there must be many others.)[3]

The reserve army of the unmarried in Western Europe

For a generation now, historians have known that in the early modern period, and perhaps before, Western Europe featured a peculiar marriage pattern (Hajnal 1965; 1982). Its main elements consisted of a late average age at first marriage for women and a high proportion of celibates. Fluctuations in time and space and between classes certainly existed, but all available data indicate quite clearly that in England, France, the Low Countries, Scandinavia, Germany, Switzerland, and eventually in much of northern Spain and northern Italy, women's age at first marriage averaged about 24 to 27 (Gaskin 1978; Flinn 1981; Knodel 1988). This meant that women generally spent the first ten to fifteen years of their reproductive years not reproducing (men refrained slightly longer). Considering other factors, such as the death of husbands and a characteristically (as yet unexplained) early retirement from childbearing, Western European women, on average, were at risk to conceive for only twelve to fifteen years of their lives, out of a biological maximum of about 35 years (Flinn 1981).[4] The extraordinary feature of this pattern was that the young of both sexes accepted a 'temporary celibacy' in life – and an economic status of pronounced inferiority to their married elders.[5]

The second element of the West European marriage pattern was its high proportion of people who never married (lifelong celibates), higher than anywhere else in the world, Japan included. In Northwestern Europe as a whole, the proportion of those who never married fluctuated around 15 per cent. Interestingly, despite the large proportion of unmarried young adults, illegitimate births before 1750 were rare, usually less than 5 per cent of total births, often much less.[6]

This pattern, generally called the European marriage pattern, prevailed in Northwestern Europe. Hajnal originally suggested a line between Leningrad (St Petersburg) and Trieste as the divisor, to the northwest of which this peculiar pattern held. Subsequent research has modified this view only slightly, suggesting several regional variants, most notably a Mediterranean pattern (Todorova 1993; Pérez Moreda and Reher 1988; Barbagli 1984). How long the pattern has held sway is open to question. The local records on which European population history is based do not begin until the fifteenth century at the earliest, and in most places only much later. Hajnal and others have suggested the marriage pattern was connected to the prevalence of nuclear family structures. The origins of both the (West) European marriage pattern and the West European propensity for nuclear family structure remain obscure.

Whatever its origins, longevity, and precise geographic extent, the West European marriage pattern produced a peculiar demographic regime, with average fertility levels and age structures quite unusual elsewhere (except Japan). The late age at marriage held fertility well below levels typical in most of the world. By foregoing ten to fifteen years of potential reproduction, West European women each had about four fewer children than they might have had. Occasional recourse to abortion and infanticide (on which more later) further checked effective fertility. Average crude birth rates in Western Europe fluctuated around 30–35 per thousand, well below those typical of societies where women are at risk to conceive throughout their entire reproductive life.[7] I shall return shortly to the economic significance of this fertility regime.

The reserve army in Japan

Japanese population history is very well known by the standards of most of the world. Nimble work by demographic historians allows a general picture of the situation in Tokugawa Japan (1603–1868), especially after about 1700 (Cornell and Hayami 1986; Saito 1992; Hanley and Yamamura 1977; Hanley and Wolf 1985; T. Smith 1977; Jannetta 1987; R. Smith 1972; Hayami and Uchida 1972; Nakane 1972; Hayami 1969; Beillevaire 1986).

In most of Japan the stem family household prevailed from about 1600.[8] Family size averaged around five, perhaps a little more early in the Tokugawa era and a little less later. Typically, but not invariably, only one child could expect to marry and take over the family farmstead. As in Western Europe, marriage and family formation normally had to wait upon inheritance (Beillevaire 1986; Nakane 1972; Hanley 1985; Cornell 1987; Kalland and Pedersen 1984; Hayami 1983). Consequently, the average age at first marriage was also high, as late as age 23–26 for women in the seventeenth and eighteenth centuries.[9] As in Western Europe, young Japanese often found themselves consigned to servitude – until in the course of the eighteenth century servitude almost disappeared – while they waited to marry and begin their own families (Hayami and Uchida 1972; Nakane 1972). The degree to which spinsterhood suppressed fertility in early modern Japan must remain an open question, but it seems probable that lifelong celibacy played a much smaller role in Japan's low fertility than in Western Europe's.

Abortion and infanticide appear to have strongly limited effective fertility in Japan. Historians now regard both practices as routine in Tokugawa Japan, not merely responses to dearth and famine. Japanese parents, it seems, consciously engaged in family planning without necessarily limiting conceptions – although they may have done that too (T. Smith 1977; Kalland and Pedersen 1984; Saito 1992). West Europeans practised abortion and infanticide as well, although, it seems, not on the same scale as the Japanese.[10]

How far back into Japanese history did this marriage pattern extend? The data again permit no clear answer. It may well be that rural peace, achieved only at the end of the sixteenth century, was a necessary precondition for nucleated families. Conditions of conspicuous insecurity oblige people to band together in clans for self-protection, and favour large families and high rates of reproduction (Bloch 1974, 1:142). The *zadruga* of the South Slavs and Northern Albanians is often interpreted in this light (Byrnes 1976). It may also be that Japanese families consciously adopted a strategy of late marriage and few children as an adaptation to the condition of recurrent famine: some evidence suggests such a change took place in northern Kyushu in the course of the eighteenth century (Kalland and Pedersen 1984).

, With late marriage, although on average perhaps not quite so late as in Western Europe, and with routine abortion and infanticide, Japanese society maintained a low effective fertility rate by the standards of other agrarian societies. Estimates show crude birth rates averaging about 25–30 per thousand in Tokugawa Japan. As in Western Europe, and indeed everywhere, these rates varied among places, over time, and between classes. Taken together, they imply fertility about 80–85 per cent of that of Western Europe in the same centuries (Hanley and Yamamura 1977, 302; T. Smith 1977, 40; Hanley 1985, 212; Kalland and Pedersen 1984, 53–4; Hayami 1985, 112).[11]

The Japanese combination of late marriage, modest rates of celibacy, and widespread abortion and infanticide suppressed effective fertility dramatically. Western Europe achieved almost the same result through even later marriage, high rates of celibacy, and (apparently) modest recourse to abortion and infanticide. Social institutions and custom governed fertility. As such it was subject to change in response to many things, but primarily to economic fortunes. Both societies could adjust their numbers, by adjusting fertility, as times improved or worsened. Or, put another way, they could adjust population to niche space. This was the great advantage conferred on societies that maintained a fertility reserve via flexible customs concerning the age of marriage – and concerning infanticide.

Before turning to the economic meaning of the reserve army of the unmarried, it is well to remember at what cost it was maintained. Like members of most armies, including Marx's reserve army of the unemployed, these young adults whether Japanese or West European did not relish their position in society, and found it a source of great frustration and resentment. They were denied, or obliged to postpone, social choices – marriage and childrearing – available to those older and richer than they.[12] The maintenance of the reserve army depended on the continued subjection of (adult) children to parents,[13] of youth to age, of poor to rich. Subjection of this sort is routine in world history: it is a necessary condition, not a sufficient one, for the existence of a reserve army.

The economic impact of the reserve army
The West European and Japanese family structures and marriage patterns[14] provided four possible benefits from the point of view of economic growth:

1.   Reduced constraints on innovation
2.   Favourable age structure and dependency ratio
3.   Comparative stability in the ratio between population and resources
4.   Derivative of 3, moderated environmental degradation.

Here I shall consider only the third point at any length. The first, the most speculative of all my suppositions, need not detain us long. In extended family situations, people typically spent much of their adult life under the control of their aged elders (not to mention lords). Heads of household exercised considerable power over decisions affecting one and all: what crops to plant, when to perform various tasks, whether or not to sell a pig. On the theory that older people are less given to experimentation, it seems likely that where extended families prevailed, new techniques of production encountered greater resistance. Even if decision making within households was not the strict preserve of household heads, but was a shared responsibility, the necessity of consensus and solidarity might check innovation and bolster tradition. Where nuclear families prevailed, young people had to shift for themselves earlier in life, even though they married later. More autonomous units (although far from fully so), they were more free to experiment, and being younger, were more likely to do so. If true, this circumstance favoured more rapid diffusion of innovations wherever nuclear families predominated. This argument is pure conjecture and not, I think, susceptible to proof. Firmer points follow.

Anyone who has raised children – or closely observed the process – can easily understand the logic of dependency ratios. (These are typically expressed as the percentage of those in a total population either too young or too old to work effectively, usually defined as those younger than fifteen or over 65, but sometimes 60.) When small children outnumber adults, it is hard to get anything done except look after the young. Social reproduction crowds out production, and thus inhibits investment and in turn further production. Exactly to what extent this happens is variable and difficult to measure. Today's societies with the highest fertility have dependency ratios of 45–48 per cent. In Tokugawa Japan the ratio was often below 30 per cent and always below 40 per cent (Hanley and Yamamura 1977, 308–10). In England in the late seventeenth century, only 28–31 per cent of the population was younger than fifteen. This was the low point of English fertility (until the twentieth century), but even at its height, in the late eighteenth and early nineteenth centuries, the proportion of those younger than fifteen never came to more than 40 per cent. 'The dependency burden in England in the recorded past was therefore lighter than in traditional societies today' (Wrigley and Schofield 1981, 218–9 and 443–50; see also R. Smith 1981, 608–11). The same was true throughout most of Western Europe, wherever young people were constrained from early marriage and wherever fertility was checked. Japan and Western Europe carried an unusually low burden of dependents.

The advantages of a light dependency ratio for economic growth are simple and straightforward. It permits more production per capita and higher living standards, and opens the door for continuous investment and the accumulation of wealth. Just how much of an economic difference a given discrepancy in dependency ratios makes is a question involving some arithmetic and several assumptions about the economic costs and benefits of children. Suffice it to say that experts agree that age structure is a significant variable affecting economic growth (Spengler 1972; Wrigley and Schofield 1981, 445–50).

Another variable critical to economic growth is the climate for investment, which depends on, among other things, predictability and stability. Risk assessment is highly complex, but other things being equal a more stable economy will enjoy higher levels of investment, as more people will be willing to trust the future. Both Western Europe and Japan had stabler economies than elsewhere, thanks to their marriage patterns and fertility reserves. Or, perhaps better put, their marriage patterns and flexible fertility (and infanticide) rates mitigated the instability in their economies. The key was the self-regulation of population in response to economic change. When times were good, young people could marry and procreate; when times were bad they had to wait – and many had to wait so long as never to procreate at all. In 1776 Adam Smith perceived the relationship: '...[T]he demand for men, like that of any other commodity, necessarily regulates the production of men; quickens it when it goes on too slowly, and stops it when it advances too fast' (Smith 1986, 183).

When landscapes were crowded and niche space rare, the marriage patterns of Western Europe and Japan restrained fertility and population growth. This restraint reduced the probability of subsistence crises resulting from overpopulation, and reduced the pervasiveness of malnutrition and deficiency diseases. The capacity for demographic self-regulation protected these societies from frequent and lengthy experience of unfavourably high ratios of people to resources: that is, overpopulation.

The reserve army of the unmarried also prevented these societies from experiencing unfavourably low ratios: that is, underpopulation. The capacity to self-regulate was especially important in times of great and frequent demographic disruption. Such times, of course, were the norm wherever human numbers depended upon agriculture and wherever settlement was dense enough to permit the circulation of infectious disease. All agrarian societies until the mid-eighteenth century (and most until the twentieth) maintained a modest surplus of births over deaths in most years. The surplus was enough that population might grow by 0.5 or 1.0 per cent per annum. But every few years demographic crises, brought on by epidemics, famine, or war – or combinations of the three – pruned back this growth, with greater or lesser severity. The mortality curves of every parish and village show great spikes, years in which mortality doubled, tripled, or increased tenfold. Indeed, had such catastrophes not repeatedly befallen all agrarian societies, and had annual population growth of 1 per cent proceeded from the dawn of agriculture to the present, the earth would now be encased in a squirming mass of human flesh expanding with a radial velocity many times greater than the speed of light (Cipolla 1962, 89). Brutal and repeated famines, epidemics and wars are the mechanisms which have checked population growth.

Crises may have come more frequently, at least in Europe, in the early modern period than before. The reasons for crises were usually crop failure or epidemic; warfare ran a distant third as a killer. Crop failure led to famine in societies that could not (or did not) transport grain quickly and cheaply. The Little Ice Age (a period of cooler average temperatures, c.1550–1850) probably saw more crop failure than had earlier centuries, although this is hard to substantiate (Grove 1988). Epidemics affected Western Europe most strongly between 1348 and 1722, years that mark the arrival of bubonic plague and its last serious outbreak (it lasted longer in Eastern Europe). These centuries comprise the golden age of pathogens in European (and Asian) history, when a welter of lethal infections returned again and again, before gradually disappearing or becoming domesticated as endemic, childhood diseases. The Little Ice Age and the golden age of pathogens overlapped during the seventeenth century, one of prolonged and repeated economic and demographic crises in most parts of Western Europe. But even in happier centuries, crisis mortality often intruded.

In Japan, crisis mortality was also a regular feature of the early modern demographic regime. Crop failure and famine visited often; perhaps more often with the Little Ice Age, during which Japanese population declined in the chilly north and grew in the warmer south. Epidemics also scythed down millions over the centuries, although they probably played a less conspicuous role in Japan than in Western Europe, chiefly because bubonic plague and typhus seem not to have significantly affected the island country until late in the nineteenth century – the first plague outbreak came only in 1899. Isolation and perhaps effective public health measures account for this good fortune in Tokugawa times (Jannetta 1987, 191–200). In comparison to Western Europe, and to most of the world, Japan enjoyed a benign mortality regime: two of the four horsemen of the apocalypse, war and pestilence, rode but rarely. Nonetheless, famine and the occasional epidemic sufficed to bring crisis mortality to Tokugawa Japan. Nowhere in the civilized world escaped it. Whenever and wherever demographic crisis hit, it radically disrupted the ratio between labour and resources.

Western Europe and Japan were better prepared than the rest of the civilized world to mitigate the disruptive effects. Demographic crises summoned the reserve army of the unmarried to active duty. Crisis mortality opened new niches, which the young rushed to fill. David Hume, writing in 1751, noted the pattern:

> History tells us frequently of plagues, that have swept away the third or fourth part of a people: Yet in a generation or two, the destruction was not perceiv'd; and the society had again acquir'd their former number. The lands, that were cultivated, the houses built, the commodities rais'd, the riches acquir'd, enabled the people who escap'd, immediately to marry, and to rear families, which supply'd the place of those who had perish'd. (Hume 1976, 3)

In a West European demographic crisis that killed 10 per cent of a population, quick recuperation could be achieved if the aging celibates (meaning 23 and older) married the new widows and widowers. A typical crisis brought reduced fertility for ten months, followed by exuberant fertility for two years (Wrigley and Schofield 1981, 359–65). Generally, in the wake of such a demographic crisis, 30–40 per cent of all marriages were remarriages.[15] In a more severe crisis, say 20 per cent mortality, the celibates could fill only half of the emptied niches, and so the young reservists were in effect called up. Age at marriage temporarily declined, and a baby boom followed. A devastating crisis, with 30 per cent mortality (rare but not unknown), would require all females down to the age of fifteen to marry in order to keep the number of families constant. This represents the limits of the possible within the West European system. At most, in a stampede to the altar involving all the available matrimonial stock, fertility could double, as it probably did in France after the Hundred Years' War (Cabourdin 1988; Dupâquier 1988a).

One well-documented example of this demographic resilience comes from Iceland, where in the early eighteenth century climatic disasters and a severe smallpox epidemic drastically reduced population. But not for long. What followed was 'intensive formation of young families, i.e., a drastic fall in the age at marriage and consequently an immediate and explosive growth of the population through the birth rate just after the crisis' (H.O. Hansen, quoted in Hajnal 1982, 478–9).

Japanese society had the same mechanism available to it. Indeed, it could rebound from crises even more quickly. The reserve army, although slightly smaller than the West European one, sprang to action in Japan with equal alacrity. Even if crises hit repeatedly, Japanese communities could accelerate the rate of family formation by lowering the age at marriage, thereby raising fertility. It is suggestive to note that in western Japan, the most prosperous part of the country until late in the nineteenth century, average age at marriage was highest (Hayami 1987, 70).

In addition, surviving couples may well have wished to expand their families in the wake of a demographic crisis. They could do so very quickly, through adoption, a routine practice in Japan. Childless couples often adopted adults and encouraged their marriage so as to perpetuate the family. Alternatively, fertile Japanese families could expand by refraining from abortion and infanticide: they could reduce (intentional) child mortality, which option may well have given Japan a more finely calibrated way of fitting population to niche space than existed through the marriage market in Western Europe. Hayami hints at this capacity for self-regulation in Japan:

> The relationship between age at marriage and economic circumstances was one of mutual interactions. ... On the one hand age at marriage was determined by demand for labor ... in the countryside; on the other hand, because of its regulatory power over population size, age at marriage also shaped economic conditions. (Hayami 1987, 71)

Although the precise mechanisms of post-crisis recovery differed slightly between Japan and Western Europe, the effects of the reserve army of the unmarried were much the same. It quickly made good losses caused by famine or epidemic, and kept the number of households more or less constant. No farms were idle for long, little land fell out of production, and very little societal income was lost: the reserve army stabilized the economy.

The reserve army could also spearhead the exploitation of newly created or discovered resources. In Japan and Western Europe such situations did not arise often, as most good land was already in use by the sixteenth century. But when they did, Japanese and West Europeans could maximize the economic benefit from the occasion, by temporarily accelerating family formation, fertility and population growth. A curious and telling example comes from Norway. In 1808 in Rogaland and Vest-Agder, herring shoals returned after a long absence. By 1815 these districts had the highest proportion of children of any areas in Norway. The herring had suddenly expanded opportunity, allowing young people to marry and reproduce, which they promptly did, leaving no niche unfilled (Drake 1969, 84–5). A similar bonanza occurred on a much larger scale with the colonization and settlement of North America: easily acquired land led to early marriage and fertility much higher than in the West European societies from which the colonists had come. In Japan in the seventeenth century, northern Kyushu was similarly a zone of rapid agricultural and demographic expansion (Kalland and Pedersen 1984, 33).

In societies where opportunity (or its absence) depended as much or more on wages than on the availability of farmsteads or fish, the average age at marriage varied in relation to trends in prices and wages. (Mortality and fertility bore some relation to such trends as well.) England more fully fits this description than anywhere else in Europe. Over 300 years of English history, marriage rates showed a sensitivity to the fluctuations in real wages.[16] In market societies as in subsistence settings, the marriage market and fertility reserve modified the swings of population that irregular mortality imposed.

The West European and Japanese marriage patterns, again through the effect of moderating population fluctuations, conferred an additional advantage on these lands: they mitigated another constraint on economic growth, environmental degradation. Great swings in population density corrode landscapes, especially those most prone to deteriorate, such as steep slopes. A burst of uninterrupted population growth typically obliged communities to bring their marginal lands under the plough (or hoe), normally hill slopes. These lands otherwise would serve as sources of fuel wood, charcoal, construction wood, roots, nuts, berries and more. Under forest, they reduced runoff and the incidence of flood. When cleared for cultivation, hill slopes invited accelerated soil erosion. The connection between land clearing and erosion is the principal mechanism whereby population pressure degrades land.

Equally costly from the environmental point of view was underpopulation. Cultivated landscapes are human artifacts, and require careful and plentiful labour to maintain. Hill slopes, especially when terraced, fall to ruin quickly if neglected, allowing soil erosion to surge with a pent-up fury. Labour shortage, as well as population overabundance, repeatedly led to degradation in landscapes with any potential for soil erosion (Le Roy Ladurie 1974, 15–17; McNeill 1992). Japan's monsoon rains, steep slopes, and extensive terracing make its rural landscape especially vulnerable to soil erosion. The environmental costs of unstable population, while considerable almost everywhere, were especially high in Japan. The importance of moderating population instability, then, was all the greater.[17]

Conclusion

Japan and Western Europe have peculiar trajectories to their economic histories. Over the long haul, and all around the world, most societies have by present standards been poor and have stayed that way (often despite great wealth enjoyed by élites). That they might not remain so indefinitely is an excellent practical reason to investigate just what permitted Western Europe and Japan to escape from permanent poverty.

The argument here – admittedly long on conjecture and short on proof – is that Western Europe and Japan featured family structures, marriage patterns and fertility regimes that allowed them to adjust population to economic conditions. In contrast, all those parts of the world where early marriage and high vital rates prevailed – 'high-pressure demographic regimes' – lacked the mechanisms to adjust fertility to circumstances. In consequence, early modern Western Europe and Tokugawa Japan enjoyed certain advantages from the point of view of fomenting economic growth: a more favourable age structure; and less pronounced population instability. The latter translated into greater economic stability and less grave environmental degradation. Through the sacrifices required of the reserve army of the unmarried – temporary or permanent celibacy – Western Europe and Japan were able (unconsciously) to accelerate capital formation and to create comparatively stable conditions for capital investment, while slowing the degradation of their landscapes. Perhaps family policy lies at the heart of political economy.

Notes

1. See, for example, emphasizing geography and environment, Jones (1981) and Crosby (1986); emphasizing science and technology, Mokyr (1990) and Landes (1969), especially pp. 13–39; emphasizing institutions and politics, North and Thomas (1973), Rosenberg and Birdzell (1986), Hall (1985), and Baechler et al. (1988); emphasizing imperialism and European rapacity, Williams (1944), and more recently, Smith (1991) among many others – see the critique of this position by O'Brien (1985); emphasizing religion and culture, Tawney (1963) and Weber (1958).
2. The economic history of China, the original home of Confucianism, suggests that while a cultural configuration such as Confucianism might conceivably be a necessary condition for sustained economic growth, it is not a sufficient one. The experience of parts of Catholic Europe imply similar qualifications to Weber's argument.
3. In making this argument I shall ride roughshod over the complexities of demographic and family history. I shall ignore exceptions to rules, variations over time and space, and among classes (my remarks are intended to apply only to the 85–95 per cent of populations that worked the land). I shall generalize relentlessly. I apologize to specialists in these fields for the simplifications which they must find oversimplifications; but with broad generalizations I hope to show how useful their work can be in addressing the large questions of world history. A recent guide to some of the complexities is Hareven (1991).
4. The early retirement from childbearing, which also characterized Japan, may have had to do with inadequate nutrition among women.
5. Celibacy here means abstinence from marriage and reproduction, not necessarily from sex. The phrase 'temporary celibacy' is Jacques Dupâquier's (1988a). The willingness of the young (or the necessity) to postpone marriage and reproduction may have led to psychological as well as demographic quirks in West European society. Friction between generations, for instance, may have been more pronounced where the young waited for the old to die or retire. Intergenerational resentment seems more ingrained in Western culture than in China, Africa, or India for example, where the elderly are typically accorded much greater respect and status than in the Western world. Perhaps neglect of the elderly is a result of the warehousing of the young. On such frictions in Japan, and cultural practices that moderated them, see Cornell (1983).
6. Dupâquier (1988b, 2:305); Wrigley and Schofield (1981, 260–62); more recently Wrigley (1988, 31) gives 5–20 per cent as the proportion never marrying for England in the sixteenth through eighteenth centuries; Flinn et al. (1977, 280–81); MacFarlane (1986, 23) gives 10–20 per cent as the proportion of women who never married in Northwestern Europe, as does Flinn (1981, 20), while Schofield (1989, 282) gives 5–10 per cent. On illegitimacy rates, Flinn (1981, 19, 25–6); Wrigley and Schofield (1981, 158); and Laslett et al. (1980). In Japan illegitimacy was not recognized before the Meiji restoration of 1868.
7. This assumes no significant use of birth control. The figures come from Flinn (1981, 25–46). Wrigley (1988, 31) gives 28–35 per thousand for England, c.1570–1770. Unrestricted

fertility, combined with early and universal marriage, produces crude birth rates above 50 per 1000.

8. Stem family households combine three or more generations in the same unit, but not married siblings. At various stages of life, Japanese typically lived in nuclear households that became stem households, then became nuclear households again, as birth, death and marriage changed the household composition.

9. Hanley and Wolf (1985, 5); Hanley (1985, 216–7). T. Smith (1977, 93) found a lower marriage age (18–19 for women), in his case study. So did Hayami and Uchida (1972, 502 and 508) – 20–21 for women. In another village study, Hayami (1985) found that in 1773–1825 women married on average at about age 24, later if they had worked away from home, earlier if not. Smith (1977, 83) admits that his village, which never counted more than 300 people, might be unrepresentative.

10. Unless one counts the tradition of employing wet-nurses as a form of infanticide. Flinn (1981, 39–42) presents data implying that West Europeans knew and intended that a large proportion of their children would die when put out to wet-nurses. Boswell (1988) has scattered information on infanticide in Europe.

11. Irene Taeuber (1958, 28–9), one of the pioneers in Japanese population history, found crude birth rates of 20–30 per thousand, but discounted these as too low to be credible for an agrarian society.

12. In the case of urban and migrant men, the sexual component of this frustration (not the social) was partly assuaged by widespread resort to prostitutes. In many towns, for instance, municipal authorities found it prudent to license houses of prostitution so as to divert the unmarried young men who deeply resented the fact that brides went to older and richer men. Watts (1984, 64); Huppert (1986); Otis (1985).

13. A Japanese proverb counsels: 'Fear earthquake, thunder, fire, and father.' Cited in Cornell (1983, 68).

14. I use the plural because, while they shared certain features, they were far from identical. In Japan, divorce ended about 10 per cent of marriages, much more than in Europe. And the age gap between spouses was also much greater in Japan than in Western Europe.

15. In western Norway in the late eighteenth century widows allegedly had difficulty burying their departed husbands before suitors made themselves known. In one 'well-known' case from Bergen diocese, a man 'whilst paying court to a new widow at the funeral feast of her late husband, learned from her that she had already promised herself to the carpenter who had come to take the measurements for his coffin!' Drake (1969, 136).

16. Wrigley and Schofield (1981, 356–453). Nuptiality followed wages, but with an unexplained lag of 20–30 years. Even in England, real wages were not a precise indicator of niche space.

17. Comparatively prudent forest policy, as well as stable population history, helped Japan to reduce environmental damage (Totman 1989).

References

Baechler, J., Hall, J.A. and Mann, M. (1988), *Europe and the Rise of Capitalism*, Oxford: Basil Blackwell.

Barbagli, M. (1984), *Sotto lo stesso tetto: Mutamenti della famiglia in Italia dal XV al XX secolo*, Bologna: Il Mulino.

Beillevaire, P. (1986), 'Le Japon, une société de la maison', in A. Burguière et al., *Histoire de la famille*, vol. 1, Paris: Armand Colin.

Bloch, M. (1974), *Feudal Society*, 2 vols, Chicago: University of Chicago Press.

Boswell, J. (1988), *The Kindness of Strangers: The Abandonment of Children in Western Europe from Late Antiquity to the Renaissance*, New York: Pantheon.

Byrnes, R.F. (1976), *Communal Families in the Balkans: The Zadruga, Essays by Philip E. Mosely and in His Honor*, South Bend: Notre Dame University Press.

Cabourdin, G. (1988), 'Qu'est-ce que c'est qu'une crise?', in J. Dupâquier et al. (eds), *Histoire de la population française*, vol. 2, Paris: Presse Universitaire de France.

Cipolla, C. (1962), *The Economic History of World Population*, Harmondsworth: Penguin.

Cornell, L.L. (1983), 'Retirement, Inheritance, and Intergenerational Conflict in Preindustrial Japan', *Journal of Family History*, 8.

Cornell, L.L. (1987), 'Hajnal and the Household in Asia: A Comparativist History of the Family in Preindustrial Japan, 1600–1879', *Journal of Family History*, 12.

Cornell, L.L. and Hayami, A. (1986), 'The Shumon Aratame Cho: Japan's Population Registers', *Journal of Family History*, 11.

Crosby, A.W. (1986), *Ecological Imperialism: The Biological Expansion of Europe. 900–1900*, Cambridge: Cambridge University Press.

Drake, M. (1969), *Population and Society in Norway. 1735–1865*, Cambridge: Cambridge University Press.

Dupâquier, J. (1988a), 'L'autorégulation de la population française (XVIe–XVIIIe siècle)', in J. Dupâquier (ed.), *Histoire de la population française*, vol. 2, Paris: Presse Universitaire de France.

Dupâquier, J. (ed.) (1988b), *Histoire de la population française*, 4 vols, Paris: Presse Universitaire de France.

Flinn, M. (1981), *The European Demographic System, 1500–1820*, Baltimore: Johns Hopkins University Press.

Flinn, M. et al. (1977), *Scottish Population History*, Cambridge: Cambridge University Press.

Gaskin, K. (1978), 'Age at First Marriage in Europe before 1850: A Summary of the Family Reconstitution Data', *Journal of Family History*, 3.

Grove, J. (1988), *The Little Ice Age*, London: Routledge.

Hajnal, J. (1965), 'European Marriage Patterns in Perspective', in D.V. Glass and D.E.C. Everseley (eds), *Population in History*, Chicago: Aldine.

Hajnal, J. (1982), 'Two Kinds of Preindustrial Household Formation', *Population and Development Review*, 8.

Hall, J. A. (1985), *Powers and Liberties*, Berkeley: University of California Press.

Hanley, S.B. (1985), 'Family and Fertility in Four Tokugawa Villages', in S.B. Hanley and A.P. Wolf (eds), *Family and Population in East Asian History*, Stanford: Stanford University Press.

Hanley, S.B. and Wolf, A.P. eds. (1985), *Family and Population in East Asian History*, Stanford: Stanford University Press.

Hanley, S. and Yamamura, K. (1977), *Economic and Demographic Change in Preindustrial Japan, 1600–1868*, Princeton: Princeton University Press.

Hareven, T.K. (1991), 'The History of the Family and the Complexity of Social Change', *American Historical Review*, 96.

Hayami, A. (1969), 'Aspects démographiques d'un village japonais, 1671–1871', *Annales: E.S.C.*, 24.

Hayami, A. (1983), 'The Myth of Primogeniture and Impartible Inheritance in Japan', *Journal of Family History*, 8.

Hayami, A. (1985), 'Rural Migration and Fertility in Tokugawa Japan: The Village of Nishijo, 1773–1868,' in S.B. Hanley and A.P. Wolf (eds) *Family and Population in East Asian History*, Stanford: Stanford University Press.

Hayami, A. (1987), 'Another *Fossa Magna*: Proportion Marrying and Age at Marriage in Late Nineteenth-Century Japan', *Journal of Family History*, 12.

Hayami, A. and Uchida, N. (1972), 'Size of Household in a Japanese Country Throughout the Tokugawa Era', in P. Laslett and R. Wall *Household and Family in Past Time*, Cambridge: Cambridge University Press.

Hume, D. (1976), 'Of the Populousness of Antient Nations', in T.R. Malthus *An Essay on the Principle of Population*, ed. P. Appleman, New York: Norton.

Huppert, G. (1986), *After the Black Death: A Social History of Early Modern Europe*, Bloomington: Indiana University Press.

Jannetta, A. (1987), *Epidemics and Mortality in Early Modern Japan*, Princeton: Princeton University Press.

Jones, E.L. (1981), *The European Miracle*, Cambridge: Cambridge University Press.

Kalland, A. and Pedersen, J. (1984), 'Famine and Population in Fukuoka Domain During the Tokugawa Period', *Journal of Japanese Studies*, 10.

Knodel, J. (1988), *Demographic Behavior in the Past*, Cambridge: Cambridge University Press.

Landes, D. (1969), *The Unbound Prometheus: Technological Change and Industrial Development in Western Europe. 1750 to the Present*, Cambridge: Cambridge University Press.

Laslett, P., Oosterveen, K. and Smith, R. (eds) (1980), *Bastardy and Its Comparative History*, Cambridge Mass.: Harvard University Press.

Le Roy Ladurie, E. (1974), *The Peasants of Languedoc*, Urbana: University of Illinois Press.

MacFarlane, A. (1986), *Marriage and Love in England: Modes of Reproduction, 1300–1840*, Oxford: Basil Blackwell.

McNeill, J.R. (1992), *The Mountains of the Mediterranean: An Environmental History*, New York: Cambridge University Press.

Mokyr, J. (1990), *The Lever of Riches: Technological Creativity and Economic Progress*, New York: Oxford University Press.

Nakane, C. (1972), 'An Interpretation of the Size and Structure of the Household in Japan Over Three Centuries', in P. Laslett, and R. Wall, (eds), *Household and Family in Past Time*, Cambridge: Cambridge University Press.

North, D.C. and Thomas, R.P. (1973), *The Rise of the Western World: A New Economic History*, Cambridge: Cambridge University Press.

O'Brien, P. (1985), 'Europe in the World Economy', in H. Bull and A. Watson (eds), *The Expansion of International Society*, Oxford: Clarendon Press.

Osamu, S. (1992), 'Infanticide, Fertility, and "Population Stagnation": The State of Tokugawa Historical Demography', *Japan Forum*, 4.

Otis, L. (1985), *Prostitution in Medieval Society*, Chicago: University of Chicago Press.

Pérez Moreda, V. and Reher, D.S. (eds) (1988), *Demografía histórica en España*, Madrid: El Arquero.

Rosenberg, N. and Birdzell, L.E. (1986), *How the West Grew Rich: The Economic Transformation of the Industrial World*, New York: Basic Books.

Rozman, G. (ed.) (1991), *The East Asian Region: Confucian Heritage and Its Modern Adaptation*, Princeton: Princeton University Press.

Saito, O. (1992), 'Infanticide, Fertility, and "Population Stagnation": The State of Tokugawa Historical Demography', *Japan Forum*, 4, no. 2, 369–81.

Schofield, R.S. (1989), 'Family Structure, Demographic Behavior, and Economic Growth', in J. Walter and R.S. Schofield (eds), *Famine, Disease, and the Social Order in Early Modern Society*, Cambridge: Cambridge University Press.

Schumpeter, J. (1954), *History of Economic Analysis*, New York: Oxford University Press.

Smith, A. (1986), *The Wealth of Nations*, Harmondsworth: Penguin.

Smith, A.K. (1991), *Creating A World Economy: Merchant Capital, Colonialism and World Trade, 1400–1825*, Boulder, Co.: Westview Press.

Smith, R.J. (1972), 'Small Families, Small Households and Residential Instability: Town and Country in "Pre-Modern" Japan', in P. Laslett and R. Wall (eds), *The Household and Family in Past Time*, Cambridge: Cambridge University Press.

Smith, R.M. (1981), 'Fertility, Economy, and Household Formation in England Over Three Centuries', *Population and Development Review*, 7.

Smith, T.C. (1977), *Nakahara: Family Farming and Population in a Japanese Village 1717–1830*, Stanford: Stanford University Press.

Spengler, J.J. (1972), 'Demographic Factors and Early Modern Economic Development', in D.V. Glass and R. Revelle (eds), *Population and Social Change*, London: Edward Arnold.

Taeuber, I. (1958), *The Population of Japan*, Princeton: Princeton University Press.

Tai H.-C. (ed.) (1989), *Confucianism and Economic Development*, Washington, DC: Washington Institute Press.

Tawney, R.H. (1963), *Religion and the Rise of Capitalism*, New York: Mentor.

Todorova, M.N. (1993), *Balkan Family Structure and the European Pattern*, Washington, DC: American University Press.

Totman, C. (1989), *The Green Archipelago*, Berkeley: University of California Press.

Vogel, E. (1992), *The Four Little Dragons: The Spread of Industrialization in East Asia*, Cambridge Mass.: Harvard University Press.

Watts, S. (1984), *A Social History of Western Europe, 1450–1720*, London: Hutchinson.

Weber, M. (1958), *The Protestant Ethic and the Spirit of Capitalism*, New York: Scribner.
Williams, E. (1944), *Capitalism and Slavery*, Chapel Hill: University of North Carolina Press.
Wrigley, E.A. (1988), *Continuity, Chance and Change: The Character of the Industrial Revolution in England*, Cambridge: Cambridge University Press.
Wrigley, E.A. and Schofield, R.S. (1981), *The Population History of England, 1541–1871*, Cambridge Mass.: Harvard University Press.

3   The roots of Latin America's backwardness

Werner Baer and Joseph L. Love

Although many Latin American countries underwent major structural transformations in the second half of the twentieth century, as evidenced by their
rapid urbanization and industrialization, their per capita incomes remained
low when compared to the advanced industrial nations, and with the possible
exception of Chile, they have not been able to produce the recent dynamism
of some Asian countries (especially South Korea and Taiwan). An additional
characteristic of the region has been the very high concentration of income
and wealth, which has persisted from colonial times to the present. Yet Latin
America hardly stagnated: in 1991 only Haiti, Nicaragua and Honduras ranked
in the lowest of the World Bank's four tiers of per capita GNP, and five
countries – in ascending order, Brazil, Venezuela, Uruguay, Mexico and
Argentina – were in the 'upper middle income' group.[1] Revised data for Chile
place it in the same category (World Bank 1994, 163, note c).

Because of the enormous scope of the period and region under discussion,
we shall confine our examination to the largest countries, Brazil, Mexico and
Argentina, plus Chile, which together were the most industrialized nations by
the early twentieth century, and remained so later. By 1992 all four were in
the top 40 per cent of GNP per capita of the 132 countries surveyed by the
World Bank in the latest *World Development Report* (1994, 162–3).

In this paper we shall assess to what extent the colonial experience, the
nature of the nineteenth-century export-oriented experience, and the way
various countries tried to catch up with the West by industrializing, explain
Latin America's relative backwardness. In our analysis we shall also attempt
to determine the extent to which this condition was externally imposed, i.e.
determined by foreign investment patterns and inducements to engage in
certain types of trade, and to what extent the backwardness was due to
internal socioeconomic factors.

The colonial inheritance

Latin America did not share the relatively egalitarian frontier experience
associated with the advance of Western settlement in the US and the British
Dominions. In Meso-America and the Andes sedentary and hierarchical in-
digenous societies were conquered by a patrimonial and legalistic regime in
Spain. The latter easily imposed its own hierarchical structure on the former.
With the early discovery of precious metals, the main interest of the Spanish

Crown in administering the colonies was to maximize their exploitation; this aim was achieved through colonial–mercantilist policies which minimized investments in infrastructure and the development of human capital. For native-born individuals, including the offspring of Spaniards, access to the highest administrative positions during the colonial regime was sharply restricted, and the best positions in commerce were held by Spanish and peninsula-connected families. The creole élites (i.e. native-born whites) therefore dedicated their efforts to exploiting agricultural labour by extra-economic means, and by the seventeenth century to acquiring large rural properties, which were not efficiently exploited. As domestic markets were small (given the low income of the rural masses), there was little incentive to invest in non-plantation agriculture. The rural élites, often being absentee owners living in towns, used their influence and income to acquire more properties, and spent a considerable share of their resources on sumptuary consumption. They were commonly indebted to merchants, who provided the only credit available for agriculture, often at usurious rates.[2]

Portuguese America (Brazil) had no significant sedentary native population, and Europeans initially found no precious metals there; Brazil was a backwater in an empire that had its most profitable colonies – most of them simply trading entrepôts – in Asia. Brazil's lack of importance resulted in a loose administrative organization of Portugal's New World colony. Sugar, the first major primary export product, was based on the direct entrepreneurial activities of landlords. This did not lead to long-term economic development, however, as sugar production was based on slave labour, using primitive technologies, which fell behind West Indian colonies by the seventeenth century. The discovery of gold in Minas Gerais at the end of that century led to a new export cycle and tended to shift economic activities from north-eastern to south-central Brazil. An indicator of the colony's new economic significance to its metropolis is the fact that the Portuguese Crown named its first Brazilian viceroy in 1720, whereas its first Indian viceroy had been appointed two hundred years earlier. But the gold boom had a negative developmental impact on Brazil, in that Portuguese authorities imposed strict mercantilistic controls over its newly rich colony. Such controls were designed to make the colony as dependent as possible on the metropolis in the later eighteenth century; manufacturing was prohibited in 1785, shutting down a not inconsiderable wrought-iron industry. Meanwhile the 'accumulation' of human capital was presumably lower than that of Spanish America, as Portugal denied Brazil both universities and printing presses, both of which institutions Spain had established in Mexico and Peru in the sixteenth century.[3]

Economic setback in the first decades of independence

Conditions of most Latin American countries in the early years of independence were not propitious for economic growth. Much of Spanish America had suffered from the destruction caused by the wars of independence – parts of Mexico, Uruguay and Venezuela were devastated. On achieving independence in the 1820s, Latin American states found themselves heavily dependent on the British government for recognition and a guarantee of their independence, and on British merchants for overseas trade.[4] These merchants took over the commodity trade by first extending credit to local producers in the early years of independence (Halperín-Donghi 1973, 49). In Mexico, per capita income, which had probably fallen in the years 1810–21 because of the civil wars and breakdown of the mining 'motor', did not recover the level of the 1830s for more than a generation, owing to continuing civil disturbances. In most of Spanish America the lack of agreement about the political 'rules of the game', the inability to pay armies and bureaucracies, and the breakdown of the mercantilist economies based on mining and plantation complexes resulted in a quarter-century or more of alternating moments of tyranny and anarchy. Unfortunately, Latin Americans had no experience in self-government, and the only colonial parliament ever to sit in the region did so during the Dutch occupation of Pernambuco (1630–54). From an economic perspective, the first four or more decades after independence were *una larga espera*, a long wait.[5] Even in Brazil, where the legitimacy of the imperial regime, continuing the Bragança line, was less frequently challenged, per capita income tended to stagnate in the nineteenth century, as foreign trade disrupted handicraft industries and dislodged local merchants; in Mexico, growth in per capita income was not sustained from one decade to the next until after 1900 (Coatsworth 1978, 82; Contador and Haddad 1975, 412).

The incapacity to achieve a trade surplus which would have enabled the countries to service the debt contracted in the 1820s forced most to default. This gave the region a reputation as a major credit risk, which kept international investment from flowing in. The availability of foreign credit would only rise dramatically in the last decades of the nineteenth century.

As Britain was Latin America's main creditor and political guarantor of independence, it insisted on favoured access to its markets. The region was swamped by British manufactured products, which both destroyed the existing industrial artisan sector and delayed the appearance of domestic industries. The emergence of the region's specialization in the export of primary products was in part imposed by Britain. If in the 1990s it is widely believed that growth and trade are closely linked, free trade and growth were not universally associated in the nineteenth century, when British and other European wares destroyed artisan industries in Latin America and elsewhere in the Third World. Before 1870–90, when several countries began to adopt policies of industrial protection, there was extensive deindustrialization in Latin America, especially in the textile industry.[6] The pattern for the commercial treaties was set by Lord Strangford in 1810, when Britain imposed a treaty on the Portuguese court, then resident in Brazil, which allowed British goods to enter the colony at a *lower* customs rate than that for Portuguese goods – and this twelve years before Brazilian independence. Nonetheless, we do not hold with those who believe that proto-industrialization, such as that of Paraguay from 1811 to 1870, could have transformed the Latin American countries into modern industrial states, if for no other reasons than the North Atlantic monopoly on rapidly evolving industrial technology and countless opportunities for smuggling.[7]

Most governments of newly independent Latin American countries were in the hands of the rural élites, which used their power to increase their landholdings at the expense of corporate bodies – first the Church and its constituent institutions, and subsequently, especially in the last quarter of the century, indigenous communities and other peasant populations. Thus the latifundium was a dynamic phenomenon, and land concentration occurred on economic frontiers as well as in areas of settled peasant populations. There was continual rise in the concentration of property and income, a process characteristic of most of the region's countries until the middle of the twentieth century or later. Given this concentration, the domestic market grew slowly, since there were few incentives to invest in sectors based on such a market.

Primary export-led growth after 1850

The rapid expansion of world trade in the second half of the nineteenth century had a notable impact on Latin America. The economies of most countries in the region became geared to the exportation of a small number of primary products – cereals and meat in the case of Argentina; coffee in Brazil; nitrates, followed by copper, for Chile; silver and various minerals in the case of Mexico. As long as the industrializing countries of Europe, and later the US, were growing rapidly, there was a strong world demand for the primary and food products that Latin American countries were exporting. The rapid growth of these export economies also attracted large capital inflows in the form of both direct investments and loans, at first mainly from Britain, but later also from France, Germany and the US. The role of most of the capital inflows was to increase the efficiency of the economies' export orientation. It was directed at the construction of railroad networks designed to bring primary products from the interior to the ports more rapidly and efficiently; mining operations (in the Andean countries and Mexico); plantations (in Central America and the coasts of Colombia and Peru); and meat-packing plants (in Argentina). Foreign capital was also invested in financial and commercial establishments to handle foreign trade and public utilities (such as power generation and distribution, the telephone systems, and urban public transportation in the main cities).[8]

It was the last quarter of the century which witnessed a real transformation of the region's export economies. The so-called second industrial revolution, associated with technological change in the production of capital goods and with the application of science to industry, brought unprecedented investment, technological innovations (steam ships driven by screw propellers, railroads made of Bessemer steel, refrigeration, barbed-wire fencing), and above all a huge new demand for capital goods inputs (e.g. copper, rubber) and consumer goods (e.g. sugar, wheat, beef, coffee).

The growth of this period, however, tended not to be developmental in nature. The benefits of the primary export economies accrued mainly to a small number of groups – large landowners, foreign owners of mines and plantations, the owners of public utilities, and a small professional class of government bureaucrats and lawyers. Much of the population continued to live at a subsistence level and little was spent on developing human capital through schooling, though Argentina was an exception: it had a rate of literacy roughly three times that of Brazil, for example, at the fall of the Brazilian monarchy in 1889.[9]

The export-led growth of the nineteenth century made the Latin American economies extremely 'dependent'. Imports consisted of foreign manufactured consumption and capital goods, while two or three primary products usually accounted for most export earnings. In an extreme case Brazil, a country covering half the South American continent, earned in the late 1920s three-quarters of its foreign exchange from a single export, coffee. Thus the Latin American economies became overly exposed to economic cycles emanating from the industrial countries, and were unable to counteract the impact of such cycles.

In the years from independence down to the Great Depression, Latin America was subject to three Kondratieff waves. The first was unfortunately timed, because the London stock market crash occurred in 1825, just as some Latin American governments were seeking foreign loans to rebuild their shattered mercantilist economies (Hernández y Sánchez-Barba 1971, 225). Others such as Argentina, however, had already contracted loans and were now defaulting. In fact, except for the years 1823–24, Spanish and Portuguese America received very modest amounts of European investment during the first half of the nineteenth century. The period 1825–50, when such investment might have occurred, roughly corresponds to the 'B' (downswing) phase of the Kondratieff wave. For a variety of reasons, of which the lack of foreign funding was probably second only to political disorder, Latin America experienced little economic growth in those years (Halperín-Donghi 1985, 304).

Chile established a stable constitutional regime in 1833, and was widely admired in Spanish America for its stability. Brazil had done so earlier (1824), but only overcame the fissiparous tendencies of its agrarian élites after 1848. Mexico and Argentina would not know stable regimes until the 1860s. Many exports which helped to make stable polities possible had their origins in the colonial period, but new ones developed in the middle decades of the nineteenth century in response to Europe's industrial and consumer needs.

Yet it was the last quarter of the century, as indicated above, which witnessed a real transformation of the region's export economies, responding to the second industrial revolution. In terms of sheer growth, the region benefited immensely more from the second Kondratieff cycle, peaking in 1870–73, than from the first; in fact, Latin America continued to receive significant amounts of foreign investment through the long depression of 1873–96. The region apparently received its largest nineteenth-century investment by decade in the 1880s, partly as a result of a strong expansion of the primary goods trade (Mörner 1977, 459–60; cf. Suter 1994, 14). Yet Latin America was integrated into the European economy at the price of consolidation of the latifundium and monocultural dependence on the world market.[10]

The transformation and dynamization of the Latin American economies occurred at different times in the histories of the national states, depending on the export commodities involved and the relative success of state building. State formation and consolidation, including the legitimation of the state for the relevant political actors, tended to secure property rights and limit transactions costs, and consequently was a necessary condition for foreign investment. Chile's Portalean State of 1833 consolidated the power of a merchant–landlord élite, and Chile was affected by overseas demand as early as the 1850s (copper exports to Europe, wheat to California). Argentina and Brazil followed in the 1860s. But the period 1870–90 provided a much more rapid ascent. These three countries, plus Mexico, now felt the full impact of the combined effects of the European economic expansion which, in the Argentine and Brazilian cases, brought in its train unprecedented levels of European immigration.

Argentina is the best exemplar of these processes. It was created as a nation – in the sense of definitively bringing the national territory under a single regime – in the third quarter of the nineteenth century. Formal political unity was achieved in 1859–61, with the accession of Buenos Aires Province to the Argentine Federation. But the governance issue was only resolved in the following two decades, with the closing of the Indian frontier in Patagonia; the suppression of the last regional revolt; and the creation of a federal district, separating the city of Buenos Aires from the province of the same name (1880).

Argentina's economic growth was spectacular. On average, exports increased 5 per cent a year between 1875 and 1914, both by quantum and by value. From 1.6 million kilos of wool in 1840, Argentina was exporting 211 million kilos per annum by the later 1890s (peak years). Profiting from the invention of refrigerated shipping, Argentina began to export frozen beef in 1894, sending abroad 328 000 tons in 1914, in which year chilled beef (a higher-grade commodity not produced in 1894) accounted for 41 000 tons. Overseas sales of canned meat in the same interval expanded ten times. Meanwhile wheat exports increased 23 times in value from 1880–84 to 1890–94. Transatlantic sales of both wheat and maize rose so rapidly that they had replaced beef as the chief exports by value on the eve of the First World War (Glade 1969, 10–11). In the words of Carlos Díaz Alejandro, 'From 1860 to 1930 Argentina grew at a rate that has few parallels in economic history, perhaps comparable only to the performance during the same period of other countries of recent settlement.'[11]

Other countries were less completely transformed than was Argentina, with the debatable exception of its small neighbour, Uruguay; but the three others treated here – Brazil, Chile and Mexico – were all profoundly affected by the forces we associate with the second industrial revolution and the age of imperialism. Brazil's gross domestic product, for example, grew at a faster annual rate (2.5 per cent) than did those of developed countries between 1920 and 1929 (Dean 1986, 685).

Land tenure patterns changed in response to international demand, and it is abundantly clear that estate owners were generally responsive to price signals (Leff 1982, 43–51; Jacobsen 1984, 488–9). The first victim of estate owners' land hunger after 1850 was the Church, controlling as much as a third of the rural real estate in early nineteenth-century Mexico. One historian has remarked in this regard that the greatest service of the state to the landowning class was the forced sale of Church property – though this was much more important in Mexico than in the three other countries considered here (Bauer 1986, 177). Yet peasants suffered too: even in remote Andean villages, peasants began to lose their land as high prices for sheep and alpaca wool brought about a diminution of peasant holdings (Jacobsen 1984, 489). Estate owners in Chile began to engross peasant lands in the 1850s and 1860s.[12] In Argentina, the latifundium arose in the nineteenth century, despite an open frontier stretching southward by the 1880s to Patagonia; likewise, the rise of the large plantation in São Paulo, Brazil, was a product of the nineteenth, and even the twentieth, centuries. In Brazil's census of 1920, only 3 per cent of the rural population owned land (although others were squatters), and of that landowning group, 10 per cent owned three-quarters of the rural property (Dean 1986, 702). In Mexico, the *hacienda* had its origins in the seventeenth century, but the Mexican Revolution of 1910 had as one principal source the vast and unprecedented alienation of community lands by *latifundistas* during the dictatorship of Porfirio Díaz (1876–1911). For Spanish America as a whole, Bauer remarks that the rural population 'probably underwent a greater change [in 1870–1930] than at any previous time ... except for the conquest....' (Bauer 1986, 185).

Labour systems associated with the export boom varied widely, but often involved coercive elements. In the case of Brazil (led by the dynamic province of São Paulo), the coffee economy bid away thousands of slaves from other provinces in the 1860s and 1870s; in the 1880s slavery gave way to European immigrant labour based on a unique mix of wages, free housing and usufruct. Elsewhere in Brazil the condition of rural labour was considerably worse, and lower classes resident on latifundia sometimes toiled in conditions resembling serfdom, rendering traditional services, including the *corvée* and the *cambão* (personal services in exchange for usufruct).[13] In Argentina, when the 'Mesopotamian' region north of Buenos Aires became one of the world's great wheat granaries, the land was subdivided and leased to Italian tenant farmers. In the Argentine case, and to a lesser extent in southern Brazil, there was a low labour-to-land ratio that resulted in relatively high rural wages.

In Chile, a rising demand for labour in the wheat-farming area of the Central Valley coupled with the expansion of large estates led to a worsening of the peasants' lot in tenancy arrangements (*inquilinaje*) in wheat farming because of land monopolization, and also increased proletarianization of the *inquilinos* and other peasants (Kay 1980, 76). Mexico had perhaps the largest variety of labour systems by the turn of the century, including illegal but *de facto* slavery for the Yaqui and Maya Indians, instances of debt servitude, share cropping, and in some places rural wage labour and tenancy (Katz 1974, 1–47). Vagrancy laws forced the proletarianization of Indians and mestizo peasants in Central America and parts of Mexico. In Argentina such laws were important in remote Tucumán, but also on the pampa, where the vanishing gaucho encountered similar legislation (Glade 1969, 37; Slatta 1983, 106–25).

Thus Latin American rural labour systems became much more highly differentiated as a result of the transformations after 1870. Whereas '...parts of Latin America, like Eastern Europe, experienced a sort of second enfeudation with the spread of a capitalist market...' (Glade 1969, 38), the immigrant-populated wheat regions of Argentina and the coffee regions of Brazil had modern labour and tenancy systems. A great contrast existed between the rural labour systems of Chile and Argentina, despite their common export booms in wheat (though the timing and markets were different), and despite Chile's impressive advances in manufacturing (see below). In Chile, the man–land ratio was considerably higher than in Argentina, the latifundist élite probably more unified, and land rents less differentiated. The last-named element was related to the striking differences between the relative independence of South European immigrants (many of whom were literate) in Argentina, and the dependent *inquilinos* in Chile, where deference to the landlords was demanded and rendered. In the view of one student, Chile followed the 'Junker route' to agricultural capitalism in the nineteenth century. Chile's rural society, it is argued, was close to *Gutswirtschaft*, while Argentina approximated *Grundherrschaft*, with its widespread rural leasing, despite a relative concentration of rural property ownership (Kay 1980, 20, 45–6; Laclau 1969, 300–308).

The nature of the process of production during and after this period is the subject of much controversy today. Those who defend a 'feudal' interpretation of the production system usually have in mind *manorialism*, which, as Marc Bloch pointed out, antedated feudalism and survived its demise (1961, I, 279; II, 442). The *hacienda* of this period is sometimes seen as poised between two worlds – the inner one of dependency and even extra-economic coercion of the labour force, and the outer one recognizably capitalistic in its response to world markets (Bartra et al. 1976, 81).

Why didn't the Latin American primary-exporting countries industrialize and diversify their economies the way the US did, after having been a primary exporter? Most Latin American countries did not experience mass immigration, which in the case of the US provided the manpower to settle the vast agricultural regions of the Midwest. The Homestead Act of 1862 also resulted in a fairly equitable distribution of the income generated by agriculture. Such income flows provided a mass market, which set the stage for the industrialization in the last years of the nineteenth century and the first decades of the twentieth century.

In Latin America, the wealth created by the primary export sector was very unevenly distributed and, given the poverty of the rural masses and thus a limited market for manufactured products, the beneficiaries of these economies (foreign investors, local landowners, and the commercial–financial establishments related to the export sector) tended to invest their capital in rural estates, commerce and foreign assets.[14] In rural areas, frontier expansion was not accompanied by enforceable Homestead Acts; rather, the latifundium was a dynamic phenomenon. In the Brazilian case, ongoing land monopolization was still observable in our own era (e.g. Souza Martins 1981 and Foweraker 1980).

There were exceptions to this picture, especially in Argentina and southern Brazil, which experienced a substantial amount of European immigration in the 1890s and the first three decades of the twentieth century. Industrial growth accompanied urbanization and immigration from the 1890s in Argentina and Brazil, and sustained industrialization seems to have begun in Chile in the 1870s.[15] In Argentina and southern Brazil immigrants provided a local market which was attractive enough to invest in textiles and food products (Gallo 1970, 49, 50, 53, 60; Dean 1969, 52) Immigrant income was heavily dependent on access to land – titles to small plots in Santa Caterina and Rio Grande do Sul, Brazil, and leases in Santa Fe, Argentina. Even in Mexico, which did not significantly benefit from immigration, urbanization and export wealth laid the basis for a national market.[16]

Yet these developments were not weighty enough to counterbalance the structure of the primary export economies. In Argentina, landowners' preference for leasing rather than selling property to immigrant settlers, combined with the absence of credit for small farmers, led to the preservation of the latifundium in wheat-farming areas as well as poor conservation policies; such experience contrasted unfavourably with that of the prairie provinces of Canada (Solberg 1987, 60–67, 142–3). In Brazil, a landowning peasantry had existed from the nineteenth century in parts of the three southernmost provinces, and the Great Depression brought about a new class of smallholders in São Paulo as coffee *fazendeiros* parcelled out their bankrupt estates (Holloway 1980, Ch. 6).

Generally speaking, however, international capital viewed late nineteenth- and early twentieth-century Latin America as one of the world's major suppliers of primary products, and its operations in the regions strengthened this specialization and land monopolization. The local oligarchies readily accepted the thesis of comparative advantage and acted accordingly, entering the 'commodity lottery' with enthusiasm.

The First World War, however, caused serious disruptions in the Latin American export economy. Grave problems followed the war in certain commodity markets, but the export boom continued in phase with the third Kondratieff wave. A major structural shift in the postwar era was the growing displacement of Britain by the US as chief lender and investor. Britain exacerbated its problems in the region by overvaluing the pound through deliberate deflation. In any case, US advances resulting from the war were evident everywhere. For instance, the Americans sent 3.5 times as many exports (by value) to Mexico as the British did in 1913, and the ratio was 10 to 1 by 1927. Great Britain led the US in the other three countries considered here in 1913, but by 1927 the latter had dislodged Britain as the leading trading partner in Chile and Brazil; and in Argentina, Britain clung to its lead by a single percentage point (Thorp 1986, 66; Suter 1994, 15). Though Great Britain's overall capital investments in the region were still larger in 1929, the US had far outstripped Britain in its postwar lending, both direct and indirect.

Import substitution industrialization (ISI)

The general absence of theoretical foundations for industrial development notwithstanding, Argentina, Brazil and Chile had made rapid industrial advances during the 1920s, in part through foreign investment in the peak years of the third Kondratieff wave. But after 1929 they faced a sustained crisis in export markets (the dollar value of Argentina's exports in 1933, for example, was one-third the 1929 figure); and despite the importance of industrialization in the 1920s, the following decade can still be understood as a period of significant structural and institutional change. In Argentina, Brazil, Chile and Mexico, convertibility and the gold standard were abandoned early in the Depression. The rise in the prices of importables, because of a fall in the terms of trade and exchange devaluation, encouraged the substitution of domestic manufactures for imported goods, as did expansionary fiscal and monetary policies. By 1935 a North American economist would hazard that 'There is probably no major section of the world in which there is a greater industrial activity relative to pre-depression years than in temperate South America', i.e. Argentina, southern Brazil, and Chile (Phelps 1935, 281). When war came in 1939, manufactures in international trade became scarce again, permitting further industrialization to the extent that capital goods, fuel and raw materials were available.

During the 1930s spokesmen for industry probably grew bolder, except perhaps those Brazilians who had initially followed the Rumanian trade theorist Mihaïl Manoilescu.[17] Note, for example, the themes chosen by Luis Colombo, the president of Argentina's Union Industrial Argentina: in 1931, he supported a moderate and 'rational' protectionism, and defended the manufacturers against the charge of promoting policies inimical to the interests of Argentine consumers; in 1933, he even-handedly justified protection for both industry and agriculture; and by 1940 he was attacking the industrial countries as having themselves violated the rules of the international division of labour by developing large agricultural establishments, only choosing to buy abroad when convenient (*Anales* 1931, 25, 27; 1933, 37; *Argentina Fabril* 1940, 3). Industrialists pointed to the vulnerability of export economies, which they more frequently dubbed 'colonial' than before. Gathering war clouds in Europe added another argument: domestic industries were necessary for an adequate national defence.[18] A basic characteristic of the period 1930–45 was an intensification of state intervention in the economy, in Latin America as elsewhere, and industrialists like other economic groups sought state assistance; they asked for subsidies, credits and increased tariff protection. The state should, they argued, aid in 'economic rationalization', i.e. cartelization, a theme of European industrialists in the 1930s (Alvarez Andrews 1936, 327–8, 385; Pupo Nogueira 1945, 18; 'Industrialización' 1945, 6).

In Argentina, Brazil, Chile and Mexico, governments began to heed the importuning of manufacturers. State aid to industry in the form of development loans tended to converge in the early years of the war. The establishment of industrial development banks was an important symbolic act, but changes in tariff structures, which have not so far been thoroughly analysed, may have been more important for growth.

The reasons for such a shift by governments are clear in retrospect: a decade of wrestling with the intractable problem of reviving traditional export markets; the relative unavailability of foreign industrial goods over virtually a fifteen-year period (1930–45); and the fact that states (and particularly the officer corps) as well as industrialists began to consider the relation between manufacturing and national defence – a process that had already begun in Chile in the late 1920s. Governments, however, moved hesitantly and inconsistently toward addressing the problems of industry. In Argentina, Luis Duhau, the minister of agriculture, in 1933 proclaimed the necessity of producing industrial goods that could no longer be imported (for lack of foreign exchange), and he pledged his government's support for the process ('Argentine Industrial Exhibition' 1933, 11, 13, 15). But in the same month the Argentine government supported the US initiative for general tariff reductions at the Pan American Union Conference in Montevideo. Earlier that year Argentina had yielded to British pressure in the Roca–Runciman pact, a trade agreement favouring British manufactures in the Argentine market in exchange for a share of the British beef market for Argentina. As late as 1940, Finance Minister Pinedo's plan for the economic development of Argentina still distinguished between 'natural' and 'artificial' industries, implying that industrial development would occur in concert with the needs of the agricultural and pastoral sectors. By the time of the colonels' coup in June 1943, intervention for industrial development had become state policy, and an industrial development bank was created in 1944. Yet even at that point support for manufacturing was far from unrestrained: the ministry of agriculture still housed the department of industry, and the minister assured Argentineans that the development of manufacturing would not threaten, but would contribute to the growth of, the country's 'mother industries', stock raising and agriculture (Masón 1944, 5–6). In the next few years, however, the Perón government would demonstrably put the interests of industrialists above those of ranchers and farmers.

In Brazil, Getúlio Vargas favoured industry – was he not the friend of all established economic interests? – but he had opposed 'artificial' industries (manufacturing) in his presidential campaign in 1930. Government loans to 'artificial' industries were still prohibited in 1937. Osvaldo Aranha, Vargas's minister of finance in 1933, even termed industries 'fictitious' if they did not use at least 70 per cent domestic raw materials (Vargas 1938; *O Estado*

1933). Vargas only became committed to rapid industrial expansion during his Estado Nôvo dictatorship (1937–45). Although he said in 1939 that he would not accept the idea of Brazil's remaining a 'semi-colonial' economy, as late as 1940, when the coffee market was still depressed after a decade of attempts to revive it, Vargas wanted to 'balance' industrial and agricultural growth. In 1941 a division for industrial development of the Bank of Brazil began to make significant loans, but from 1941 through 1945 the bank only disbursed an annual average of 17.5 per cent of its private sector loans to manufacturing concerns (Vargas 1940, 91; 1941, 179; Villela 1973, 352). Nonetheless, in the 1940s the government showed a commitment to industrialization by obtaining support from the Roosevelt administration for a state-operated steel complex at Volta Redonda, Rio de Janeiro. The mills opened in 1946 as Latin America's largest steel plant.

In Mexico, industrialization in the 1930s made impressive advances even while agrarian reform was at the top of Lázaro Cárdenas's agenda. It was not, however, the result of government policy. Nacional Financiera, a partly government-owned development bank, had been established in 1934, but only became seriously committed to manufacturing after its reorganization at the end of 1940, when the new pro-industry administration of Avila Camacho took office. During the Second World War, the pace quickened (Haber 1989, 176–7; Villareal 1976, 43–5; Izquierdo 1964, 243; Navarrete R. 1967, 119; Ramírez 1986, 62–7). In Chile, nominal government support for industrial development began with the creation of an institute of industrial credit in 1928. Ten years later the Popular Front government of Pedro Aguirre Cerda established CORFO, the government development corporation. But in 1940 the sum budgeted for the development of manufacturing was less than each of those for agriculture, mining, energy and public housing (Presidente 1940, 21–2, 95).

The somewhat 'unintended' industrialization of the larger Latin American countries and a partial acceptance of it by the United States government was reflected at the Chapultepec conference of the Pan American Union (1945). The meeting's resolutions gave a qualified benediction to the industrialization process in Latin America ('Industrialización' 1945, 30). At the end of war, therefore, it was clear that industrialization had greatly advanced in the region.

Thus ISI as a government policy began hesitantly in the later 1930s, *faute de mieux*, in the absence of sufficient foreign exchange to buy foreign manufactures. Explicit in the 1949 *Survey* by the UN Economic Commission for Latin America (ECLA) was the thesis that industrialization in Latin America had historically occurred in periods of world crisis; that is, ECLA viewed development as occurring through the agency of 'external shocks', in Celso Furtado's phrase.[19] For the Brazilian case, Furtado pointed to rapid industrial growth in the Depression, partly due to 'the socialization of losses' through exchange devaluation, which nonetheless helped maintain domestic demand.[20] In Brazil, Furtado viewed expansionary fiscal and monetary policies for the coffee industry during the Depression as a form of unwitting Keynesianism. Yet as a 'spontaneous' process ISI had already begun during the nineteenth century in the four countries examined here, and it had accelerated in the years before the First World War. The level of technology was generally behind that of the developed countries, but Mexico, close to capital markets and sources of equipment, was an exception.[21] In any event, industrialization, it is now understood, was especially dynamic in the 1920s; so much so that the 1920s rather than the 1930s are now viewed as the critical moment of industrial development.[22] A now widely held view is that investment in industry (capacity) grew in line with export earnings for the period 1900–45, while output (but not capacity) tended to rise during the 'shocks', when imports had to be curtailed. Capacity could not grow appreciably during the Depression for lack of exchange credits to buy capital goods and inputs, nor during the world wars because of the unavailability of capital goods and fuels from the belligerent powers.[23]

At any rate ISI accelerated in the 1930s, and foreign exchange earnings facilitated the process, contrary to the original 'external shocks' theory.[24] ISI, which intensified in the first two decades after the Second World War, was supposed to provide for its defenders a base for rapid economic development through the establishment of a diversified economic structure. In addition, it was supposed to arrest the transfer of resources from Latin America to advanced industrial countries by counteracting the decline of the terms of trade.[25]

The strategy consisted of protection, attraction of foreign investments to manufacturing, stimulation of local manufacturing enterprises, creation of complementary state enterprises, and the establishment of development banks. The immediate success of postwar ISI was found in its stimulation of periods of high rates of growth, in the changed structure of the economy – that is, the growing share of industry in GDP – and in the creation of a skilled labour force. In the initial decades of ISI (varying with the country at issue), manufacturing, industrial employment, and per capita income tended to expand briskly.

The way ISI was actually implemented was censured by ECLA, which had originally championed ISI. In 1963, Raúl Prebisch, the outgoing executive secretary of ECLA, denounced the actual pattern of industrialization in Latin America, pointing out that the exaggerated pattern of protection had allowed grossly inefficient industries to arise. Latin America had, on average, the highest tariffs in the world, depriving it of economies of scale and opportunities to specialize for export (Prebisch 1963, 71). Given the small size of national markets, as early as 1959 ECLA had also championed the development of a Latin American common market, but such efforts at integration would only bear fruit over the next several decades. In retrospect, in articulating a theory and implicit ideology in favour of ISI and then pointing the way to correcting its excesses, ECLA may have had the right policies but an inadequate instrument for their execution: for ECLA, the national state was the vehicle of reform, and perhaps the agency put too great a faith in the capacity of the state to implement disinterested policies. The patrimonial residues in modern Latin American 'stateness' are significant. Gunnar Myrdal's notion of the 'soft state', (1970, 208–52) whose principal capacity is the employment of functionaries, should make us wary of inferring that the state's failure to implement the projects of powerful economic interests necessarily results from any competing development programme of politicians or bureaucrats. In addition, ECLA implicitly placed its faith in Latin America's national bourgeoisies, and several sociological studies conducted in the mid-1960s revealed scepticism about the ability of such groups to take charge of their national states at the expense of traditional landed and commercial groups (F. Cardoso 1964; 1966, 147; 1971 [data collected in 1963, 1965–66] 1, 103, 146, 158, 215; Cuneo 1967, 129, 172, 192; Véliz 1965, 7–8). Such considerations, along with the stuttering process of import substitution and the new prominence of multinational corporations, paved the way for dependency analysis. Did the Latin American nations have 'soft bourgeoisies' as well as 'soft states'?

At any rate, the way in which ISI was carried out had serious negative consequences. The cost structure of most industries was high because of low labour productivity and, given the small market, the lack of economies of scale. In Argentina, Brazil, Chile and Mexico, for two decades little attention was paid to diversifying exports and, given overvalued exchange rates, even traditional exports were placed at a disadvantage. Most disappointingly, ISI did not provide the jobs needed to effectively employ the rapidly growing urban population. The Latin American problem in recent decades was compounded not only by the world's highest regional rate of population growth in the 1950s and 1960s, but also by even higher rates of urbanization. Most of the rural–urban migrants only found employment in marginal formal and informal service activities. However, Víctor Tokman, an economist at PREALC, an ECLA-associated agency, demonstrated that, compared to the historical experience of the developed countries, the problem of insufficient employment opportunities in Latin America owed less to excessive population growth and a low rate of expansion in industry than to a failure of the service sector to absorb the 'informally' employed into activities of higher productivity (1982, 126). In any event, one would expect industrial labour absorption to be considerably less than that of nineteenth-century, labour-intensive industrialization.[26] Finally, in the Chile and Argentina of recent decades a process which some writers call a 'premature deindustrialization' and a return to primary activities may have compounded the problem (Kay 1989, 221–2).

The relative capital intensity of the sectors affected by ISI also helps explain the continued skewness and even worsening of the region's income distribution. Since industry was the country's most dynamic growth sector, its high capital/labour ratio resulted in much of the increment of the gross domestic product going to non-labour factors of production. Accompanying ISI were government policies to transfer income from the agricultural sector to industry through exchange rate discrimination and other controls; such policies in the 1950s and 1960s tended to shrink the sectors that produced the vital foreign exchange for the capital goods and fuels for further industrial growth.

In general, during the middle decades of the century, the state took over public utilities and natural resource exploitation, leaving foreign capital to develop the manufacturing sector, typically employing advanced technology with high capital densities. The Mexican government liberalized its rules on foreign investment in 1946, and Chile, Argentina and Brazil all took similar steps in 1955 (Thorp 1994, 138–9). The US provided the largest share of this direct investment, half of which was in manufacturing by 1976 (Calcagno 1980, 35). In Brazil, the state's share of gross domestic product had risen dramatically in the 1960s and 1970s. By 1979, 28 of Brazil's 30 largest non-financial firms were publicly owned (Trebat 1983, 59).

In the post-ISI period remedies for the region's problems were of limited effect, e.g. efforts to diversify exports by eliminating overvalued exchange rates and/or providing special incentives to non-traditional exports, such as steel subsidies in Argentina and Brazil. Although new exports began to appear in the late 1960s – soya beans and footwear in the Brazilian case – there was insufficient attention to export innovation until the 1980s. Meanwhile, during much of the 1970s and 1980s, Latin American economic actors became involved in a distributional struggle, fuelling inflation, which further hampered and distorted growth and development. Nonetheless, Latin America's per capita income would probably have been much lower without ISI, and the growing share of industrial products in its export profile (see below) would have been impossible.

Following the 'lost decade' of the 1980s, in which Latin America's per capita income decreased by 0.8 per cent a year, it is still important to recall that Latin America's economy was anything but stagnant in the earlier years of the current half-century: from 1950 to 1981, the region's economy grew at 5.3 per cent per year, and income per capita – in a region with the world's highest population growth rates until the mid-1960s – expanded at 2.6 per cent a year; the real GDP of Latin America expanded five times in this period. From 1950 to 1981 industrialization remained the chief transforming force: Brazil and Mexico in this period expanded their industrial output ten times, while Argentina and Chile tripled theirs (Ffrench-Davis et al. 1994, 159–60, 165, 197, 247).

Of course this strong if not spectacular growth was closely associated with the growth of the world economy and international trade, and it seems that Latin America's great mistake was continued dependence on commodity trade:[27] The developed countries' imports of manufactures grew at 12 per cent a year, whereas their imports of commodities grew at only 7 per cent a year from 1960 to 1973; in the 1980s, while the developed countries' imports of manufactures grew at 11 per cent per year, their imports of primary goods fell below 2 per cent (Ffrench-Davis et al. 1994, 165, 167).

The problems of the 1980s had their roots in the previous decade, as declining rates of productivity growth in the US led to an overvalued dollar, then floating exchange rates and inflation, compounded by the 1973 oil shock. The recycling of 'petrodollars' by overliquid private banks in the US and elsewhere in the remainder of the decade proved irresistible to Latin American clients, as loans were made at *negative* real interest rates in the 1970s. Many countries of the region had decided to borrow to avoid having to curtail economic growth associated with higher energy prices. Brazil, for instance, engaged in 'debt-led growth' in the 1970s, using borrowed re-sources to invest in new import-substituting sectors (such as the capital goods industry) and in non-traditional exports. Mexico, which benefited from the oil shock, borrowed heavily to expand oil extraction and to establish a large petrochemical complex (Baer 1995, Ch. 6; Ramírez 1989, Ch. 5). The inter-est rate shock of the early 1980s resulted in real rates which were more than three times as high as those of the 1950s and 1960s.[28] The Mexican debt moratorium of 1982 caused the closing of financial markets to most of Latin America and forced most countries into adjustment programmes. As a result, during the 1980s many Latin American countries made larger transfers as a share of GDP than the reparations payments of Germany after the First World War (Ffrench-Davis, et al. 1994, 246).

Although orthodox economists point to the 'high-performing' countries of East Asia – Japan, Korea, Malaysia, Indonesia, Singapore, Thailand and Taiwan – as successful examples of the application of liberal policies, a revisionist monographic literature has established that governments played important roles in development through market intervention in Japan, Korea and Taiwan.[29] Moreover, the same seven 'high-performing' countries that achieved three times the growth rates of Latin America and South Asia between 1960 and 1985 – and five times those of Sub-Saharan Africa – also performed considerably better than the latter areas with regard to income distribution among social groups, partly because of state policy, including land reform in Japan, Korea and Taiwan (World Bank 1993, 2). One of the themes development economists now stress is the importance of human, as opposed to physical, capital, and the extension of primary education in the East Asian high performers was, for the World Bank, 'by far the largest single contributor to…[their] predicted growth rates' (World Bank 1993, 52).

The success of the Asian Tigers could hardly be ignored in Latin America. For the Brazilian economist Winston Fritsch, the recurrent external disequilibrium that concerned Raúl Prebisch in the 1940s and 1950s could be overcome in the 1990s not by less trade, but more, given the ever-rising share of manufactures in the world market, and the limits of a strategy of compression of imports. Latin American nations should follow a policy of generalized liberalization of trade combined with protection of nascent industries, especially manufactures, based on criteria of efficiency and competitiveness in the international market (Fritsch 1991, 407, 414). Here 'neostructuralism' reconciles the structuralist tradition, emphasizing industrialization, with the mounting evidence linking economic growth with international trade.[30]

In fact, Latin American countries have been implementing the exports of industrial goods for some time. Exports of manufactures rose at 11.3 per cent a year from 1960 to 1973, and at 15 per cent a year between 1977 and 1990, so that the region's exports of manufactures are 25 times larger than in the early 1950s. Brazil diversified trade the most, so that the sale of manufactures accounted for 52 per cent of Brazilian exports by 1990. Automobiles and related products surpassed the value of coffee sales in Brazil's export profile in the 1980s (Ffrench-Davis et al. 1994, 205).

A considerably different path was pursued by Chile, despite the fact that its guiding post-ISI policies, like Brazil's, were set by a military regime. For Chile in the 1970s, anti-communist and anti-populist politics was accompanied by economic policies that would have as their top priorities the elimination of inflation and balance-of-payments deficits through monetarist stabilization policies and export orientation, as recommended by the International Monetary Fund. Indeed, neoclassical orthodoxy, not the policies of ECLA, provided the signposts for the 1970s and later for most of Latin America.

This situation was most obvious in Chile. The new government, like the new military dictatorships in Argentina and Uruguay, faced three-digit inflation, balance-of-payments crises and social conflict. Furthermore, after 1973 the international economy was in recession: the volume of world trade from 1965 to 1973 grew at an average of 9 per cent a year, but fell to 4 per cent for the rest of the decade. In the earlier period, underdeveloped countries' share of world trade had been 6.4 per cent, but fell to 3.4 per cent in 1974, and protectionism was rising in the West (Foxley 1983, 33–5). To the extent that growth continued, it depended in large part on foreign borrowing, a policy only sustainable until the 1979 recession.

Nowhere was monetarism applied with greater determination than in Chile, where the Chicago School was dominant.[31] Under General Augusto Pinochet, that country was the flagship for a set of policies which can be characterized as a kind of 'conservative structuralism'. The main policy objective was the restructuring or even 'destructuring' of the Chilean economy, as it existed under the socialist government of Salvador Allende. Chile was to be opened to world trade, and protectionism ended; state agencies were to be disbanded or sold to the private sector; and wages were to be compressed. These goals were accomplished: by 1979, Chile's average level of protection was only 10 per cent, as contrasted with 94 per cent in 1973, and with 41 per cent in the authoritarian Brazil of the later 1960s.[32] By 1980, the Chilean government had reduced the number of state entities from 507 in 1973 to fifteen. By the later 1970s wages had dropped 25–35 per cent below those of 1970. Yet at the end of the 1970s or the early 1980s, the results were mixed, or even largely negative. Despite vigorous growth in the latter years of the 1970s, the creation of new exports, and the diminution of inflation, these achievements occurred at the expense of a decrease in industrial employment and a fall in industry's share of GDP; high rates of overall unemployment; a reversal of agrarian reform; and a greater concentration of income distribution and of ownership of major enterprises. All in all, Chile's neoconservative experiment was probably more successful up to 1980 than Argentina's and Uruguay's, though exports grew rapidly in all three (Foxley 1983, 44, 61, 67, 76, 78–81, 122–4, 188).

In the 1980s, however, Chile achieved some real policy successes that were admired in conservative circles elsewhere. Although the orthodox stabilization policy of 1978–82 resulted in lower wages and massive unemployment (up to 26 per cent), the Pinochet government's deficit of 9 per cent of GDP moved to a 3 per cent surplus, while inflation remained moderate between 1984 and 1988. The GDP itself grew rapidly in the last years of the decade, though Chile's industrial sector did not grow at all in the years 1980–86, and income concentration, compared to the late 1960s, continued to increase into the 1980s. Chile achieved greater export competitiveness by lowering wages more than by technological innovation (Corbo and Solimano 1991, 78; Ffrench-Davis and Muñoz 1991, 13; Meller 1991, 1545–7, 1555).

By the 1990s the neoliberalism practised by Chile had spread throughout the region; not only the governments of the four countries examined – though Brazil lagged behind the others – but also many others engaged in various types of orthodox stabilization measures, and pursued programmes of privatization and liberalization. The 'lost decade' of the 1980s seems to have been followed by a period of falling rates of inflation, large inflows of foreign capital (much of it speculative), and a return to economic growth. It was not clear, however, whether the turn to neoliberalism would improve or worsen the lot of the Latin American masses.

Conclusion

The fitful performance of the Latin American economies relative to the dynamism of the West has deep historical roots. We have shown how the organization of the primary export economies of the region, which were inherited from colonial times and were vastly expanded in the nineteenth century, was responsible for a high degree of concentration of property and income. The great expansion of exports was not accompanied by institutions and practices to develop human capital, with the partial exception of Argentina; thus Latin America entered the twentieth century as an array of highly stratified societies, with small numbers emulating the lifestyles of the advanced West and the masses living at or near a state of subsistence. Between them lay a thin but growing stratum of middle sectors in the four Latin American countries considered here in some detail.

Import substitution industrialization in this century occurred within a context of social backwardness and extremely rapid rural–urban migration. The new industrial sectors' technology did not permit a high absorption of labour, and thus the growth resulting from ISI was unevenly distributed, at times even worsening the income distribution in the region.

Although most of Latin America's population is presently urbanized and industry's contribution to the national product is over three times greater than that of agriculture, the region is still relatively underdeveloped because of the continuing concentration of property and income combined with severely limited educational opportunities for the majority of the population. The recent policy shifts in the region, emphasizing privatization of state enterprises, have the potential of expanding the tax base available to states with more focused mandates to improve health and education. True, the 'lessons' of East Asia may be limited in their applicability to the 'late, late industrializers'; but the Asian experience, which frequently included government intervention in economy and society, seems to show that vigorous growth can be combined with a more equitable sharing of the fruits of economic progress. 'Growth by concentration', as Celso Furtado styles the Latin American experience, is not the only way.

Notes
1. Plus the US dependency Puerto Rico and the West Indian island-state, Trinidad and Tobago (World Bank 1994, 162–3, 221).
2. For a conspectus of the Spanish American economy, see Lockhart and Schwartz (1983, Chs 4, 5 and 9).
3. For a survey of the Brazilian colonial economy, see ibid., Chs 6, 7, and 10.

4. At the end of the Napoleonic Wars, Britain not only had the world's largest merchant marine, but its navy was four times larger than that of its nearest rival, France.
5. Halperín's phrase in *Historia* (1970, 134).
6. See Bairoch (1993, 90). Bairoch generalizes that '...in the nineteenth century, the liberal trade experience in the Third World was a complete failure' (171). On Latin America, see Glade (1969, 196–7).
7. See Batou (1990). Although Francia achieved an agrarian revolution and national self-sufficiency, there were only 1,000 industrial workers – one for every 750 inhabitants – by the mid-1860s.
     Did Egypt, Paraguay, or any other country studied offer 'a coherent model of state-led industrialization before the Japan of Meiji'? Though Batou believes the matter is an open question, it seems unlikely to us. He gives scant attention to disparities in the size of domestic markets of his several countries when compared to Japan's, and perhaps under-values 'human capital': Japan had the highest literacy rate anywhere outside Western Europe and North America around 1850. Further, in focusing on the autocratic state as the potential demiurge of development, Batou discounts the possibility of a transformation of feudal structures and class alliances, central to Barrington Moore's explanation of Japan's success. See Moore (1966).
8. For some details, see Rippy (1959) and Marichal (1989).
9. Brazil's rate of literacy was 15 per cent in 1890, and Argentina's 46 per cent in 1895. See Ludwig (1985, 132) and Vázquez-Presedo (1971, 27). However, the Brazilian figure is for all ages, including 0–4, and that of Argentina, for those aged six and older.
10. Hernández y Sánchez Barba (1971, 230–31). Nonetheless, these estates were highly differentiated across the region as to the modernity of their technology, business practices, and labour relations.
11. Díaz Alejandro (1970, 2). In 1895 Michael Mulhall believed Argentina's per capita income was higher than that of several West European countries. Mulhall, cited in ibid., p. 1, note 1.
12. Inferred from Bauer and Johnson (1977, 88–9).
13. Extra-economic coercion in Brazilian agriculture was still widely observable in 1993. See 'Forced Labor' (30 Nov. 1993).
14. For Argentina: Inferred from Díaz Alejandro (1970, 6) and Oddone (1967). For Chile, see Mamalakis (1976, 79–80). For Mexico, Haber notes the preponderant role of foreigners in industrial development (1989, 80–82). For Brazil, Dean (1969) credits Paulista coffee planters with investments in railroads, but views immigrant importers as more important in developing early manufacturing.
15. Palma (1979) has shown that industrial development was extensive between 1875 and 1900, despite a literature that emphasizes lost opportunities for modernization under the regime of a traditional landed oligarchy. He found that import substitution industrialization was already well underway in Chile by 1914, and was reaching its limits by 1934, much earlier than in other countries. He also found a correlation between export growth and the growth of manufacturing before the First World War, but not later. Palma for Chile, like Dean for Brazil, argues that export expansion was a precondition for industrialization.
16. '[D]uring the twenty years between 1890 and 1920 Mexican manufacturing was transformed. Large, vertically integrated firms replaced the small shops and artisan producers...,' using new technology and machinery (Haber 1989).
17. Manoilescu (1929). His leading champion in Brazil was the industrialist and economic historian Roberto Simonsen. See Simonsen (1931, 58, 91). On Manoilescu's influence in the Ibero-American world, see Love (1996, Chs 7 and 9).
18. In 1942 Enrique Zañartu Prieto defended 'autarky' in Chile, but in vague terms. See Zañartu Prieto (1946, 243).
19. See United Nations (1950, 97), citing the case of Argentina, and Furtado (1950, 28).
20. See Furtado (1950). For a similar thesis about the socialization of losses through exchange depreciation and government maintenance of aggregate demand, see United Nations (1951, 60, 171–2).

21. See note 16 on Mexico above. By contrast, for Brazil Stein noted that there was a shortage of capital in the textile industry owing to a narrow group of investors, and that 'Approximately half of Brazil's cotton textile equipment in 1945 was installed and in operation in 1915' (1957, 25, 103).
22. For a summary of Furtado's arguments and the subsequent debate in Brazil, see Suzigan (1986, 21–73). Also see C. Cardoso and Brignoli (1979, 197) summarizing a literature on Mexico, Argentina, Brazil and Chile, and p. 199; see also the essays in Thorp (1984, passim); and Lewis (1986, 287, 320).
23. On Brazil, see Baer and Villela (1973, 217–34).
24. Bulmer-Thomas (1994, 101–2). Argentina, the author notes, was the exception.
25. See United Nations (1950). Raúl Prebisch was the author of this essay–manifesto that began the 'structuralist' school. According to Prebisch (and Hans Singer), at the international level, unequal exchange derived from differential productivities between industrial Centre and agricultural Periphery in the world market, combined with different institutional arrangements in capital and labour markets. Technological progress in manufacturing, in any case, was shown in a rise in incomes in developed countries, while that in the production of food and raw materials in underdeveloped countries was expressed in a fall in prices. The explanation of contrasting effects of technological progress was found in the disparate income elasticities of demand for primary and industrial goods. Since consumers of manufactured goods in world trade tended to live in underdeveloped countries, and the contrary was true for consumers of raw materials, the latter group had the best of both worlds, while the former had the worst. On the origins of Prebisch's theories, see Love, (1996, Ch. 8).
26. Relevant for the 'classical' experience as well is the fact that much of Europe's surplus labour did not have to be absorbed because of emigration.
27. With some exceptions: see text below on Brazil.
28. As an index, the London inter-bank offer rate averaged 5 per cent in 1950–71; it fell to –5.3 per cent in 1972–80, and then rose to 14.6 per cent in 1981–87. Ffrench-Davis et al. (1994, 231).
29. World Bank (1993, 83). On the same page the bank takes a middle position, arguing for a limited 'market-friendly' interventionism 'to ensure adequate investment in people, provision of a competitive climate for enterprise, openness to international trade, and stable macroeconomic management'.
30. On the linkage, see, for example, Levine and Renelt (1992, 942–63); and Esfahani (1991, 93–116). Levine and Renelt examined data for 119 countries, and Esfahani considered data for 31 semi-industrialized countries. Esfahani emphasizes that the correlation between export and GDP performance has mainly to do with exports' mitigation of import 'shortages', which restrict the growth of output in these countries.
31. Valdés (1989) offers a full study.
32. Foxley (1983, 2, 16, 58, 71). Figures exclude duties on automobiles.

References

Alvarez Andrews, O. (1936), *Historia del desarrollo industrial de Chile*, Santiago: Sociedad de Fomento Fabril.

Anales de la Unión Industrial Argentina, año 44 (Dec., 1931).

Argentina Fabril [successor to *Anales*, previous item] año 53 (Jan., 1940).

'Argentine Industrial Exhibition, The' (Dec., 1933) *Review of the River Plate*, 22.

Baer, W. (1995), *The Brazilian Economy: Growth and Development*, 4th edn, New York: Praeger.

Baer, W. and Villela, A.V. (1973), 'Industrial Growth and Industrialization: Revisions in the Stages of Brazil's Economic Development', *Journal of Developing Areas*, 7, 2.

Bairoch, P. (1993), *Economics and World History: Myths and Paradoxes*, Chicago: University of Chicago Press.

Bartra, R., et al. (1976), *Modos de producción en América Latina*, Lima: Delva.

Batou, J. (1990), *Cent ans de résistance au sous-developpement: L'industrialisation de l'Amérique Latine et du Moyen-Orient face au défi européen: 1770–1870*. Geneva: Droz.

Bauer, A.J., and Johnson, A.H. (1977), 'Land and Labour in Rural Chile, 1850–1935', in K. Duncan and I. Rutledge (eds), *Land and Labour in Latin America*, Cambridge: Cambridge University Press.

Bauer, A.J. (1986), 'Rural Spanish America, 1870–1930', in L. Bethell (ed.), *Cambridge History of Latin America* [hereafter *CHLA*], vol. 4, Cambridge: Cambridge University Press.

Bloch, M. (1961), *Feudal Society*, Chicago: University of Chicago Press.

Bruno, M. et al. (1991), *Lessons of Economic Stabilization and its Aftermath*, Cambridge, Mass.: MIT Press.

Bulmer-Thomas, V. (1994), 'The Latin American Economies, 1929–1939', in L. Bethell (ed.), *CHLA*, vol. 6, Cambridge: Cambridge University Press.

Calcagno, A.E. (1980), *Informe sobre las inversiones directas extranjeras en América Latina*, Santiago de Chile, Naciones Unidas: Comisión Económica para América Latina.

Cardoso, C.F.S., and Brignoli, H.P. (1979), *Historia económica de América Latina*, vol. 2, Barcelona: Crítica.

Cardoso, F.H. (1964), *Empresário industrial e desenvolvimento econômico no Brasil*, São Paulo: Difusão Europeia do Livro.

Cardoso, F.H. (1966), 'The Entrepreneurial Elites of Latin America', *Studies in Comparative International Development*, 2.

Cardoso, F.H. (1971), *Ideologías de la burguesía industrial en sociedades dependientes (Argentina y Brasil)*, México, D.F., Siglo Veintiuno.

Coatsworth, J. (1978), 'Obstacles to Economic Growth in Nineteenth-century Mexico', *American Historical Review*, 83, 1.

Contador, C.R. and Haddad, C.L. (1975), 'Produto real, moeda e preços: A experiência brasileira no período 1861–1970', *Revista Brasileira de Estatística*, 36, 143.

Corbo, V. and Solimano, A. (1991), 'Chile's Experience with Stabilization Revisited', in Bruno et al. (1991).

Cuneo, D. (1967), *Comportimiento y crisis de la clase empresarial*, Buenos Aires: Pleamar.

Dean, W. (1969), *The Industrialization of São Paulo, 1880–1945*, Austin: University of Texas Press.

Dean, W. (1986), 'The Brazilian Economy, 1870–1930', in L. Bethell (ed.), *CHLA*, vol. 5, Cambridge: Cambridge University Press.

Díaz Alejandro, C.F. (1970), *Essays on the Economic History of the Argentine Republic*, New Haven, Conn.: Yale University Press.

Esfahani, H.S. (1991), 'Exports, Imports, and Economic Growth in Semi-Industrialized Countries', *Journal of Development Economics*, 35.

Ffrench-Davis, R. and Muñoz, O. (1991), 'Latin American Economic Development and the International Environment', in P. Meller (ed.), *The Latin America Development Debate*, Boulder, Co.: Westview Press.

Ffrench-Davis, R., Muñoz, O. and Palma, J.G. (1994), 'The Latin American Economies, 1950–1990', in L. Bethell (ed.), *CHLA*, vol. 6, Cambridge: Cambridge University Press.

'Forced Labor in Brazil Re-visited: On-site Investigations Document That Practice Continues' (30 Nov. 1993), *Americas Watch: A Division of Human Rights Watch*, 5, 12.

Foweraker, J. (1980) *The Struggle for Land: A Political Economy of the Pioneer Frontier in Brazil from 1930 to the Present Day*, Cambridge: Cambridge University Press.

Estado de S. Paulo, O. 8 March 1933.

Foxley, A. (1983), *Latin American Experiments in Neo-Conservative Economics*. Berkeley: University of California Press.

Fritsch, W. (1991), 'El nuevo marco internacional: Desafios y oportunidades', in O. Sunkel (ed.), *El desarrollo desde dentro: Un enfoque neoestructuralista para la América Latina*, México, D.F., Fondo de Cultura Económica.

Furtado, C. (1950), 'Características gerais da economia brasileira', *Revista Brasileira de Economia* 4, 1.

Gallo, E. (1970), 'Agrarian Expansion and Industrial Development in Argentina, 1880–1930', in R. Carr (ed.), *Latin American Affairs*, London: Oxford University Press.

Glade, W.P. (1969), *The Latin American Economies: A Study of their Institutional Evolution*, New York: American Book–Van Nostrand.

Haber, S.J. (1989) *Industrialization and Underdevelopment: The Industrialization of Mexico, 1890–1940*, Stanford: Stanford University Press.

Halperín-Donghi, T. (1970), *Historia contemporánea de América Latina*, 2nd edn, Madrid: Alianza Editorial.

Halperín-Donghi, T. (1973), *The Aftermath of Revolution in Latin America*, New York: Harper and Row.

Halperín-Donghi, T. (1985), 'Economy and Society in Post-independence Latin America', in L. Bethell (ed.), *CHLA*, vol. 3, Cambridge: Cambridge University Press.

Hernández y Sánchez-Barba, M. (1971), 'Ciclos Kondratieff y modelos de frustración económica Ibero-americana (Siglo XIX)', *Revista da la Universidad de Madrid*, 20, 78.

Holloway, T.H. (1980), *Immigrants on the Land: Coffee and Society in São Paulo, 1886–1934*, Chapel Hill: University of North Carolina Press. 'Industrialización' (1945), editorial, *Revista Económica* (Mexico), 8, 10.

Izquierdo, R. (1964), 'Protectionism in Mexico', in R. Vernon (ed.), *Public Policy and Private Enterprise in Mexico*, Cambridge, Mass.: Harvard University Press.

Jacobsen, N. (1984), 'Cycles and Booms in Latin American Export Agriculture', *Review* [of the Fernand Braudel Center], 7, 3.

Katz, F. (1974), 'Labor Conditions on Haciendas in Porfirian Mexico', *Hispanic American Historical Review*, 54, 1.

Kay, C. (1980), *El sistema señorial europeo y la hacienda latinoamericana*. México, D.F., Ediciones Era.

Kay, C. (1989), *Latin American Theories of Development and Underdevelopment*, London: Routledge.

Laclau, E. (1969), 'Modos de producción, sistemas económicos y población excedente: Aproximación histórica a los casos argentino y chileno', *Revista Latinoamericana de Sociología* 5, 2.

Leff, N. (1982), *Underdevelopment and Development in Brazil*, London: Allen & Unwin.

Levine, R. and Renelt, D. (1992), 'A Sensitivity Analysis of Cross-Country Growth Regressions', *American Economic Review*, 82, 4.

Lewis, C. (1986), 'Industry in Latin America before 1930', in L. Bethell (ed.), *CHLA*, vol. 5. Cambridge: Cambridge University Press.

Lockhart, J. and Schwartz, S.B. (1983), *Early Latin America: A History of Colonial Spanish America and Brazil*, Cambridge: Cambridge University Press.

Love, J.L. (1996), *Crafting the Third World: Theorizing Underdevelopment in Rumania and Brazil*, Stanford: Stanford University Press, forthcoming.

Ludwig, A.K. (1985), *Brazil: A Handbook of Historical Statistics*, Boston: G.K. Hall.

Mamalakis, M.J. (1976), *The Growth and Structure of the Chilean Economy*. New Haven, Conn.: Yale University Press.

Manoilescu, M. (1929), *Théorie du protectionnisme et de l'échange international*, Paris: Felix Alcan.

Marichal, C. (1989), *A Century of Latin American Debt Crises in Latin America*, Princeton, NJ: Princeton University Press.

Masón, D. (1944), 'Introducción' to M. Abarca, *La industrialización de la Argentina*, Buenos Aires: Ministerio de Agricultura.

Meller, P. (1991), 'Adjustment and Social Costs in Chile during the 1980s', *World Development*, 19, 11.

Moore, Barrington, Jr (1966), *Social Origins of Dictatorship and Democracy*, Boston: Beacon Press.

Mörner, M. (1977), 'Latin American "Landlords" and "Peasants" and the Outer World during the National Period', in K. Duncan and I. Rutledge (eds), *Land and Labour in Latin America*, Cambridge: Cambridge University Press.

Myrdal, G. (1970), *The Challenge of World Poverty: A World Anti-Poverty Program in Outline*, New York: Pantheon.

Navarrete R.A. (1967), 'The Financing of Economic Development', in E. Pérez López et al., *Mexico's Recent Economic Growth: The Mexican View*, tr. Marjory Urquidi, Austin: University of Texas Press.

'Necesitamos una política económica de industrialización' (1940) editorial, *Revista de Economía y Finanzas* (Peru), 16, 92.

Oddone, J. (1967), *La burguesía terrateniente argentina*, 3rd edn, Buenos Aires: Ediciones Populares Argentinas.

Palma, J.G. (1979), 'Growth and Structure of Chilean Manufacturing Industry from 1830 to 1935', PhD diss., Oxford University.

Phelps, D.M. (1935), 'Industrial Expansion in Temperate South America', *American Economic Review*, 25.

Prebisch, R. (1963), *Towards a Dynamic Development Policy for Latin America*, New York: United Nations Economic Commission for Latin America.

Presidente de la República (de Chile, Pedro Aguirre Cerda) (1940), *Mensaje...en la apertura...del Congreso Nacional 21 de Mayo de 1940*, Santiago, Chile.

Pupo Nogueira, O. (1945), 'A propósito da modernização de uma grande indústria', *Revista Industrial de S. Paulo*, año 1, 6.

Ramírez, M.D. (1989), *Mexico's Economic Crisis: Its Origins and Consequences*, New York: Praeger.

Ramírez, M.D. (1986), *Development Banking in Mexico: The Case of the Nacional Financiera, S.A.*, New York: Praeger.

Rippy, J.F. (1959) *British Investments in Latin America, 1822–1949*, Minneapolis: University of Minnesota Press.

Simonsen, R. (1931), *Crises, Finances and Industry*, São Paulo: Limitada.

Slatta, R.W. (1983), *Gauchos and the Vanishing Frontier*, Lincoln: University of Nebraska Press.

Solberg, C. (1987), *The Prairie and the Pampas: Agrarian Policy in Canada and Argentina, 1880–1930*, Stanford: Stanford University Press.

Souza Martins, J. de (1981), *Os camponeses e a política no Brasil*, Petrópolis: Vozes.

Stein, S.J. (1957), *The Brazilian Cotton Manufacture: Textile Enterprise in an Underdeveloped Area, 1850–1950*, Cambridge, Mass.: Harvard University Press.

Suter, C. (1994), 'Cyclical Fluctuations in Foreign Investment 1850–1930: The Historical Debate and the Latin American Case', in C. Marichal (ed.), *Foreign Investment in Latin America: Impact on Economic Development, 1850–1930* (Proceedings: Eleventh International Economic History Congress), Milan: Universita Bocconi.

Suzigan, W. (1986), *Indústria brasileira: Origem e desenvolvimento*, São Paulo: Brasiliense.

Thorp, R. (1986), 'Latin America and the International Economy from the First World War to the World Depression', in L. Bethell (ed.), *CHLA*, vol. 4, Cambridge: Cambridge University Press.

Thorp, R. (1994), 'The Latin American Economies, 1939–c.1950', in L. Bethell (ed.), *CHLA*, vol. 6, Cambridge: Cambridge University Press.

Thorp, R. (ed.) (1984), *Latin America in the 1930s: The Role of the Periphery in World Crisis*, London: Macmillan.

Tokman, V. (1982), 'Unequal Development and the Absorption of Labour: Latin America 1950–1980', *CEPAL Review*, 17.

Trebat, T.J. (1983), *Brazil's State-Owned Enterprises: A Case Study of the State as Entrepreneur*, Cambridge: Cambridge University Press.

Unión Industrial Argentina (May, 1946) *Revista*, año 57.

United Nations Economic Commission for Latin America (1951 [Sp. orig., 1950]), *Economic Survey of Latin America: 1949*, Santiago, Chile: United Nations.

United Nations Economic Commission for Latin America (1950 [Sp. orig., 1949]), *The Economic Development of Latin America and Its Principal Problems*, Santiago, Chile: United Nations.

Valdés, J.G. (1989), *La escuela de Chicago: Operación Chile*, Buenos Aires: Grupo Editorial Zeta.

Vargas, G. (1938, 1940, 1941), *A nova política do Brasil*, I, VI, VIII, Rio de Janeiro: José Olympio.

Vázquez-Presedo, V. (1971), *Estadísticas históricas argentinas (comparadas)*, Buenos Aires: Macchi.

Véliz, C. (1965), 'Introduction', in C. Véliz (ed.), *Obstacles to Change in Latin America*, London: Oxford University Press.

Villareal, R. (1976), *El desequilibrio externo en la industrialización de México (1929–75): un enfoque estructuralista*, México, D.F., Fondo de Cultura Económica.

Villela, Annibal V. and Suzigan, W. (1973), *Política do governo e crescimento da economia brasileira, 1889–1945*, Rio de Janeiro: IPEA.

World Bank (1993), *The East Asian Miracle: Economic Growth and Public Policy*, New York: Oxford University Press.

World Bank (1994), *World Development Report: 1994*, New York: Oxford University Press.

Zañartu Prieto, E. (1946), *Tratado de economía política*, 2nd edn, Santiago, Chile: Zig Zag.

4   Economic growth in Europe's Third World: Central and Eastern Europe, 1870–1989*

David F. Good

Introduction

In analyses of long-term economic growth on a global scale, most European countries rank among the rich nations of the world. Cross-national comparisons of income certainly justify this, but they also point to the sharp disparities in levels of development *within* Europe, especially the substantial lag of the economies along its southern and eastern periphery.

The collapse of the Soviet Union has increased awareness of these disparities. The initial euphoria that accompanied the end of the cold war has given way to a more sober recognition of the monumental task confronting the former East bloc states. Even those who are inclined to view the region's current relative backwardness purely as a legacy of communism are aware that its foundations actually lie deep in the past, not simply in the post-1945 era. For centuries much of the region fell on the low end of the economic gradient that descended eastward and southward from the highly developed regions of Northwestern Europe.[1] The persistence of this long-standing gradient makes Europe itself a useful focal point for examining the larger issue of 'Why the West grew rich.'[2]

Some glaring gaps in the growing literature on the economic history of the former East bloc make this exercise difficult. The most bothersome is the lack of usable data to assess the region's long-term economic performance. My recent study (Good 1994a), begins filling the gap by providing estimates of income for the pre-1914 period on the present-day territories of the Habsburg successor states, including the recent successor states to Yugoslavia and Czechoslovakia. Here I extend these estimates to non-Habsburg Eastern Europe, link them to existing income estimates for the post-1950 period, and combine them with comparable data for Western Europe to measure and interpret the long-term performance of Central and Eastern Europe.

The data

My analysis relies on country-level estimates of GDP per capita for the benchmark years 1870, 1890, 1910, 1950, 1973 and 1987.[3] The task of

*The author wishes to thank David Ryden for valuable research assistance and the Graduate School of the University of Minnesota for generous financial support.

building such a data set faces three problems. The first is the difficulty of making international income comparisons. Here I rely heavily on data from Angus Maddison (1989; 1990; 1991). In deriving his long-term series on national income, Maddison avoids the well-known problems in using exchange rates to convert GDP in different national currencies into a single currency by adopting the solution of the International Comparison Project (ICP).[4] The ICP approach, which is now used by all major international statistical offices, is to use purchasing power parities rather than exchange rates to convert GDP into a common currency unit, typically the international or US dollar. My estimates start with Maddison's GDP data for 1980, which are based on the recent ICP-type estimates of Eurostat/OECD.[5] The 1980 levels for each country were projected back to the benchmark dates with Maddison's indexes of GDP, which he derived from the work of country specialists, and then were adjusted with his population figures to arrive at GDP per capita.[6] This method was used for all the OECD countries of Western Europe (except Austria) in all benchmark years and for the former East bloc economies and Austria for 1950, 1973 and 1987 only.

The second problem stems from the recent dismemberment of Czechoslovakia and Yugoslavia: how to generate a long-term time series of GDP for their successor states. For the post-Second World War period, data exist on the distribution of income among the republics of former Czechoslovakia and former Yugoslavia. For the two pre-1992 republics (post-1992 states) of Czechoslovakia, Capek and Sazama (1993) have republic-level GDP per capita for the relevant benchmark years that can be applied to the corresponding GDP per capita levels for Czechoslovakia as estimated above. For the pre-1989 republics (post-1989 successor states) of Yugoslavia Nikolič (1992) and Miljkovič (1992) have republic-level GDP per capita in the relevant benchmark years for Slovenia, Croatia, Bosnia-Hercegovina and Serbia (and Vojvodina as an autonomous region of Serbia) that can be applied to the corresponding GDP per capita for Yugoslavia as estimated above.

The third problem is the lack of data for pre-1914 Central and Eastern Europe. There are estimates for the two quasi-states of the Habsburg Empire, Austria and Hungary, but only scattered estimates for the immediate prewar years for the Habsburg successor states. For the area under Habsburg control, the estimates rely on my recent study (1994a). Estimates of income for the pre-1914 independent states of Serbia, Romania and Bulgaria, and for Bosnia-Hercegovina (occupied by the Habsburg Empire, but not formally part of it), rely on the same method and on official government statistics kindly supplied by Michael Palairet.

The estimates of GDP per capita for 27 European countries for the benchmark years 1870, 1910, 1950, 1973 and 1987 appear in Table 4.1.

Table 4.1   GDP per capita in Europe in 1980, international dollars

	1870	1890	1910	1950	1973	1987
Northwest						
UK	1993.2	2493.1	2867.5	4164.4	7413.8	9369.3
Belgium	1538.1	1969.9	2335.7	3114.4	6936.7	8770.8
France	1150.6	1421.2	1748.3	3038.2	7559.3	9546.1
Germany	951.8	1256.5	1754.9	2508.1	7594.7	9929.7
Netherlands	1559.2	1940.0	2238.4	3554.5	7754.3	9130.0
Switzerland	1294.0	1637.6	2089.4	4589.3	9217.3	10332.8
Nordic						
Denmark	1210.5	1524.9	2239.5	3894.8	7844.8	10018.3
Finland	700.5	848.5	1171.3	2613.3	6813.3	9497.7
Norway	900.5	1117.7	1418.9	3435.7	7071.7	11806.1
Sweden	960.1	1204.1	1719.8	3874.0	8237.2	10500.6
Mediterranean						
Italy	915.6	1008.9	1432.7	2103.7	6383.6	9017.3
Greece	NA	NA	743.2	971.8	3857.8	4700.2
Portugal	568.3	NA	639.4	1096.4	3792.8	4658.6
Spain	853.4	NA	1473.8	1682.6	5300.8	6404.6
Central and East						
Austria	1045.3	1333.7	1812.8	2122.8	6434.5	8715.3
Hungary	531.7	789.1	1253.2	1847.4	3971.0	4883.9
Czech Republic	869.0	1186.7	1633.7	2909.0	5461.4	6534.7
Slovakia	502.9	720.5	1029.8	1785.4	4714.2	5613.6
Slovenia	584.2	785.2	1136.6	1631.1	5657.7	8154.9
Croatia	377.1	506.2	785.8	1165.1	3536.1	5291.3
Vojvodina	444.3	626.4	922.9	1003.0	3281.5	5184.4
Bosnia-Herceg.	NA	NA	533.2	861.1	1867.1	3051.7
Serbia	271.6	532.1	650.9	982.7	2715.7	4086.0
Romania	382.1	557.7	827.1	865.3	2555.5	3767.7
Poland	419.7	574.5	762.6	1827.3	4014.4	4067.9
Bulgaria	NA	516.4	668.7	1095.9	3624.4	4448.9
Ger. Dem. Repub.	NA	NA	NA	1769.4	5358.7	7703.7

Sources and notes
1. Western Europe, all benchmark years, and Central and Eastern Europe, 1950, 1973 and 1987: derived from data in Maddison (1989; 1990; 1991).
2. Central and Eastern Europe, 1870, 1890 and 1910: adapted from data in Good (1994a) and (1993) except for Bosnia, Serbia and Bulgaria, which uses the methodology of Good (1994a) and government statistics supplied by Michael Palairet. For details see the text and an appendix that is available on request from the author. See also note 3, p. 79.

The economic lag of central and Eastern Europe in historical perspective

With the estimates of Table 4.1, we can generate evidence on the two proximate determinants of Eastern Europe's current lag within Europe – the initial lag of the region in 1870 and its relative growth rate between 1870 and 1987.

Table 4.1 confirms clearly that the current lag of the region was already deeply entrenched in the nineteenth century. We do not know how rapidly the regions of Central and Eastern Europe grew in the decades before 1870, but we can say that they failed to keep pace with the economies of Western Europe. In that year GDP per capita exceeded the level of Germany, at $952 the lowest in Western Europe, only on the territory of present-day Austria, which had attained a level of $1 045. On the territories of the other present-day states in the region, GDP per capita ranged between $272 in Serbia and $869 in the Czech Republic.

Using standard definitions of Europe's regions,[7] the data in Table 4.2 suggest that Central and Eastern Europe grew relatively rapidly after 1870. Over the entire period 1870–1987, the region grew faster than the European average and at roughly the same rate as Nordic Europe. The pattern varied somewhat over time. Before the First World War it was the fastest growing region; between 1910 and 1950 it grew relatively slowly, ahead only of the Mediterranean; and after the Second World War it was the second fastest growing region, ahead of the Mediterranean region, but behind the Nordic region.

The lag of Central and Eastern Europe and the convergence debate

Although these comparative growth rates suggest that the Central and Eastern European economies performed rather well over the past century or so, they do not constitute totally unambiguous evidence. The reason is that the two proximate determinants of the region's current lag – its level of development in 1870 and its subsequent rate of economic growth – may be highly interrelated. This notion goes back at least to Alexander Gerschenkron (1962) who argued that low-income economies could grow rapidly in a 'great spurt' of industrialization as they exploited certain advantages of backwardness. The same idea lies at the core of recent debates among economists and economic historians on global trends in productivity, in particular whether productivity (and income) levels among countries are likely to converge over time (Abramovitz 1986; Baumol et al. 1989; Barro 1991; Barro and Sala i Martin 1991; Dowrick and Nguyen 1989; Evans and Karras 1993; Alam 1992; Quah 1993; and Williamson 1991).

The fundamental idea is that a productivity (income) differential between followers and an economic leader represents a gap that *could* be closed by relatively rapid rates of growth. The potential for closing is inherent in the

Table 4.2 Annual growth rates of GDP per capita in four regions of Europe, 1870–1987

Region	1870–1910	1910–50	1950–87	1950–73	1973–87	1870–1987
NW	1.105	1.175	2.758	3.532	1.485	1.652
NORDIC	1.354	1.908	3.018	3.407	2.379	2.070
MED	0.927	0.828	3.929	5.301	1.674	1.825
CEE	1.783	1.007	3.521	4.367	2.133	2.037
EURI	1.420	1.177	3.247	4.062	1.908	1.915
EURII	1.420	1.157	3.338	4.178	1.957	1.915

NW: Belgium, France, Germany, UK, Netherlands and Switzerland
NORDIC: Denmark, Finland, Norway and Sweden
MED: Greece, Portugal and Spain
CEE: Austria, Hungary, Czech Republic, Slovakia, Slovenia, Croatia, Vojvodina (Serbian province), Bosnia-Hercegovina, Serbia, Romania, Poland, Bulgaria and the German Democratic Republic.
EURI: The simple average of the 23 cases that have data for all time periods, that is, the above cases excluding Greece, Bosnia-Hercegovina, Bulgaria and (after 1945) the German Democratic Republic.
EURII: The simple average of the maximum number of cases for which data are available: 1870–1910 – the 23 cases of EURI; 1910–50 – 26 cases, that is, the above without the German Democratic Republic; 1950–87 and its two sub-periods – all 27 cases.

Sources and notes: Computed from data in Table 4.1. See also note 3, p. 79.

69

high marginal rate of return on capital in low-income countries, the transfer of technology that follows from its character as a public good, and the changing tastes of consumers in high-income economies away from material output to service-oriented output. In the catch-up phase the relatively rapid growth in low-income economies allows them to converge on the leader.

This line of argument implies that the relatively high rates of economic growth in Central and Eastern Europe from 1870 to 1987 may simply reflect the low initial income levels, that is, the region's relative backwardness. It suggests the value of comparing the growth rates of economies there with those of other European latecomers. Sweden provides a useful standard because in 1870 it, too, was relatively backward within Europe, yet it now has one of the highest income levels in the world. Table 4.3 presents evidence for the comparison. The absolute levels of GDP per capita in Table 4.1 have been converted into index numbers where the level for Sweden equals 100 in each of five benchmark years – 1870, 1890, 1910, 1950 and 1987. The benchmark dates set off three distinct periods – the pre-world war era 1870–1910, the period from 1910 to 1950 that includes the two world wars and the Great Depression, and the cold war era, 1950–87.

The data show that in 1870 Sweden was relatively backward compared to the high-income economies of Western Europe – the United Kingdom, France, Belgium and the Netherlands – but relatively advanced compared to the economies of Central and Eastern Europe. Within Central and Eastern Europe only Austria had a higher per capita income than Sweden. In the period 1870–1910, the relative position of the region improved: index numbers for nine of ten present-day states rose, which implies that they grew somewhat faster than Sweden. In the subsequent period, the pattern was reversed, compared to Sweden the small states of Central and Eastern Europe grew slowly as is shown by their falling index numbers. For example, Austria's GDP per capita, which had been about five per cent higher than Sweden's in 1910, stood at barely half the Swedish level in 1950. In the cold war era, the pre-First World War pattern returned; in ten of thirteen cases the index numbers for the states of Central and Eastern Europe rose, which means that they gained some ground on Sweden. Over the entire period 1870–1987, six of the ten present-day states in the region grew faster than Sweden (rising index numbers) while four of the ten grew more slowly (falling index numbers). In the end, the net effect was to leave unchanged the relative position of the region with respect to Sweden. In 1987 no country in Central and Eastern Europe (including Austria) had an income per capita higher than Sweden and six of the thirteen still had levels of income per capita less than half the level of Sweden.

Table 4.3   Relative income levels in Europe, 1870–1987. Indexes of GDP per capita (Sweden=100; present-day boundaries)

Country	1870	1890	1910	1950	1973	1987
Northwest						
UK	207.6	207.1	166.7	107.5	90.0	89.2
Belgium	160.2	163.6	135.8	80.4	84.2	83.5
Netherlands	162.4	161.1	130.2	91.8	94.1	86.9
France	119.8	118.0	101.7	78.4	91.8	90.9
Germany	99.1	104.4	102.0	64.7	92.2	94.6
Switzerland	134.8	136.0	121.5	118.5	111.9	98.4
Nordic						
Denmark	126.1	126.6	130.2	100.5	95.2	95.4
Finland	73.0	70.5	68.1	67.5	82.7	90.4
Norway	93.8	92.8	82.5	88.7	85.9	112.4
SWEDEN	**100.0**	**100.0**	**100.0**	**100.0**	**100.0**	**100.0**
Mediterranean						
Italy	95.4	83.8	83.3	54.3	77.5	85.9
Greece	–	–	43.2	25.1	46.8	44.8
Portugal	59.2	–	37.2	28.3	46.0	44.4
Spain	88.9	–	85.7	43.4	64.4	61.0
Central and East						
Austria	108.9	110.8	105.4	54.8	78.1	83.0
Czech Republic	90.5	98.6	95.0	75.1	66.3	62.2
Slovakia	52.4	59.8	59.9	46.1	57.2	53.5
Hungary	55.4	65.5	72.9	47.7	48.2	46.5
Slovenia	60.8	65.2	66.1	42.1	68.7	77.7
Croatia	39.3	42.0	45.7	30.1	42.9	50.4
Vojvodina	46.3	52.0	53.7	25.9	39.8	49.4
Bosnia-Hercegovina	–	–	31.0	22.2	22.7	29.1
Serbia	28.3	44.2	37.8	25.4	33.0	38.9
Poland*	43.7	47.7	44.3	47.2	48.7	38.7
Romania*	39.8	46.3	48.1	22.3	31.0	35.9
Bulgaria	–	42.9	38.9	28.3	44.0	42.4
German Dem. Repub.	–	–	–	45.7	65.1	73.4

Note: *For 1870, 1890 and 1910 the GDP per capita levels in Poland and Romania are for those portions of the present-day states that fell within the boundary of the Habsburg Empire. For Poland and Romania in 1950, 1973 and 1987 the GDP per capita levels are for the entire state, not just the Habsburg portions.

Sources: Calculated from Table 4.1. See also note 3, p. 79.

Central and Eastern Europe and convergence: a formal test
The evidence shows that the economies of Central and Eastern Europe were not able to grow rapidly enough to overcome much of their initial lag with respect to latecomer Sweden. In the context of the literature on convergence, it raises the more general question: given the potential for 'catching-up' inherent in the relative backwardness of Central and Eastern Europe in 1870, did the economies of the region grow rapidly or slowly over the subsequent 120 years?

The high potential for catch-up in low-income economies implies that in a cross-sectional sample of countries, rates of economic growth should be inversely related to initial levels of GDP; the lower the initial level, the more rapid the rate of growth. Empirical tests of the convergence model have, not surprisingly, yielded mixed results.[8] My purpose here is not to address directly the convergence debate with empirical evidence, but to use the approach's fundamental insight – that an economy's potential rate of growth is related to its starting level – in assessing the long-term economic performance in Central and Eastern Europe.

I set up the analysis by estimating equations for a sample of European countries where the growth rate of GDP per capita is a function of two variables – the initial level of GDP and a variable EAST equal to 1 for countries in Central and Eastern Europe and 0 for all others. The estimated coefficient of the first variable indicates whether incomes converged across the sample of countries. A negative sign would mean that low-income economies grew relatively fast and began to catch up with high-income economies; a positive sign would indicate that low-income economies grew relatively slowly and fell further behind high-income economies. The coefficient of the EAST variable indicates whether the economies of Central and Eastern Europe grew more rapidly (if the sign is positive) or more slowly (if the sign is negative) than would be predicted by their initial level of income.

The regression results are in Table 4.4. For the period as a whole, 1870–1987, they show strong evidence of income convergence within Europe. In Equations 1a and 1b the regression coefficients are negative and statistically significant at the 0.01 level; the lower the level of GDP per capita in 1870, the higher the rate of growth in the period 1870–1987. Within this overall pattern of catch-up between 1870 and 1987, however, the economies of Central and Eastern Europe tended to grow more slowly than would have been expected from their low initial levels of income. The signs on the EAST variable in Equations 1c and 1d are negative, although the level of statistical significance at 0.15 is not high.

The patterns differ within the four sub-periods – 1870–1910, 1910–50, 1950–73 and 1973–87. These correspond to the 'phases of capitalist growth' identified by Maddison (1991, Ch. 4). His phases are not stages in the Marxian

Table 4.4 *Assessing the economic performance of Central and Eastern Europe: regressions based on the convergence model*

			Independent variables				
Eq.	Dep. var.	N	Const.	GDP	LGDP	EAST	R^2
1a	GR7087	23	2.3390*	−0.00049*			.677
1b		23	4.4271*		−0.3777*		.574
1c		23	2.4858*	−0.000587*		−0.130††	.700
1d		23	5.2787*		−0.4951*	−0.163††	.603
2a	GR7010	23	1.9841*	−0.000644*			.380
2b		23	5.3158*		−0.58565*		.452
2c		23	1.4296*	−0.000255		0.4913*	.536
2d		23	3.0181**		−0.26878	0.4364**	.548
3a	GR1050	26	1.0557*	−0.000073			.036
3b		26	0.1998		0.13410		.030
3c		26	1.4379	−0.000089		−0.3420	.019
3d		26	1.7888		−0.06820	−0.3150	.023
4a	GR5087	26	4.4440*	−0.000490*			.556
4b		26	10.9900*		−1.0080*		.522
4c		26	5.0219*	−0.00064*		−0.5202**	.624
4d		26	13.1320*		−1.2621*	−0.4431†	.567
5a	GR5073	26	5.6041*	−0.00063*			.546
5b		26	13.5910*		−1.2400*		.463
5c		26	6.5150*	−0.00086*		−0.8204*	.560
5d		26	16.7690*		−1.6170*	−0.6575**	.526
6a	GR7387	26	2.7728*	−0.00015†			.075
6b		26	9.0130**		−0.8250**		.120
6c		26	2.9590*	−0.00021†		+0.3377	.057
6d		26	11.4240**		−1.1274**	+0.3659	.110

Levels of statistical significance: * = 0.01 level; ** = 0.05 level: † = 0.10 level; †† = 0.15 level.

Sources and notes:
Variables computed from data in Table 4.1. See also note 3, p. 79.
Key to variables:
GR7010: growth rate of GDP per capita, 1870–1910
GR1050: growth rate of GDP per capita, 1910–50
GR5087: growth rate of GDP per capita, 1950–87
GR5073: growth rate of GDP per capita, 1950–73
GR7387: growth rate of GDP per capita, 1973–87
GDP: GDP per capita in initial year
LGDP: log of GDP
EAST: dummy variable = 1 for countries of Central and Eastern Europe (see text and Table 4.1 for inclusions); = 0 for all other countries.

or Rostovian sense, but represent, according to Maddison, distinct periods characterized by sharp turning points and changes in the 'momentum of growth'. The growth rates in Table 4.2 show the changes in momentum in the sense discussed by Maddison. For Europe as a whole, growth was moderate in the period 1870–1910, slow in the period 1910–50, and rapid in the period 1950–87, with the oil price shock marking off a period of unusually rapid growth before 1973 and a slowdown after this.

In the era of moderate growth before the First World War, low-income economies began to 'catch up' with high-income economies; the coefficients of Equations 2a and 2b are negative and statistically significant at the 0.01 level. Within this overall pattern of convergence, the economies of Central and Eastern Europe performed well. They grew rapidly not only compared to other European economies, but also compared to what would have been expected from their low starting point. The coefficients of the EAST variable are positive and statistically significant at the 0.01 (Equation 2c) and 0.05 (Equation 2d) levels.

The experience in the era of slow growth from 1910 to 1950 was sharply different. According to the coefficients of Equations 3a and 3b, incomes did not converge in Europe during this period; growth rates were unrelated to initial levels of GDP per capita in 1910. In addition, the signs on the EAST variable in Equations 3c and 3d are negative, but not statistically significant, which means that there was no difference between growth rates among the economies of Central and Eastern Europe and the rest of Europe.

Income convergence resumed in the cold war era of rapid growth from 1950 to 1987; the signs on the income per capita variable in Equations 4a and 4b are negative and statistically significant. The oil price shock of 1973 ushered in both a growth slowdown in all European economies and a weakening of the trend toward convergence; the signs on the income per capita variable are smaller and their statistical significance is somewhat weaker in the period 1973–87 (Equations 6a and 6b) than in the period 1950–73 (Equations 5a and 5b).

For the period as a whole, Equations 4c and 4d show that at the same level of initial income in 1950, the economies of Central and Eastern Europe grew more slowly than the rest of Europe, the sign on the EAST variable is negative and significant at the 0.05 and the 0.10 levels. The results for the two sub-periods bounded by the oil shock show that experience in the two sub-periods was not uniform and, in fact, runs counter to conventional wisdom. A look at the growth rates in Table 4.2 indicates that the region's economies initially did well, but then sputtered; annual growth was 4.37 per cent before 1973 and 2.13 per cent after 1973. In the pre-1973 era of rapid growth, however, rates of growth in Central and Eastern Europe were not as fast as would have been expected from the initial income levels: the signs on the

EAST variable in Equations 5c and 5d are negative and statistically significant at the 0.01 and 0.05 levels. In contrast, growth rates in the region during the post-1973 era of slower growth tended to be somewhat faster than would have been expected from the 1973 levels of income: the signs of the EAST variable in Equations 6c and 6d are positive, although the statistical significance is not high.

Interpreting the patterns
Taken as a whole, the quantitative results show that since the late nineteenth century, the individual economies of Central and Eastern Europe have entered the path of modern economic growth at different times and at different rates. As a group their rate of economic growth compared to other countries was relatively high. But these high growth rates must be evaluated in the light of the region's relative economic backwardness in the late nineteenth century. Considering the high growth potential inherent in the large gap between the region and the world's economic leaders, first the UK and then the US, the region grew somewhat more slowly than would have been predicted by initial income levels. So the current lag of the region reflects both the low level in 1870 and the relatively slow pace since then.

Explaining these two patterns is, of course, no simple task. There is space here for only a brief survey of the main issues. The literature on the substantial lag of Eastern Europe by 1870 is sizeable.[9] There is little chance of documenting quantitatively the point when development levels in Eastern Europe and Western Europe began to diverge, although the period most certainly lies deep in the past, perhaps in the middle ages. The sources of the divergence are, of course, even less well understood, but they are obviously rooted in deep-seated differences in culture, society and politics along the West to East European economic gradient. In the early modern period, the economies of Eastern Europe operated within the institutions of the 'second' serfdom, which also implied weak central governments *vis-à-vis* the rights and privileges of a strong nobility, and within a rigid ideological climate constrained by Catholicism in the region's western portions and by Orthodoxy in the region's eastern portions. In the same era, the economies of Western Europe flourished within an institutional environment characterized by the rapid flowering of capitalist relations, by strong mercantilist states with programmes of economic development, and by a more fragmented religious climate associated with the Reformation and its various Protestant offshoots. As productivity rose in Western Europe and stagnated in Eastern Europe, the west to east economic gradient began to steepen. By 1870 it had reached the proportions observable in the income estimates of Table 4.1 and the index numbers of Table 4.3.

The literature on the economic history of Eastern Europe over the last century and a half is also sizeable and falls into three separate traditions based on chronology and thematic focus. One tradition covers the period 1870 to 1910 and deals with the economic development of the region under Habsburg imperial rule. The standard, more negative view typified in the older works of Jaszi (1961) and Gerschenkron (1977) has been challenged by more positive assessments that rely on a variety of quantitative evidence.[10] By stimulating increasing interregional flows of capital, labour and tradeable goods, economic integration within the Habsburg lands and Habsburg contact with the independent Balkan states fostered the eastward spread of modern economic growth within Central and Eastern Europe. The evidence presented here supports this newer body of work: incomes within the present-day boundaries of the Habsburg successor states grew more rapidly in the late nineteenth century than would have been predicted by their low initial levels.[11]

A quite distinct, second strand of the literature covers the period from 1910 to 1950 (Berend and Ránki 1974, Lampe and Jackson 1982, and Kaser and Radice 1986). The main theme is state building among the successor states of the Habsburg, Russian and Ottoman Empires in the larger context of the First World War, the Great Depression, and the Second World War. As in most of Europe, this was an era of economic instability and stagnation in Central and Eastern Europe. While the mechanisms are not clear, specialists point to the profound structural weaknesses in the region after imperial collapse and the rise of protectionism as new states instituted their own tariff regimes (März 1981). These weaknesses in turn led to the fall of Vienna's Creditanstalt, which had been the dominant institutional force in the region's capital market under imperial rule. The bank's fall triggered a financial crisis that ultimately lengthened and deepened the worldwide depression. The data tend to give some support for this assessment of economic weakness in Central and Eastern Europe. Despite rapid growth in the late nineteenth century, the lag of the region within Europe on the eve of the First World War was still substantial. Of course, most European economies tended to slow down in the period of the world wars and the Great Depression. But considering the income levels prevailing in 1910, the rate of growth in Central and Eastern Europe should have been faster than it actually was.

The third separate branch of the literature covers the cold war era from 1950 to 1987. It focuses on the economic consequences of communism within the overall debate on the relative performance of capitalism and socialism as economic systems. Most assessments are overwhelmingly negative: they regard the communist era as a kind of missed opportunity for Central and Eastern Europe.[12] The sources of the missed opportunity were both internal and external. In part they lay in the institutional mechanisms of state socialism even in its reformed versions – the system's striking inability to provide incentives for 'positive-sum' productivity-raising behaviour and its rigidity in face of changing external circumstances. In part the causes lay in the region's fundamental isolation from the more dynamic Western econo-mies, which persisted despite some opening up in the 1980s. With only limited access to Western markets and capital, the region could not tap the sources of economic growth that continued to fuel the closing of the gap between Western Europe and the US. Obviously the internal and external factors are related. In the early years the closed nature of the economic system and the self-sufficiency of the East bloc were mutually reinforcing. The internationalization of the socialist economies in the 1970s sought to restart their sputtering growth engines; ultimately it may have undermined the system itself. A less commonly held variant offers a more generous view: that communism served its purpose in the early post-1945 years by promot-ing rapid modernization but then its rigidities acted as an obstacle to growth and eventually led to the wholesale collapse of state socialism throughout Central and Eastern Europe.[13]

My analysis provides some statistical support for the overall negative assessment. Although the economies of the region grew rapidly during the cold war, rates of economic growth should have been even more rapid given the low income levels in 1950.[14] But the idea that the state-socialist growth engines did well initially and then sputtered must be viewed against the tendency for Central and Eastern Europe to underperform the convergence model before the oil price shock of 1973 and outperform it after 1973. Despite unprecedentedly rapid rates of growth from 1950 to 1973, the small states of Central and Eastern Europe grew more slowly than would have been predicted by their income levels prevailing in 1950. After 1973 growth rates slowed dramatically in the region to about half those of the pre-1973 period. Yet given the income levels of 1973, growth rates in the region were higher than would have been predicted by the income levels of 1973.[15]

Despite variations within individual sub-periods, the overall pattern seems clear. The region of Central and Eastern Europe grew rapidly between 1870 and 1987, but considering its relative backwardness in 1870, the subsequent rate of growth after 1870 was somewhat slow. To arrive at a satisfactory explanation, it is necessary to synthesize the rather disparate literatures on the region's economic history. The synthesis would show that the explanation lies ultimately in the pattern of state building and economy building that has characterized 'the lands between' Germany and Russia, especially in the last century or so.

Since the mid-1800s, the political economy of the region seems to have been reinvented every half century in the wake of destabilizing external shocks. The first shock came in the late nineteenth century as the uneven spread of modern economic growth through Central and Eastern Europe uprooted traditional agrarian societies and fostered the growth of nationalism (often economic-based) within multinational empires. The First World War delivered the second shock: successor states were created from the fallen Russian and Habsburg Empires in much the same way that war had led to the fragmentation and ultimate collapse of the decaying Ottoman Empire during the nineteenth century. The Second World War delivered the third shock as all the small states of the region except Austria were incorporated into the Soviet Empire with the fall of the iron curtain. Now the region labours in the aftermath of a fourth major shock – the collapse of the Soviet imperial system that began in 1989. Each of these shocks set off significant changes in the region's underlying pattern of state building and/or economy building, including its domestic institutions and international economic relations. The transitional periods were painful and marked by economic difficulties, social conflict and political instability. These dramatic twists and turns alone may explain much of the region's tendency toward relatively slow convergence on the higher-income economies of Europe after 1870.[16]

Of course, the radical nature of these changes should not be overemphasized, nor should the shocks that preceded them be regarded strictly as exogenous. Reflecting choices made in prior eras, institutional and ideological legacies persist and shape decision making in successive generations, which gives history its path-dependent character (Arthur 1988; David 1985; and North 1990). In explaining the patterns of economic development in Central and Eastern Europe, it is important to account for this by identifying both the continuities and the sharp breaks in the region's political economy. Some Western specialists have been doing precisely this in their analysis of the current transition (Stark 1992 and Murrell 1992). They argue that current efforts to transform these planned economies into full-blown, Western-style market economies represent a grand design of social engineering on the scale of the communist experiment itself. In the communist case, the grand design was ultimately constrained and shaped by legacies from the past, that is, it was path-dependent. Path dependence led to different patterns of reform in the initial grand design[17] and perhaps to the ultimate breakdown in the experiment itself. It now shapes the different paths during the current transition and may determine the ultimate outcome.

But 'failed' efforts at social engineering have a long history in the region; they accompanied and in large measure were important factors in the previous destabilizing shocks: nation building under imperial rule in the context of great power politics was a major factor in the outbreak of the First World War; state-building efforts among the imperial successor states in the context of international diplomacy played a key role in the events that led to the Second World War.

This brief survey of economic history in Central and Eastern Europe suggests caution in assessing the economic future of Europe's Third World.

Previous efforts at reinventing the region's political economy have certainly fostered modern economic growth, but the pace of catch-up has been somewhat slow considering the potential inherent in the relative backwardness of the region a century ago. As in the past, the region's ability to tap this potential and begin catching up with the rest of Europe will depend both on internal and external factors, and on the interaction of the two. If the post-1989 transition loses legitimacy, economic growth in the region will be hampered by a new round of political instability. If the peoples of the region are left on the doorstep of a fortress EU, then economic growth will be hampered by a new kind of neo-cold war isolation, which will in turn heat the fires of domestic political instability.

In both respects the case of Austria is instructive.[18] Among the small states in Central and Eastern Europe, no country in the interwar period suffered more from the region's devastating cycles of political economy than Austria. But the country miraculously escaped the cycle after the Second World War and is now a full-fledged member of the EU. The Austrian case provides some hope that the cycle can also be broken for its neighbouring states of the former East bloc.

Notes

1. For surveys of the region's economic history, see Chirot (1989), Good (1984), Kaser and Radice (1986), and Lampe and Jackson (1982).
2. Of course, levels of income per capita in the former East bloc are high compared to most developing economies in Africa, Asia and even Latin America, which makes facile analogies between Eastern Europe and the Third World highly suspect.
3. Tables 4.1 and 4.3 present the most recent estimates, which were carried out in the final phase of typesetting. They differ slightly from the data set used in the calculations for Tables 4.2 and 4.4 because of minor revisions in the underlying statistics and small computational errors, but do not alter the main conclusions. For details on the estimates see the separate appendix available from the author on request.
4. For a useful summary of the ICP approach see Kravis (1986). For more detail see Kravis et al. (1978) and Summers and Heston (1988).
5. Maddison (1991) provides updated estimates based on ICP data for 1985, but not for the countries of Eastern Europe and the Mediterranean (Portugal, Spain and Greece). Because of my interest in the European 'periphery', I have relied on the ICP 1980 data in his (1990) volume, which contains a detailed discussion of sources in Table A-2.
6. For a full discussion of the sources underlying the GDP indexes for each country see Maddison (1991, 201–205; 220–21) and Maddison (1990, Table A-l). Maddison has adjusted these GDP indexes to eliminate the effects of boundary changes. He acknowledges the problems in using the indexes, but notes that their weighting systems are updated from time to time and that each national series is composed of differently weighted sub-periods that are linked together. See Maddison (1989, 196) and Maddison (1990, 96–7). Over the years he has periodically updated these indexes as country specialists improve their long-term estimates of GDP. For the pre-1914 period, the GDP indexes are relatively more reliable for the UK, France, Germany, Italy and the Scandinavian countries than for Belgium, the Netherlands, Switzerland and Russia. See Maddison (1990, 101 and 104).
7. See notes for Table 4.2. Because of historic ties to its neighbours in the former East bloc, I include Austria as part of Central and Eastern Europe. I list Vojvodina separately from

Serbia because of its pre-First World War status as Habsburg territory and its post-1945 status as an autonomous province within Serbia.

8. The relationship is strong using a small sample of already developed economies in the post-1945 period or state-level data for the US. Studies that use an enlarged sample of present-day developing economies or extend the analysis to include pre-1945 data show little or no evidence of income convergence. Some economists have argued that these tests of convergence have serious flaws from a statistical point of view (see Friedman 1992 and Quah 1993). But assuming that the tests are valid, the results are, of course, open to different interpretations. Proponents of neo-Marxist or dependency theory would view the lack of 'fit' as evidence that a convergence of incomes over time is not inevitable. For a summary of these traditions see Brewer (1980). Within the neoclassical tradition, the lag of the actual rate of growth in low-income economies behind potential may be explained by obstacles that impede the long-term tendency toward convergence. These may be economic factors relating to the openness of the economy or market size, or institutional factors relating to the social capacity to innovate, the nature of human capital, or the pattern of property rights. Incorporating measures of these factors into regression equations has improved the 'fit', that is, explained some variation in growth rates beyond that explained by the initial level only.

9. See, for example, the citations in note 1.

10. See, for example, Eddie (1989), Good (1984), Gross (1966), Huertas (1977), Katus (1970), Kausel (1979), Komlos (1983), Mosser (1980), and Rudolph (1976).

11. But see the recent conclusions of John Lampe (1989). From fragmentary data he argues that 'the experience of the southern and eastern Habsburg periphery suggests that these borderlands did not share fully in the monarchy's fairly impressive economic growth and integration between 1815–1914.' The estimates here and in Good (1994a) indicate that Lampe's conclusion holds for the first half of the nineteenth century, but not for the second half. They are also consistent with the work of John Hanson (1986) who argues from export data that existing studies greatly underestimate pre-1914 levels of GDP in both the Third World and in Eastern Europe.

12. See, for example, the contributions of Lee Alston, Scott Eddie, Michael Palairet, and Jan Stankovsky in Good (1994b).

13. See, for example, the contribution of Ivan Berend in Good (1994b).

14. In contrast, Frederic Pryor (1985) found that growth rates in post-1945 East European economies were not slower even after adjusting for differences in initial levels of income. Apart from differences in underlying data, these results are not strictly comparable with mine. His sample of Western countries included all OECD countries, not just European members, while his sample of Eastern European countries included the Soviet Union, but not the successor states to former Czechoslovakia and former Yugoslavia.

15. Again my results differ from those of Frederic Pryor, which he published in his recent (1994) article. Using the same sample of OECD and Eastern European countries from his (1985) study, he found a greater deceleration of income after the early 1970s in the East bloc than in the group of OECD countries.

16. This idea was suggested to me by Ellen Comisso.

17. See Johnson (1989).

18. On this theme see Matis (1991) and Kramer and Butschek (1985).

References

Abramovitz, M. (1986), 'Catching Up, Forging Ahead, and Falling Behind', *Journal of Economic History*, 46.

Alam, M.S. (1992), 'Convergence in Developed Countries: An Empirical Investigation', *Weltwirtschaftliches Archiv*, 128.

Arthur, W.B. (1988), 'Self-Reinforcing Mechanisms in Economics', in P.W. Anderson, K.J. Arrow and D. Pines (eds), *The Economy as an Evolving Complex System*, Reading, Mass.: Addison-Wesley.

Barro, R.J. (1991), 'Economic Growth in a Cross Section of Countries', *Quarterly Journal of Economics*, 106.

Barro, R.J. and Sala i Martin, X. (1991), 'Convergence across States and Regions', *Brookings Papers on Economic Activity*, 1.

Baumol, W.J. (1986), 'Productivity Growth, Convergence, and Welfare: What the Long-Run Data Show', *American Economic Review*, 76.

Baumol, W.J., Blackman, S.A.B. and Wolff, E.N. (1989), *Productivity and American Leadership: The Long View*, Cambridge, Mass: MIT Press, 1989.

Berend, I. and Ránki, G. (1974), *Economic Development in East-Central Europe in the 19th and 20th Centuries*, New York: Columbia University Press.

Brewer, A. (1980), *Marxist Theories of Imperialism*, London: Routledge & Kegan Paul.

Capek, A. and Sazama, G.W. (1993), 'Czech and Slovak Economic Relations', *Europe–Asia Studies*, 45: 211–35.

Chirot, D. (ed.) (1989), *The Origins of Backwardness in Eastern Europe: Economics and Politics from the Middle Ages until the Twentieth Century*, Berkeley: University of California Press.

Crafts, N.F.R. (1983), 'Gross National Product in Europe 1870–1910: Some New Estimates', *Explorations in Economic History*, 20.

David, P. (1985), 'Clio and the Economics of QWERTY', *American Economic Review*, 75.

Dowrick, S. and Nguyen, D.-T. (1989), 'OECD Comparative Growth 1950–85: Catch-Up and Convergence', *American Economic Review*, 79.

Eddie, S. (1989), 'Economic Policy and Economic Development in Austria-Hungary, 1867–1913', in *The Cambridge Economic History of Europe*, vol. 8.

Evans, P. and Karras, G. (1993), 'Do standards of living converge? Some cross-country evidence', *Economic Letters*, 43.

Friedman, M. (1992), 'Communication: Do Old Fallacies Ever Die?', *Journal of Economic Literature*, 30.

Gerschenkron, A. (1962), *Economic Backwardness in Historical Perspective*, Cambridge, Mass: Harvard University Press.

Gerschenkron, A. (1977), *An Economic Spurt that Failed*, Princeton, NJ: Princeton University Press.

Good, D.F. (1984), *The Economic Rise of the Habsburg Empire 1750–1914*, Berkeley: University of California Press.

Good, D.F. (1993), 'Estimating Pre-1914 Incomes in the Post-1919 Successor States of the Habsburg Empire: Supplementary Notes and Tables', unpublished manuscript.

Good, D.F. (1994a), 'The Economic Lag of Central and Eastern Europe: Income Estimates for the Habsburg Successor States, 1870–1910', *Journal of Economic History*, 54.

Good, D.F. (ed.) (1994b), *Economic Transformations in East and Central Europe: Legacies from the Past and Policies for the Future*, London and New York: Routledge.

Gross, N. (1966), 'Industrialization in the Nineteenth Century', PhD diss., University of California, Berkeley.

Hanson, J.R. II (1986), 'Export Shares in the European Periphery and the Third World before World War I: Questionable Data, Facile Analogies', *Explorations in Economic History*, 23.

Huertas, T. (1977), *Economic Growth and Economic Policy in a Multinational Setting*, New York: Arno Press.

Jaszi, O. (1961), *The Dissolution of the Habsburg Monarchy*, Chicago: University of Chicago Press.

Johnson, P.M. (1989), *Redesigning the Communist Economy: The Politics of Economic Reform in Eastern Europe*, Boulder, Co.: East European Monographs.

Kaser, M.C. and Radice, E.A. (eds) (1986), *The Economic History of Eastern Europe 1919-1975*, Vol. I, Oxford: Oxford University Press.

Katus, L. (1970), 'Economic Growth in Hungary During the Age of Dualism 1867–1913: A Quantitative Analysis', in E. Pamlenyi (ed.), *Social and Economic Researches on the History of East-Central Europe*, Budapest: Akademei Kiado.

Kausel, A. (1979), 'Österreichs Volkseinkommen 1830 bis 1913', in *Geschichte und Ergebnisse der zentralen amtlichen Statistik in Österreich 1829–1979*, Vienna: Österreichisches statistisches Zentralamt.

Komlos, J. (1983), *The Habsburg Monarchy as a Customs Union: Economic Development in Austria–Hungary in the Nineteenth-Century*, Princeton: Princeton University Press.

Kramer, H. and Butschek, F. (1985), *Vom Nachzügler zum Vorbild(?). Österreichische Wirtschaft 1945 bis 1985*, Stuttgart: Gustav Fischer.

Kravis, I. (1986), 'The Three Faces of the International Comparison Project', *Research Observer*, 1.

Kravis, I., Heston, A. and Summers, R. (1978), 'Real GNP Per Capita for More than One Hundred Countries', *Economic Journal*, 88.

Lampe, J. (1989), 'Imperial Borderlands or Capitalist Periphery? Redefining Balkan Backwardness, 1520–1914', in Chirot (1989).

Lampe, J. and Jackson, M. (1982), *Balkan Economic History 1550–1950: From Imperial Borderlands to Developing Nations*, Bloomington: Indiana University Press.

Landes, D. (1969), *The Unbound Prometheus*, Cambridge: Cambridge University Press.

Maddison, A. (1989), *The World Economy in the 20th Century*, Paris: OECD.

Maddison, A. (1990), 'Measuring European Growth: The Core and the Periphery', in E. Aerts and N. Valério (eds), *Growth and Stagnation in the Mediterranean World in the 19th and 20th Centuries*, Leuven: Leuven University Press.

Maddison, A. (1991), *Dynamic Forces in Capitalist Development*, London and New York: Oxford University Press.

März, E. (1981), *Österreichische Bankpolitik in der Zeit der grossen Wende 1913–1923*, Vienna: Verlag für Geschichte und Politik.

Matis, H. (1991), 'Österreichs Wirtschaftsgeschichte - ein Modell für Osteuropa?' *Österreich in Geschichte und Literatur*, 35.

Miljkovič, D. (1992), 'The Economic Development Level of the Former (SFR) Yugoslavia Compared to the Countries of Europe 1985–1991', *Yugoslav Survey*.

Mosser, A. (1980), *Die Industrieaktiengesellschaften in Österreich 1880–1913*. Vienna: Verlag der österreichischen Akademie der Wissenschaften.

Murrell, P. (1992), 'Conservative Political Philosophy and the Strategy of Economic Transition', *East European Politics and Society*, 6.

Nikolič, M. (1992), 'Economic Development of the First and Second Yugoslavia (1918–1990), *Yugoslav Survey*.

North, D.C. (1990), *Institutions, Institutional Change and Economic Performance*, Cambridge: Cambridge University Press.

Palairet, M. (1993), 'The Habsburg Industrial Achievement in Bosnia-Hercegovina, 1878–1914: An Economic Spurt That Succeeded?' *Austrian History Yearbook*, 24.

Pryor, F. (1985), 'Growth and Fluctuations of Production in O.E.C.D and East European Countries', *World Politics*, 37.

Pryor, F. (1994), 'Growth Deceleration and Transactions Costs: A Note', *Journal of Economic Behavior and Organization*, 25.

Quah, D. (1993), 'Galton's Fallacy and Tests of the Convergence Hypothesis', *Scandinavian Journal of Economics*, 95.

Rostow, W.W. (ed.) (1963), *The Economics of Take-Off into Sustained Growth*, London: Macmillan.

Rudolph, R. (1976), *Banking and Industrialization in Austria–Hungary*, Cambridge: Cambridge University Press.

Stark, D. (1992), 'Path Dependence and Privatization Strategies in East Central Europe', *East European Politics and Societies*, 6.

Summers, R. and Heston, A. (1988), 'A New Set of International Comparisons of Real Product and Price Levels: Estimates for 130 Countries, 1950–1985', *The Review of Income and Wealth*, 34.

UN/Eurostat (1986), *World Comparisons of Purchasing Power and Real Product for 1980*, New York: UN.

Williamson, J.G. (1991), 'Productivity and American Leadership: A Review Article', *Journal of Economic Literature*, 29.

5 Macroeconomic populism and economic failure in Africa since 1960

Stuart Jones

655

The economic failure of Africa in the second half of the twentieth century has been widespread and persistent. It has not been a local phenomenon. The collapse started in West Africa in the days of Nkrumah, spread to East Africa and has now reached Southern Africa. By the 1980s Sub-Saharan Africa had entered on a period of negative economic growth. Between 1980 and 1987 the GDP of the region was falling at the rate of 1.3 per cent a year and per capita GDP was declining at the rate of 4.5 per cent a year (Hodd 1991, 20). Even oil-rich Nigeria and gold-rich South Africa, geographically far apart and experiencing quite different economic conditions, had joined the Sub-Saharan Africa club of failing economies.

Failure on this scale is both disturbing and challenging: the former because it provides ammunition to advocates of ethnic interpretations of what has gone wrong; the latter because it challenges economic historians and economists to identify the causes so that solutions may be found to what are clearly deep-rooted economic problems. A continental failure of these proportions suggests that there may be general causes at work affecting the continent as a whole as well as more specific ones at work in individual countries. Implicit in this interpretation is the notion that Africanization and the abandonment of Western norms and Western ways of doing things create obstacles to modern economic growth.

Two approaches to the problem will be adopted in this paper. First there will be an attempt to identify the causes of economic growth in the West and to determine whether they are present in modern Africa, and second, there will be an attempt to identify the specific causes of African economic failure.

Causes of Western economic growth
Explanations of the rise of the West implicitly and sometimes explicitly argue that efficient economic organization is the key to economic growth (North and Thomas 1973). This is uncontroversial. How to achieve this illusive goal is less clear as all the Sub-Saharan states have learned in recent years. What is clear is that the relatively efficient economic organization of early modern Europe owed much to the existence of clearly defined property rights, to its geographical uniqueness and to the progress of technology. While the first of

these may be crucial to getting the growth process under way it is argued here that it should be seen as a consequence of environmental factors peculiar to Western Europe. Environmental factors and the role of technology may therefore be identified as the main causes of economic growth.

Both attach importance to solving supply-side problems but the environmentalists place very special emphasis on demand. This may be seen most clearly in *The European Miracle* (Jones 1981) in which the author argues that in Europe the absence of large river valleys containing great concentrations of people together with its particular geography prevented the rise of centralizing autocracies that acted as revenue pumps. Such revenue pumps encouraged expenditures on grandiose projects or wasteful military spending and by their very existence restricted the growth of the market. In Europe the decentralized structure that succeeded the Roman Empire acted as an impediment to tax collection. It permitted within the framework of Latin Christendom the evolution of relatively liberal states in which the role of the individual could develop and be recognized. The Renaissance and the Protestant Reformation built on these foundations and subsequent political and constitutional developments in both the Netherlands and England reinforced them. Liberal constitutional governments created the conditions in which property rights were defined and secured and in which efficient economic organization could take place. It was no accident that economic growth flourished in the Netherlands and England and stagnated or declined in Italy and France. Efficient economic organization within a very special set of political circumstances made possible by environmental factors distinguished the economy of early modern Europe from that of other continents.

Europe moreover was blessed with abundant natural resources. It possessed plentiful rainfall, fertile river-valleys and broad plains, while its deeply indented coastline sheltered many small harbours fed by rivers suitable for navigation. Minerals too were abundant and could be transported by water. Trade was vigorous and not excessively taxed. Yet it was on an agricultural foundation that the economic growth took place. Agricultural progress was most evident in those parts of Europe where property rights were clearly defined and where inefficient peasant producers could be replaced by more efficient tenant farmers. Tenant farming, responding to signals coming out of the market, was the means by which agricultural productivity was raised and this happened long after the nuclear family had replaced the extended family in Western Europe.

In Africa conditions were very different. Most parts of the continent are not blessed with regular and plentiful rainfall. Droughts are common. Nor is Africa blessed with large numbers of river valleys that combine fertile soil with facilities for transport. The continent's mineral endowment is more abundant and its efficient economic exploitation began in the nineteenth century when the colonial state played a central role in the economic trans-formation of tropical Africa (Munro 1984, 30). Economic development accel-erated in the middle decades of the twentieth century with the rapid expan-sion of copper mining in Central Africa, the opening of new gold mines in South Africa and the discovery of oil in West Africa. By the third quarter of the twentieth century the known resource base of Africa had increased sub-stantially.

How therefore can we explain the failure that took shape in this period? What has changed? What has made post-1960 Africa so different from the Africa that experienced sustained economic growth in the late 1940s and 1950s? The answer is clear. The disadvantageous political and environmental factors that had for so long held back economic development were strength-ened by the new political structures that were taking shape throughout the continent. The transplanting to Africa of politics based in Western Europe had introduced into Africa liberal structures that rewarded individual enter-prise while keeping corruption to a minimum. British and French colonies in effect were extensions into Africa of the same liberal structures that made possible sustained economic growth in Western Europe. The granting of independence and the emergence of local African regimes that were not liberal and which were heavily influenced by collectivist ideas radically changed the situation.

Collective ownership of the land acted as a major obstacle to agricultural development in many parts of Africa at a time when state marketing monopo-lies were drawing wealth from agriculture to finance inefficient socialist projects in the secondary sector and to support bloated bureaucracies. Gov-ernment policies made it difficult if not impossible for African countries to experience agriculture-led growth after independence. Institutional failure has been the main cause of Africa's economic failure. The governments and the institutions they created did not produce conditions favourable to eco-nomic growth. This decline began before the long period of worldwide sus-tained economic growth came to an end in 1973, though since then the changed international environment has made the task more difficult for all developing countries including those in Southeast Asia.

African states all too often have wanted to have their cake and eat it. They have wanted to have Western standards of living and Western incomes while introducing African ways of doing things that conflicted with economic effi-ciency. Inheriting West European types of constitutional governments, they converted them into Latin American type populist regimes regardless of the fact that macroeconomic populism has disastrous economic and social conse-quences. Populist regimes in both Latin America and Africa have been char-acterized by expanding government spending, cheap credit, sharp wage in-creases, quantitative import restrictions and overvalued exchange rates (Mohr

1993, 39). These conditions were very different from those prevailing in Western Europe and North America and without exception brought growth to a halt and harmed the very people that were supposed to be benefiting from such policies.

The second general explanation of growth that might throw light on the African experience is the one which attributes the key role to technology. Arthur Lewis gave his imprimatur to it even though he accepts that trade was an engine of growth in the late nineteenth century (Lewis 1978, 74). The era of the industrial revolution had seen Western Europe and North America move decisively ahead of the rest of the world in the level of technology employed in mining, manufacturing and transport. The nineteenth century saw the pace of change accelerate and this pattern has been conspicuous in the second half of the twentieth century. It has therefore been easy for economists to identify technology as the main cause of economic growth. Schmookler was arguing for this back in 1966 (Schmookler 1966), but according to Maddison there is no evidence that the postwar acceleration in the growth rate was the result of a faster pace of technological innovation. The frontier of technology lay predominantly in the US economy whose pace of productivity growth did not increase. The acceleration of growth outside the US is basically explicable in terms of a reduction in the technological gap (Maddison 1982, 124).

Not all countries were able to reduce this gap by importing technology because conditions in the recipient countries differed very considerably. While Western Europe and Japan narrowed the gap between themselves and the US, that between Sub-Saharan Africa and the developed West widened. Technology transplant requires a high stock of skills which was lacking in much of Africa plus an expanding economy that could utilize modern technology. Only in portions of South Africa were the conditions conducive to the successful rooting of imported technology on a large scale and even here those conditions were deteriorating in the 1980s. Elsewhere some catching up could take place – the borrowing of yesterday's technology – but in general the conditions were not favourable to productivity-raising innovation and much of the growth that occurred was simply the result of more inputs producing more outputs.

Much of Africa in the third quarter of this century was far behind the socioeconomic level of Europe in the 1880s. Even in an industry as unsophisticated as cotton spinning the conditions did not exist for the introduction of the most modern technology. That took place in Germany, Switzerland and Japan, not in Africa; and where governments pushed the introduction of a textile industry as in Kenya and South Africa productivity was such that the infant industries had to be protected by high tariff barriers that raised costs to the consumer and reduced the market for other manufactured goods.

Modern technology requires capital and that capital needs to be employed efficiently. Meanwhile as businesses have grown larger and more complex the management of them has also become more complex and specialized management skills have become relatively more important. If the Massachusetts Institute of Technology symbolizes progress in technology then the Harvard Business School around the corner symbolizes putting it to productive use. In Africa managerial skills have been in short supply and managerial weakness has been conspicuous. Chartered accountants, business managers and production engineers cannot be produced overnight in a backward economy which is why capital imported into an underdeveloped economy is seldom as productive as that in Japan or Germany. The modern business corporation emerged in America according to Alfred Chandler in order to manage complex manufacturing enterprises and their very large cash flows (Chandler 1977). Technology does not operate in a vacuum and unless the firms incorporating it are well managed and make profits it will not be an engine of growth.

The ending of the Western framework

In post-colonial Africa the reproduction of West European conditions in the political and economic spheres came to an abrupt end in the early 1960s (Hopkins 1973, 171). Relatively liberal market-oriented economies bearing light layers of government gave way to illiberal socialist-leaning regimes that spawned bloated bureaucracies. A decline in efficiency inevitably occurred. In such conditions technology could be imported yet all too often this was not a response to market forces but the result of ideologically motivated political intervention pandering to vested interests. Capital-intensive glamour projects were undertaken in preference to labour-intensive ones when the dominant factor endowments would suggest the opposite. After 1960 the conditions that had made economic growth possible in Western Europe and North America and which had been introduced into Africa by the colonial powers no longer existed and growth that had flourished in such conditions began to weaken. Instability replaced stability and the climate of confidence changed (Hodd 1991, 33).

At the general level this thesis provides an explanation of why African economies have performed so poorly in the years since independence. Critics of this thesis, however, may ask why illiberal regimes in Southeast Asia have been able to succeed when those in Africa failed. Two explanations are possible: either special circumstances applied to Southeast Asian countries that enabled them to go on growing despite experiencing a different set of political and social conditions from liberal Western countries, or unusually unfavourable conditions afflicted African countries after 1960. Special circumstances certainly applied to Southeast Asia and Africa. The former lie outside the scope of this paper; the latter may be summed up in the term macroeconomic populism. Newly independent regimes, already nationalist in sympathy in their struggle against colonialism, readily succumbed to the blandishments of socialism and, as Hitler so ably demonstrated, the mixture of socialism and nationalism produces an explosive force that can be devastating.

It certainly has been devastating in Africa where African governments have been responsible for massive economic failure. Exogenous factors may have exacerbated weaknesses in African economies as the terms of trade turned against primary producers, but the main source of the malaise should be sought within Africa. Repeated harping on the legacy of colonialism – a favourite pastime of Nyerere – is positively harmful for it enables those responsible for economic failure to evade responsibility for their actions (Ayittey 1989, 4). Contrast the whining of Nyerere with the response of the South Korean government to its plight in 1960. The former inherited a reasonably solid infrastructure, a growing economy and a legacy of reasonably good colonial government, yet twenty years after Tanzania had gained independence Nyerere's response to the debt crisis was to argue that 'The situation is a neo-colonial one and African economies are not going to change until the neo-colonial relationship is changed' (Ayittey 1989, 8). This is meaningless and compares unfavourably with the record of South Korea which did not experience reasonably good colonial government. It was plundered by Japan for 40 years and then devastated by the Korean War that saw much of the country fought over four times within the space of two years, first by North Koreans then by the Americans, by the Chinese and lastly by the Americans again. In 1960 South Korea was much poorer than Tanganyika; but instead of blaming colonialism and holding out the begging bowl the South Korean government set about reforming agriculture by breaking up the great estates into small peasant farms. Nyerere did the opposite. He destroyed the peasant farms and drove the occupants into Stalin-style collective farms. The South Korean government invested heavily in education especially technological education. African governments neglected it and failed to divert sufficient funds either into technological education or into ordinary secondary education. One-party states presided over by socialist dictators systematically destroyed the economies of Ghana, Zambia and Tanganyika. Macroeconomic populism in the guise of African socialism has wrought more harm on the peoples of Africa than its counterpart in Latin America has upon the peoples of that continent.

The failure of African economies since 1960 cannot be attributed simply to poor factor endowments, to the effects of colonialism or to more difficult international economic conditions, all of which apply equally to South Korea, Taiwan, Hong Kong and Singapore; nor in the case of Africa may the failure be laid at the door of droughts of unusual intensity, for there is little evidence that natural calamities were more severe after 1960 than they were before 1960 when economic growth was vigorous and widespread. The cause of Africa's failure lies in the failure of African governments to maintain the conditions that made growth possible. It was a political failure of continental proportions; and at the heart of this failure was economic policy.

The adoption and implementation of policies inimical to economic growth were exacerbated by the expanded role afforded to the state, by the creation of bloated bureaucracies and by an acceleration in the rate of population growth (Ravenhill 1986, 27). Many African governments have tended to take away the competitive advantage that a rapidly expanding population might have brought by raising minimum wages to levels that make export-led growth spear-headed by the secondary sector impossible. By denying the existence of comparative advantage in an increasingly competitive international economy they were able to adopt and to maintain policies that brought them into conflict with the market. For many years the rapid growth of the international economy accompanied by a steady flow of foreign aid enabled harmful policies to be adopted and maintained longer than would otherwise have been the case. If African economies grew it was likely to be despite the actions of their governments rather than because of them.

Macroeconomic populism, the cause of this monumental economic failure, was characterized by the failure to establish clearly defined and secure private property rights that would encourage individual enterprise. It embraced the following policies: overvalued exchange rates, substantial increases in government expenditure, import controls, unjustified wage increases and food subsidies designed to benefit the urban poor (that might threaten weak governments) at the expense of the agricultural sector. Macroeconomic populism was urban-based with self-perpetuating oligarchies handing out subsidies to their urban supporters. Not surprisingly agriculture was neglected, as were infrastructure projects with a long time threshold, while industrial policies were often so unreal that only politicians of the calibre of a Kaunda or Nyerere could think that they would succeed. Popularized by Mussolini and further developed by Hitler, the explosive mixture of nationalism and socialism that forms the basis of macroeconomic populism has exerted a baleful influence over much of Africa, Asia and Latin America. Indeed, if African economies were underdeveloped, as many neo-Marxists would have us believe, it is arguable that this was done not by the colonial governments of yesteryear but by the liberated governments of the later twentieth century which all too often had become interests opposed to growth (Ravenhill 1986, 26). 'Africa's economic crisis is above all a political crisis.'

The impact of harmful policies was in many instances made worse by Western aid which provided incompetent governments with the means of implementing policies that were damaging their economies. This unhappy state of affairs was partly a consequence of the cold war and partly a reaction to feelings of guilt by leaders in the developed economies. Between 1970 and 1985 Western donors poured $16 billion into Tanzania to support 'an arrogant single party bureaucracy', 'the persecution of anyone seeking to provide a service for profit' and a 'Stalinist type of collectivisation of agriculture' (*The Economist*, 24 August 1991). The World Bank too has consistently supported Third World dictatorships.

This view has been admitted by the Bank in an internal report drawn up in 1990. During the presidency of Robert McNamara, the Bank viewed Tanzania 'as coming close to being a model developing country', and in the words of its own report 'Tanzania's unprecedented access to concessionary flows of external capital has allowed it ... to maintain a high rate of largely ill-conceived and uneconomical industrial investment' (Georgeson and Holman 1994). When the burgeoning economic crisis at last forced the Bank to review its policies and the government of Tanzania to introduce some market-driven reforms, Nyerere retired. The World Bank's experience with Tanzania highlights the failure of responsible institutions to criticize recipient governments and their tacit acceptance of corruption at high levels in the governments with which they were dealing.

This view is also supported by *The Economist* (24 August 1991) which has argued forcibly that Western aid donors and in particular the Nordic countries have contributed to perpetuating the suffering of millions of persons in four ways: by financing dictatorships, by financing uneconomic projects, by helping bankrupt governments to stay in power and by helping to destroy previously viable economies.

The failure of African governments to adopt policies likely to bring about satisfactory economic growth is linked to the replacement of the relatively liberal market-oriented governments by arbitrary self-perpetuating oligarchies. Indeed the experience of Sub-Saharan Africa since 1960 provides much evidence in support of Mancur Olson's thesis outlined in *The Rise and Decline of Nations*. He argues convincingly that the larger the political unit the less likely it is that collusive coalitions of vested interests will be able to manipulate the organs of state in their own interest. Medieval towns that were controlled by guilds gave way to the larger nation state and, in the nineteenth-century era of free trade, British colonialism opened Africa to a worldwide market larger than any previously known – a market in which collusive coalitions of the kind referred to by Olson were at their weakest (Olson 1982, 119). Independence had the effect of shrinking the horizons and immeasurably strengthening the influence of local vested interests. Olson accepts that economic growth will normally occur but argues that historically collusive coalitions have usually slowed it down and often brought it to a halt by placing their own selfish interests before the good of the whole body politic. This is what has happened in much of Africa in the second half of the twentieth century. Corrupt and repressive regimes were allowed to continue for so long because the cold war enabled them to play off East against West or vice versa. This applied to both pro-Western and pro-Soviet regimes. Both Mobuto in Zaire and Menghistu in Ethiopia were allowed to pursue policies that made efficient economic organization impossible in their respective countries. Others deluded themselves into believing that in African socialism or macroeconomic populism they had found an alternative way to growth. Indeed they had the begging bowl approach that kept alive the illusion that their policies were working, but this source of growth was already becoming increasingly hard to obtain before the collapse of the Soviet Union brought it to an end. By the 1990s the only internationally acceptable path to growth was a market-driven one and the Sub-Saharan countries were back to the position of the late 1950s.

The demographic factor
Policy failure in Africa has been accompanied by unparalleled population growth and the continent is in danger of heading towards a Malthusian condition with its population increasing at an annual rate of 3.2 per cent (Hodd 1991, 8). This rate of growth, moreover, has been accelerating in the second half of this century (Wolfson 1985, 94). In South Africa the rate of increase is said to be decreasing, but only after an increase of 120 per cent in 30 years. Kenya's track record is even worse than that of South Africa. Its rate of increase shot up from 3.4 per cent in the 1960s to 4.2 per cent in the 1980s (World Bank 1990, 292), surpassed only by the Ivory Coast, which hit a peak of 4.3 per cent a year in the 1970s (World Bank 1990, 146). Growth in the order of this magnitude makes per capita economic growth virtually impossible. It is a phenomenon previously unknown in the history of the world. Nor have the rulers of African states usually had the statesmanship to acknowledge the existence of the problem. In South Africa no leading black politician is yet prepared to support birth control, yet they parade around the country talking of free schooling and free housing without apparently understanding that such benefits have to be paid for and can be crippling to a poor country with its population structure skewed in favour of the young. In Zimbabwe Mugabe, the ideologue, initially closed down all the family planning clinics, but then 'did have the sense to reopen them a year or so later. Roman Catholicism and Islam coupled with traditional male chauvinism account for the tardy recognition of the problem in Africa.

Africa's high rate of population growth was accompanied by rapid urbanization. In the late nineteenth century the costs of rapid urbanization forced even the dynamic economy of the US to rely on an inflow of overseas capital in order to maintain growth (Lewis 1978a, 149). At that time the US had an urban growth rate of 3.7 per cent. Modern African states have far greater urban growth rates, so that even with model governments they would have difficulty in maintaining growth. The problem is a very real one. To absorb the population increase of the rural areas the urban population needs to grow at rates that threaten to consume an ever larger proportion of domestic savings and to make African countries ever more dependent upon overseas capital. Yet in the period 1960–90 many of these countries placed obstacles in the way of productive foreign investment or channelled aid into unproductive enterprise.

Other disadvantages flow from a high rate of population growth. It not only places pressure on agricultural resources and the infrastructure, it also requires high savings and investment ratios just to maintain the existing per capita stock (Livingstone and Ord 1980, 32). In the rural areas, too, the land simply cannot support the number of people trying to scratch a living from it. Scarce trees are chopped down for fuel in a way that aggravates the problem of soil erosion. A form of agriculture that was fashioned for temporary cultivation has become permanent, while the amount of available unused land has dwindled. In much of East, Central and Southern Africa, where wealth has been measured in cattle rather than in fields, overgrazing has seriously damaged the land. Population pressure is the direct cause of many of modern Africa's economic problems. This has been brought about by a reduction in the death rate consequent upon the introduction of Western medicine and a more efficient food distribution system rather than by an increase in the birth rate.

The failure of African governments to face up to the population problem has had serious economic consequences for Sub-Saharan Africa. Since the 1960s the growth rate of the Sub-Saharan economies has been declining. From an annual 4 per cent in the 1970s it almost halved to 2.1 per cent in the period 1980–91 for those countries producing statistics (World Bank 1993, Tables 1 and 2). The growth rate would be even lower if the statistics of Zaire, Zambia, Uganda, Angola, Liberia and Guinea had been included.

The fact that Zambia, formerly one of the most prosperous economies in Africa, could not even produce statistics for the 1980s is evidence of the mismanagement of the one-party Kaunda regime. Uganda apparently was still suffering from the effect of the Amin dictatorship and the collapse of its infrastructure. Zaire was on the brink of total disintegration and Angola and Liberia were afflicted by war.

This average growth rate of 2.1 per cent for Sub-Saharan Africa presents an overoptimistic picture of what was happening to the economies as a whole, for it translates into disaster when converted into per capita growth rates. Table 5.1 gives the details of this for the recording countries and shows

Table 5.1 *The annual growth rate of GDP and per capita GDP in Sub-Saharan Africa, 1980–91*

Country	GDP	Per capita GDP
Benin	2.4	−0.9
Botswana	9.8	5.6
Burkina Faso	4.0	1.2
Burundi	3.7	1.3
Cameroon	1.4	−1.0
Central African Republic	1.4	−1.4
Chad	5.5	3.8
Congo	3.3	−1.2
Cote d'Ivoire	−0.5	−4.6
Ethiopia	1.6	−1.6
Gabon	0.2	−4.2
Ghana	3.2	−0.3
Guinea Bissau	2.4	1.1
Kenya	4.2	−0.3
Lesotho	5.5	−0.5
Madagascar	1.5	−2.5
Malawi	3.1	0.1
Mali	2.5	−0.1
Mozambique	−0.1	−1.1
Namibia	1.0	−1.2
Niger	−1.0	−4.1
Nigeria	1.9	−2.3
Rwanda	0.6	−2.4
Senegal	3.1	0.1
Sierra Leone	1.1	−1.6
South Africa	1.3	0.7
Tanzania	2.9	−0.8
Togo	1.8	−1.3
Zimbabwe	3.1	−0.2
Sub-Saharan Africa	2.1	−1.2

Source: World Bank (1993)

how the positive growth rate of 2.1 per cent annually for the GDP converts into a negative one of −1.2 per cent on a per capita basis. Only eight economies achieved positive growth and some of these were the result of bounce-back from earlier disasters in the 1970s. This applied to Chad, Zimbabwe and

Guinea Bissau. The most impressive achievement is that of Botswana, which experienced a GDP growth rate of 9.8 per cent and a per capita growth rate of 5.6 per cent a year. This however was from a low base and was entirely caused by South African investment consequent upon the diamond discoveries. Foreign investment had made possible the growth. Some of the largest declines occurred in francophone Africa, where overvalued currencies and impractical policies were finally catching up with countries that had long been relying on French financial and technical assistance. Niger, Cote d'Ivoire and Gabon all experienced per capita declines of over 4 per cent in the 1980s. Even Zimbabwe's bounce-back growth rate of 3.1 per cent a year converts into a decline of 0.2 per cent on a per capita basis, which no doubt has contributed to Mugabe's modifying some of his earlier macroeconomic populist policies. In total, 21 of the recording countries experienced economic decline in the 1980s – a total that rises to 27 if the six non-recording countries are included.

The economic record

At the general level the main policy failure lies in the inability to maintain a constitutional framework in which market forces could operate efficiently, that is in the rejection of the colonial inheritance. Yet at the local and individual level macroeconomic populism has been responsible for countless numbers of individual blunders that have wrought great damage upon much of Africa. It is to the evidence of this that we now turn in the sectoral analysis that follows.

Policy failure has been most conspicuous in agriculture. In the words of Eicher: 'studies carried out over the past two decades provide solid evidence that African states are using negative pricing and taxation policies to pump the economic surplus out of agriculture' (Eicher 1986, 161). This exploitation of agriculture has been accompanied by 'persistent attempts to renovate or prop up non-viable collective institutions in rural Sub-Saharan Africa – attempts with which donors are intimately associated'. This can only stifle the growth of indigenous private intermediaries (Berg 1985, 143). Indeed it was precisely these kinds of policy that permitted Sweden and Canada, the chief aid donors, to help finance the destruction of peasant houses and the ploughing in of peasant crops in Tanzania (Wickins 1986, 291).

Such policies were encouraged by Western aid donors because in the post-1945 era 'development economics and its concomitant prescriptions for policy and planning were usually considered a separate field with greater scope for dirigism' (Maddison 1989, 108). 'It has become a major axiom of the mainstream development literature that comprehensive central planning is indispensable for the progress of poor countries' (Bauer 1986, 1). Socialist dictators then set about reconstructing their economies and especially agriculture by developing further the socialist-oriented institutions already established by the former colonial authorities. Pre-eminent among these were the state marketing boards that flourished in the last years of colonialism (Berg 1985, 137). According to Faucher and Schneider, between 1961 and 1980 pricing policies hurt farmers in fourteen of nineteen countries studied (Faucher and Schneider 1985, 59). Overvalued currencies further hurt agriculture by restricting exports in Ghana, Nigeria and Zaire (Faucher and Schneider 1985, 54). The prevailing ideological bias in favour of industrialization as the way to economic growth also encouraged governments to neglect agriculture (Faucher and Schneider 1985, 62). In the 1970s the results of this neglect became apparent. In that decade Sub-Saharan Africa's annual increase in food production (optimistically estimated) grew at the rate of 1.7 per cent a year, about half the rate at which the population was growing (Ravenhill 1986, 9); and Africa, which had been a net food exporter in 1960, had become a net food importer. Marketing parastatals played a significant role in bringing about this situation as a politically rational policy of creating patronage led to economically irrational bloated public sectors in which the signals coming out of the market were ignored (Ravenhill 1986, 12; Faucher and Schneider 1985, 55). This need not have happened. When the right conditions were present, African farmers increased their output substantially as in Kenya in the 1950s (Munro 1984, 60), though already the pressure of population was bringing about a decline in both the size and fertility of smallholdings (Mosley 1983, 86).

Development in other parts of the primary sector has been helped by Africa's mineral resources. Development however is not automatic. It requires a demand for the mineral products and the ability to meet this demand competitively. Traditional supply-side constraints had been overcome with the creation of secure property rights and an adequate legal structure, by the development of a modern transport network, by the provision of an acceptable currency, by the creation of business corporations that could work to long time horizons and by the kind of economic policy that adopted an intelligent and enlightened approach to foreign investment and taxation. Mining not surprisingly boomed in the 1950s and early 1960s, that is until it came into conflict with misguided economic and political policies.

Kaunda's Zambia provides a textbook case of what not to do. There in the space of less than a generation Kaunda transformed one of Africa's wealthiest countries into a basket case by nationalizing the two main copper-mining companies and neglecting agriculture. Nationalizing the copper mines hurt Zambia in four different ways. First, it used up the country's foreign exchange reserves and incidentally provided Oppenheimer with the funds to launch Minorco as Anglo-American's overseas investment arm. Then, as the quality of the management deteriorated in the nationalized mines, profits dwindled and the mines' contribution to the fiscus fell away. Third, when this trend accelerated before the world copper surplus, the impoverished Zambian taxpayer had to begin subsidizing the mines and the latter, which had only a few years earlier been the main source of government revenue, became a drain on the economy. Last, nationalization led to a fall in the state's income tax receipts for, under the new regime, settlers were replaced with ex-patriots who were paid a portion of their salaries overseas that was not subject to Zambian taxation. While the case of Zambia and neighbouring Zaire may be exceptional, their experience in the 1970s and 1980s illustrates vividly how bad management inspired by macroeconomic populism outweighed the advantages of favourable factor endowments and wrought havoc upon once prosperous economies.

The rise in the price of petroleum was also a mixed blessing for Africa. Only in part of the north and west is Africa endowed with substantial petroleum deposits. As a result, the Arab-induced increases in the price of oil in 1973 and 1979 benefited Algeria, Tunisia, Libya, Nigeria, Gabon and Angola, but inflicted severe hardship on the rest of the continent. The cost of Ghana's oil imports quadrupled, Zambia's more than doubled and the Ivory Coast, which had paid 3 809 francs for its fuel imports in 1972, found itself faced with a bill for 31 043 francs in 1974 (Wickins 1986, 280). Such a dramatic change in relative prices threw current accounts into deficit and encouraged governments to borrow to overcome their immediate balance-of-payments difficulties. This had a number of harmful consequences. Bureaucrats and politicians imposed stringent import controls that damaged domestic industry while careless borrowing inflicted severe damage on state finances. Both of these contributed towards bringing growth to a halt, a development that was aggravated by the world economic recession of 1974. The days of cheap oil were over and with them the growth that had depended on the low price of fuel; but in the long run the oil price rise was not the main cause of African economic failure. Had movements in the petroleum price been the main determinant of economic growth then South-east Asia, Japan, Korea, Taiwan and Hong Kong would have experienced comparable difficulties. In Africa, though, the increase in the price of oil does seem to have strengthened the macroeconomic tendencies that were already present in the one-party and military dictatorships that were strewn across the continent.

The failure of industrial policies did not have as harmful an impact on African economies as the disastrous agricultural policies because they involved a much smaller proportion of the population. However macroeconomic populism did involve pandering to trade unions and the introduction of high minimum wages in economies that needed labour-intensive industries. These policies made it very difficult for African manufactured goods to compete on world markets. Industrial policy from Kenya in the east and

Nigeria in the west to South Africa at the tip of the continent focused on import substitution with tariff protection and it had the same effect on Africa that it had on India after 1923. It led to a loss of export markets and, by raising the price to domestic consumers, further eroded the domestic market for manufactured goods in economies where per capita incomes were still low. Macroeconomic populism, whether of the black nationalist variety or that of the Afrikaners, had the same effect. It encouraged the growth of capital-intensive industries rather than labour-intensive ones in economies with large supplies of labour. In Kenya for example this led to foreign multinational chemical companies building large synthetic fibre plants that could not compete with the more efficient ones in Europe and Asia; and in South Africa it led to a number of petrochemical projects of dubious economic viability and to a nuclear power station. Labour-intensive enterprises have been unable to compete on world markets because of the low productivity of African labour while capital-intensive enterprises have been unable to compete because of the higher capital costs in Africa and the less efficient use of capital by the parastatals that have dotted the landscape of the secondary sector.

An alternative strategy based on industrialization for the home market was much more difficult to achieve because of the large subsistence sector in much of Africa and the ever present policy north of the Zambezi of using agriculture as a milch-cow. The home market in most countries was too small to sustain viable manufacturing industries without government help. Government intervention of the positive kind all too often tended to favour five-year plans and showy projects. The legacy of Stalin may have done more harm to African economies whose infrastructure could not cope with sophisticated and grandiose projects than it has done to the Indian economy following the same route to development.

Despite the evidence of widespread mismanagement in agriculture, mining and manufacturing it is in the tertiary sector that some of the greatest failures have occurred. Foreign trade has not on the whole been a dynamic characteristic of post-independence Africa which has not experienced export-led growth. This is in sharp contrast to the post-independence experience of Southeast Asian countries. Driven by the trade winds of export-led growth the Southeast Asian economies sailed into an era of unparalleled prosperity while Sub-Saharan economies floundered in the doldrums of economic stagnation. Misguided economic policies (Wickins 1986, 286; Rimmer 1984, 259–60; Langdon 1986, 181–212) and mismanaged currencies have been responsible for this unhappy state of affairs.

The experience of Nigeria affords clear evidence of this policy failure. Before 1970 agricultural exports had been the engine of growth and then when they failed after 1970 oil came to the rescue; but by the later 1980s not even this bonanza could counter the harmful policies. Macroeconomic populism had made it impossible for Africa to supply world markets on competitive terms (Ravenhill 1986, 3), yet in Nigeria's first development plan the importance of exports was recognized if targets were to be met (Ekundare 1973, 388). Unfortunately this recognition of the vital role of exports and world markets was not accompanied by policies designed to accomplish it. Instead governments embarked on a programme of social engineering that was as harmful in Nigeria as the Verwoerd policies were in South Africa. These policies also depended on rising oil exports and the continued high price of oil. Policy failure was admitted by Brigadier Sani Abacha at the time of his coup in 1983 when he declared:

> You are all living witnesses to the grave economic predicament ... which an inept and corrupt leadership has imposed on our beloved nation ... Our economy has been hopelessly mismanaged. We have become a debtor and beggar nation. There is inadequacy of food at reasonable prices ... Health services are in a shambles as our hospitals are reduced to mere counselling clinics without drugs, water or equipment. Our education system is deteriorating at an alarming rate. Unemployment figures including graduates have reached embarrassing and unacceptable levels. (*The Economist*, 21 August 1993)

Sadly, recognition of the problem did not lead to its solution and in the eight years after Babangida took power in 1985 Nigeria's decline continued. In 1993 the budget deficit was 10 per cent of GDP, the external debt consumer a quarter of foreign exchange earnings, inflation was still close to 100 per cent per annum and real incomes had fallen to 10 per cent of their 1985 level (*The Economist*, 21 August 1993). Access to and manipulation of the government spending process had become the golden gateway to fortune (*The Economist*, 21 August 1991). The oil wealth did not go into priming the pump for economic growth. It went into prestige projects and consumption because the macroeconomic measures requiring fiscal and monetary discipline were not implemented.

Economies that depended upon a single commodity for their exports all experienced difficulties in this period. Among them were Nigeria, Ghana, Zaire and Zambia, all of which were badly hit when commodity prices fell. In this respect developing countries in Africa were more vulnerable than those elsewhere because of the high proportion of output that was exported, on average 25 per cent, as opposed to 20 per cent in developing countries as a whole (Hodd 1991, 13). These difficulties were compounded by deteriorating terms of trade after the early 1970s which had the effect of accentuating the impact of unwise policies. The fall in real commodity prices by over half from the high levels in 1950 was made even more glaring by the failure to achieve a significant increase in the export of manufactured goods. Export-led growth of the kind experienced by almost all African countries in the 1950s and by the Ivory Coast until the 1980s was becoming impossible to achieve with primary products. It had failed with manufactured products (Ravenhill 1986, 4).

In much of Sub-Saharan Africa the growth of domestic economies had been determined by the performance of the export sector. In West Africa, under the British and French, long-distance trade had continued to cross political divisions. Political independence brought an end to this state of affairs (Hopkins 1973, 252) and this inevitably reduced the size of the market and made it more difficult to achieve economies of scale. Import controls, exchange controls, price controls and nationalization, together with the mismanagement or neglect of transport, all further reduced the likelihood of achieving export-led growth. Yet Africa in 1987 managed to export 25 per cent of its output (Hodd 1991, 123).

All these difficulties paled into insignificance before the mismanagement of the currency and the fiscus (Hodd 1991, 16, 35; Ravenhill 1986, 22; Rothchild and Boadi 1986, 263; Eicher 1986, 161; Please and Amoako 1986, 141–2; World Bank 1990, 140, 222, 292, 395, 610; *The Economist*, 7 July 1990; 8 May 1993). Grandiose ideas on the role of the state, often reinforced by socialist ideology, encouraged many of the newly independent states to engage in reckless spending that led to budgetary deficits and to an ever increasing reliance upon borrowing and foreign aid. The inevitable result was inflation, inefficiency and corruption from South Africa in the south to Kenya in the east and Nigeria in the west. Mismanagement of central banks and an attachment to overvalued exchange rates further compounded the problem. By 1987 the 34 Sub-Saharan states analysed by Hodd were relying on foreign aid to provide 8 per cent of their GDP (Hodd 1991, 16) and aid per head was over four times that of other developing countries.

Inflation accompanied by overvalued currencies was the most serious obstacle to economic growth in regions that had long relied on export-led growth to be the driving force behind development. According to Faucher and Schneider, between 1973 and 1991 real exchange rates in Sub-Saharan Africa appreciated by 44 per cent. Jeanneney (1985) has examined the effects of overvalued currencies in Senegal, Madagascar and Guinea and the difficulties experienced in implementing successful devaluation policies. When deficits on current account are the result of price distortions devaluations do not provide solutions to the problem. That the problem is very widespread is clear from Hodd, who finds most Sub-Saharan countries guilty of maintaining overvalued currencies. When market forces finally triumph the process is painful. Ghana's currency fell from 2.75 to the dollar in 1982 to 306 to the dollar in 1989 (Hodd 1986, 35, 36, 55, 69, 83, 95, 101, 114, 118, 142, 158, 181, 207, 255, 279, 324, 327; Ravenhill and Eicher 1986, 161; Wickins 1986, 3; World Bank 1990).

Overvalued currencies were the response of inexperienced and ideologically motivated politicians to growing balance-of-payments problems in the face of increasing government expenditure. Low-income countries cannot afford the high taxation that is a privilege of the wealthy countries, as exemplified in seventeenth-century Netherlands or twentieth-century Scandinavia. Consequently although Sub-Saharan African governments in the 1980s spent a smaller proportion of their countries' GNPs than did the developed world, 24 per cent as opposed to 29 per cent (Hodd 1991, 17), the burden was considerable and made worse by the manner in which it was spent. Forty per cent of central government spending was absorbed by administrative costs compared with 25 per cent in other developing countries and much of the remaining 60 per cent represented spending of questionable value.

This increase in government spending was the result of macroeconomic populism being adopted by African governments in the 1960s. Hodd (1986, 35) has succinctly enumerated the steps they took along this road:

1. Marketing boards with monopolies over cash crop purchasing established or retained as a means of taxing agriculture.
2. Industrialization seen as a path to rapid development and manufacturing plants set up with monopolies with tariff protection and with state ownership.
3. Foreign investment discouraged and foreign assets nationalized.
4. Price controls introduced.
5. Exchange rates fixed by the government.
6. Import controls by means of licences, quantitative controls and foreign exchange rationing.
7. Non-food cash crops neglected.
8. An increase in spending on pet projects and on the bureaucracy.

In the 1970s government intervention increased still further (Wickins 1986, 299), despite the obvious failure of the 'bureaucratic entrepreneur' and the increased opportunities for corruption that followed hard on the heels of the increasing state intervention in the economy. Macroeconomic populism was characterized by an increasing lack of realism in the 1970s. This was most evident in Nigeria's development plans (Wickins 1986, 283; Tims 1974, 3) because of the size of the resources at the command of Nigerian governments; but it may also be seen in the experience of Zaire. Nor did African governments learn from their mistakes as 'everywhere even in the face of economic stagnation governments spent more and more' (Wickins 1986, 302).

This increase in government spending without a corresponding increase in government revenues inexorably led to rising budget deficits. This was particularly true of the smaller West African countries, Zambia, Sierra Leone and Ghana (International Monetary Fund 1975, 49, 126, 423). Nigeria's government deficit grew until 1971, when the expanding oil revenues pushed the budget into surplus (International Monetary Fund 1975, 327; Tims 1974, 17). This intermission lasted only a few years and by 1975 the internal deficit was back again. The share of government consumption in total GDP rose from 13 per cent in 1960 to 20 per cent in 1975 (Wickins 1986, 302). Had this been in profitable investment the economies might have benefited, but all too often government enterprises in transport, manufacturing and marketing were burdens upon the taxpayers and consumers. At the same time expenditure on armaments was rising rapidly so that the changeover from colonial rule to independence was likely to be accompanied by a multiple impact on government spending: bureaucratic growth, unprofitable investment and increased military expenditures. By the 1980s government budgetary deficits in Africa were running at 33 per cent of GDP as opposed to 7.7 per cent in other developing countries (Hodd 1991, 17). Because Sub-Saharan countries tended to be more heavily indebted than other developing countries Jacky Mathonet concluded that 'domestic economic policies have been relatively more important than exogenous factors in the development of the debt crisis' (Mathonet 1985, 237).

The difficulties associated with managing an internal debt were frequently compounded by the even greater difficulties that accompanied the growth of external debt. The two of course were interrelated as macroeconomic populism encouraged foreign borrowing in order to accelerate the pace of development. While the cold war lasted African states were able to get away with this by playing the West off against the Soviet Bloc: but with the collapse of the Soviet Union and communism as a credible alternative route to economic development international lenders are becoming much more discriminating. IMF-designed structural adjustment programmes are now the order of the day; but in the 1960s through to the 1980s this was not the case and debt servicing became a major constraint, consuming a growing proportion of many countries' export earnings. Though only a small proportion of total world debt (12 per cent in 1987), Africa's debt formed a much greater proportion of Africa's GDP. The gap was widening between individual gain and social gain and those persons favoured by the political–military élites prospered at the expense of the general public. Financial mismanagement clearly lies at the heart of Africa's economic problems.

Financial mismanagement lay behind the declining investment rate that was a notable feature of the African economies in the 1980s. Between 1980 and 1987 gross investment was contracting by 8.3 per cent a year and Africa was trailing other developing countries (Hodd 1991, 22). Ideas of capital shortage that had been popular in the 1960s gave way in the 1980s to ones on the absence of entrepreneurs and an inability to absorb capital Livingstone and Ord 1980, 22). As a result, the crucial difference between the developed and the less developed countries is now seen to lie in their capacity to create wealth rather than in their stock of capital. In effect this demoted the role of capital and promoted the role of the entrepreneur, thereby shifting the emphasis from impersonal capital to people and to the nature of the society that produced them. If this line of thinking is correct then ethnic and cultural differences may be recognized as playing an important role in economic development. These differences may affect attitudes towards land ownership, nepotism, tax evasion, the handing out of government contracts and family size. The apparent failure of African economies to reap the benefits of technological progress in the decades since independence has been explained by Maddison who observed as early as 1966 that 'the productivity opportunities offered by technical progress cannot be exploited unless the capital stock per worker is renewed and expanded' (Maddison 1982, 109).

This failure to maintain the capital stock can be seen clearly in the transport networks of Africa. Both roads and railways have suffered from a lack of capital investment since independence and from a lack of trained personnel to operate the railway systems efficiently. In 1988 the South African Development Coordination Council listed 192 projects requiring an investment of 11 billion rand and agreed that 39 per cent of this was to be implemented, costing $1 686.5 million. It did not of course represent new investment. It was to be money spent on repairing damaged or neglected tracks in Angola, Mozambique and Tanzania. So inefficient was the port of Dar-es-Salaam that importers avoided it and by the 1970s it had become primarily an export port for bulk products that did not have to fear theft and could also bear the cost of the long delays. After his purchase of British surplus locomotives in the 1970s that could not be used on the narrow Zambian gauge, Kaunda made no major investment in his landlocked country's railways. The situation in Zaire was worse. There, the shippers' response to uncontrolled pilfering was to weld the wagon doors immediately after placing goods in them. Investment in maintenance did not occur and when there was new investment, for example, when the World Bank funded cranes for loading containers, the volume of business did not warrant their installation (Kennedy 1988, 5, 14, 72, 87). Even Zimbabwe neglected maintenance of its railways and by the late 1980s over half the country's rolling stock was out of commission and the Mugabe government had to resort to borrowing stock from South Africa. Throughout Africa little or no attempt has been made to train management because the new regimes accorded management a low priority. Training did not figure on the agenda of macroeconomic populism.

Conclusion

Macroeconomic populism appealed to the semi-educated and ignorant who wanted simple solutions to complex problems. It appealed particularly to the underprivileged and deprived and the new generation of African politicians proved adept at exploiting these sentiments. When they themselves failed to deliver the goods they could continue to blame colonialism for their own shortcomings. Above all, such a policy permitted their constituencies to feel that they were the victims of circumstances and that African underdevelopment was somehow the consequence of Western capitalism and colonialism. Personal responsibility for the consequences of actions was evaded and failing politicians were able to remain in power or were replaced by even more incompetent generals. While the cold war lasted they were able to play off West and East in the quest for aid and the Nordic countries in particular helped to perpetuate the suffering of many of Africa's people by helping to prop up corrupt and brutal dictatorships. The West too supported unacceptable regimes, particularly the French in Central Africa and the Americans in Zaire.

Macroeconomic populism led to a huge increase in government interference in the economy that brought an end to the era of Western liberalism that had provided the framework for growth before 1960, and with that end came an end to efficient economic organization. This was epitomized in Zambia, once a relatively wealthy state by African standards. 'The main cause of its decline has been its government's interventionism' (*The Economist*, 7 July 1990). The same was true of Ghana where in the 1970s General Acheampong was primarily responsible for his country's economic crisis (Rothchild and Boadi 1986, 263). Economic pluralism cannot be separated from political pluralism. Autocratic regimes in Africa have been unable to emulate the Tigers of Southeast Asia and, given their track record, it is unlikely that they will be able to do so in the future. A more liberal market-oriented approach to development provides the only hope of limiting the corruption of African governments and there are signs that this is slowly being realized. Whether even the most liberal of market economies, operating in an expanding international economy, will be able to deliver sustained economic growth at a time when much of the continent's population is increasing at a rate of over 3 per cent a year remains to be seen. What is clear is that macroeconomic populism has been the principal cause of economic failure in Africa in the years since 1960 – the opposite of Asia's experience since 1973 where, according to Maddison, prudent macroeconomic management has been the order of the day (Maddison 1989, 97).

References

Ayittey, G.B.V.A. (1989), 'The Political Economy of Reform in Africa', *Journal of Economic Growth*, 3.

Bauer, P.T. (1986), 'Market Order and State Planning in Economic Development', *Journal of Economic Growth*, 1.

Berg, E. (1985), 'The potentials of the private sector in sub-Saharan Africa', in Rose (1985).

Bethel, T. (1987), 'The Ethics of Private Property Rights', *Journal of Economic Growth*, 2.

Bethel, T. (1989), 'Review of Paul Kennedy, *The Rise and Fall of the Great Powers*', *Journal of Economic Growth*, 3.

Chandler, A.D. Jr (1977), *The Visible Hand; the Managerial Revolution in American Business*, Cambridge, Mass.: Harvard University Press.

Eicher, C.V. (1986), 'Facing up to Africa's Food Crisis', in Ravenhill (1986).

Ekundare, R.O.E. (1973), *An Economic History of Nigeria, 1860–1963*, London: Methuen.

Faucher, J.-J. and Schneider, H. (1985), 'Agricultural Crisis: structural constraints, prices and other policy issues', in Rose (1985).

Georgeson, H. and Holman, M. (1994), 'World Bank laments past role in Tanzania', *Business Day*, 1 August.

Hodd, M. (1991), *The Economics of Africa*, Dartmouth: Dartmouth Publishing Company.

Hopkins, A.G. (1973), *An Economic History of West Africa*, New York: Columbia University Press.

Hutchful, E. (1987), *The IMF and Ghana: the Confidential Record*, London: Institute of African Alternatives.

International Monetary Fund (1975), *Surveys of African Economies*, 6. Washington, DC: International Monetary Fund.

Jeanneney, S.G. (1985), 'Foreign Exchange Policy and Economic Performance: A Study of Senegal, Madagascar and Guinea', in Rose (1985).

Jones, E.L. (1981), *The European Miracle*, Cambridge: Cambridge University Press.

Kennedy, T.L. (1988), *Transport in Southern Africa*, Braamfontein, Johannesburg: Institute of International Affairs.

Langdon, S. (1986), 'Industrial dependence and export manufacturing in Kenya', in Ravenhill (1986).

Lewis, W.A. (1978a), *Growth and Fluctuations 1870–1913*, London: Allen & Unwin.

Lewis, W.A. (1978b), *The Evolution of the International Economic Order*, Princeton: Princeton University Press.

Livingstone, I. and Ord, H.W. (1980), *Economics for Eastern Africa*, London: Heinemann.

Maddison, A. (1982), *Phases of Capitalist Development*, Oxford: Clarendon Press.

Maddison, A. (1989), *The World Economy in the Twentieth Century*, Paris: OECD.

Mathonet, J. (1985), 'The impact of external factors and domestic policies on external debt', in Rose (ed.).

Mohr, P. (1993), 'Can South Africa avoid macroeconomic populism?' paper presented to the biennial conference of The Economic Society of South Africa, Pretoria.

Mosley, P. (1983), *The Settler Economies, Studies in the Economic History of Kenya and Southern Rhodesia, 1900–1963*, Cambridge: Cambridge University Press.

Munro, J.F. (1984), *Britain in Tropical Africa*, London: Macmillan.

North, D.C. and Thomas, R.P. (1973), *The Rise of the Western World*, Cambridge: Cambridge University Press.

Olson, M. (1982), *The Rise and Decline of Nations*, New Haven: Yale University Press.

Please, S. and Amoako, K.Y. (1986), 'OAU, ECA and the World Bank: Do They Really Disagree?' in Ravenhill (ed.) (1986), pp. 127–48.

Ravenhill, J. (ed) (1986), *Africa in Economic Crisis*, New York: Columbia University Press.

Rimmer, D. (1984), *The Economies of West Africa*, London: Weidenfeld and Nicolson.

Rose, T. (ed), (1985), *Crisis and Recovery in Sub-Saharan Africa*, Brighton: OECD Development Centre, University of Sussex.

Rothchild, D. and Boadi, E.G. (1986), 'Ghana's economic decline and development strategies', in Ravenhill (1986).

Schmookler, J. (1966), *Invention and Economic Growth*, Cambridge, Mass.: Harvard University Press.

Tims, W. (1974), *Nigeria: Options for Long-term Development*, London: World Bank.

Wick, P. (1989), 'Ivory Coast recession', *Journal of Economic Growth*, 3.

Wickins, P. (1986), *Africa 1880–1980: an Economic History*, Cape Town: Oxford University Press.

Wolfson, M. (1985), 'Population and poverty in Sub-Saharan Africa' in Rose (1985).

World Bank (1990), *Trends in Developing Countries*, Washington, DC: World Bank.

World Bank (1993), *World Development Report 1993*, Oxford: Oxford University Press.

6   Asian stagnation: real or relative?
A.J.H. Latham

It is often assumed that the Third World countries of Asia are poor because they have been exploited in the past, and have been denied resources in recent times. This paper will argue that, on the contrary, the colonial period was a period of dynamism and modernization, and that the backwardness of these countries today is due to their own failure to grasp opportunities available to them after the depressed years of the 1930s and the Pacific War. Most of them did make some progress after 1950, but little compared to the success of Japan. Their relative backwardness is of their own making.

The growth record
Maddison has provided useful estimates of growth in Asia relative to the 'world' economy (Maddison 1989, 14–15). More recently, estimates of GDP per capita in Asia prepared by van der Eng give a good insight into economic

Table 6.1   Relative indices of GDP per capita in Asia, 1870–1990 (Japan = 100)

	1870	1900	1929	1950	1973	1990
Japan	100	100	100	100	100	100
Singapore	–	–	–	188	75	109
Taiwan	–	66	57	49	31	49
South Korea	–	78	79	46	24	45
Malaya/Malaysia	–	82	160	151	43	43
Thailand	110	82	52	53	21	27
China	–	68	45	34	12	19
Sri Lanka	–	–	60	68	18	16
Indonesia	119	85	84	60	17	16
Philippines	–	101	92	78	22	14
Pakistan	96	70	43	66	14	12
India	96	70	43	33	7	6
Bangladesh	96	70	43	66	7	5
Burma	–	72	54	25	6	4

Source: van der Eng 1994, 102.

differences between the various Asian countries. The weakening position of many Asian countries relative to Japan can be seen from the data in Table 6.1.

Whilst Singapore has a higher per capita product than Japan, with 109 per cent, the others have less than half the Japanese level, and eight, including the giants India and China, have less than 20 per cent. As for China, there has to be some doubt about the figure of 19 per cent. In another exercise undertaken by van der Eng, he utilizes estimates of the average standard of living given by the International Comparison Project (ICP) which express the value of a standard basket of goods and services in international and national activity. On this basis, China is only accorded a figure of 4 per cent compared with Japan (van der Eng 1994, 8). To add to the confusion, Minami gives a figure of $290 for per capita income in China in 1987, compared with $15,950 for Japan, a mere 1.8 per cent (Minami 1994, 9). The statistical basis for these exercises in Asia is very much weaker than for most Western countries, due to the undeveloped nature of their statistical services.

Table 6.2   *Growth of per capita GDP in Asia, 1870–1990 (percentages per annum)*

	1870–1900	1900–29	1929–50	1950–73	1973–90
Japan	1.4	1.7	0.1	8.0	3.7
Singapore	–	–	–	7.1[a]	6.0
Taiwan	–	1.2	–0.7	5.9	6.6
South Korea	–	1.8	–2.4	5.1	7.4
Malaya/Malaysia	–	4.1	–0.2	2.2	3.8
Thailand	0.4	0.2	0.2	3.8	5.2
China	–	0.4	–1.3	3.5	6.3
Sri Lanka	–	–	0.7	2.0	3.0
Indonesia	0.4[b]	1.7	–1.5	2.4	3.1
Philippines	–	1.4	–0.8	2.4	1.0
Pakistan	0.3	0.0	–0.5	0.3	2.9
India	0.3	0.0	–0.5	1.4	2.6
Bangladesh	0.3	0.0	–0.5	–0.4	1.7
Burma	–	0.8	–3.6	1.7	1.4

Notes:
Calculated as compound growth rates from three-year averages centred around the years shown.
[a]   1960–73
[b]   1880–1900

Source: as for Table 1.

From Table 6.2 it can be observed that the big growth disparity between Japan and the rest of Asia (with the exception of Singapore) opened up between 1950 and 1973. In every case the gap with Japan widens markedly, being particularly pronounced in the case of India, Pakistan, Bangladesh and Sri Lanka. Indonesia, the Philippines and China also saw a big gap emerge. This was due to the dynamism which Japan exhibited in this period and the slow growth of the other countries.

An examination of the growth rates experienced by these countries supports the view that the differences in per capita GNP between them are largely due to their growth rates since 1950. In the Japanese case (pop. 124.3 million), the high growth rate of 8 per cent per annum between 1950 and 1973 is crucial. All the countries, with the exception of Singapore (pop. 2.9 million), lost ground in comparison with Japan over this period. But the relatively good position of Taiwan (pop. 20.8 million) and South Korea (pop. 43.6 million) is due to the high growth they too experienced after 1950, particularly after 1973. But it is important to note that all the countries saw positive growth in this period, and not one can be said to have been stagnating, even though they were losing ground relative to Japan. Both Malaysia (pop. 18.6 million) and Thailand (pop. 184.3 million) experienced satisfactory growth, and so did Indonesia (pop. 184.3 million). The Philippines (pop. 64.2 million) fared less well, and have the distinction of recording the lowest growth rate after 1973. Moreover, the low starting base for many had the effect of accentuating the absolute gap with Japan. This was particularly true of the Asian giants India (pop. 882.5 million) and China (pop. 1 166 million).

These figures reveal positive growth in all the listed countries after 1950 and it is only relative to Japan that stagnation appeared to take place. What is more the countries of Asia did not stagnate in 1870–1900 or in 1900–29, and it is only the traumatic period 1929–50 of the Depression and the Pacific War that stagnation and indeed regression can be said to have taken place.

The colonial period
To turn to the nineteenth century, the absence of statistical material emphasizes the undeveloped nature of many of these countries. The fact that it is the colonial countries of British India and Indonesia (Dutch East Indies) which have adequate figures for this period emphasizes the modernizing force of colonialism. The exceptions are Thailand and Japan. British India is of course one of the two Asian giants, but the other, China, is sadly lacking in adequate material at this time. One other major colonial territory, French Indo-China, is not included in these exercises although there is a fair amount of information at least for these years. That this became a disaster area after the French left is clear, and the difficulties which have hit Vietnam, Laos and Cambodia since 1950 are only too obvious.

Certainly the countries of Asia were not stagnating in the nineteenth century. On the basis of the figures given, British India was growing at the rate of 0.3 per cent per annum in 1870–1900. This is a low figure, but elsewhere Mukherjee suggests that per capita incomes in India were growing from 1857–63 to 1881–89. Then growth of income was checked and fell back slightly due to famine, to be resumed from 1906–14 (Mukherjee 1969, 61). The progress is supported by circumstantial evidence including improvement in railways and telegraphic communications, the increased number of educational institutions, the increase in exports and imports, the growth of government revenue and the development of modern industry, particularly the cotton and coal industries. When checks occurred in the growth of per capita income, particularly in the 1890s, known famines were largely responsible (Mukherjee 1969, 37–122). The relatively low growth overall is due largely to climatic factors, not to any deleterious effect of British colonial policy. What is certain is that nationalist and Marxist images of drain and exploitation have to be discarded. Recent research has shown that the view that the Indian cotton industry was systematically wrecked to make room for imports of British textiles is simply wrong. India was not deindustrialized and manipulated into being a primary exporter so as to produce a trade surplus to finance a colonial drain expropriated by Britain. On the contrary, colonial policy ensured that a substantial trade surplus was able to service the substantial debts incurred in financing infrastructural advance, of which railways and telegraphs were central. The economic policy of the British colonial government was a model of successful development policy, with trade surpluses financing development without recourse to reckless foreign borrowing. What borrowing took place was properly financed via the trade surplus. Even after service payments on debt had been covered there was a net inflow of silver and gold indicating success for a country with a currency based first on silver, then from 1893 on gold (Latham 1978a, 33–51). Far from suffering deindustrialization India saw substantial industrialization, both in the cotton industry in Bombay and the jute industry in Calcutta, the former being almost entirely Indian-owned. In 1875 there were 48 modern cotton mills in Bombay, and by 1913–14 there were 264 mills employing over a quarter of a million people. This can hardly be said to be deindustrialization! So successful was the cotton industry that it drove British yarn out of the Chinese market (Bhattacharyya 1972, 99–104). Kawakatsu and Farnie confirm this picture (Kawakatsu 1986, 639; Farnie and Kawakatsu 1994, 10–11).

China by comparison seems to have fared less well. No estimates are available for the period before 1900, because of the lack of adequate statistical material. Feuerwerker states baldly that precise quantitative information is not available and probably cannot be satisfactorily derived for pre-republican China (Feuerwerker 1969, 1–2). Lack of such information is an indication of China's relative backwardness. Although she was a major borrower from abroad (Remer 1933, 76), modernization made little progress before 1914. Railway construction lagged far behind India, for in 1913 she had only 6 158 miles compared to India's 33,850 (*Railway Year Book* 1916, 48–9). India had an internal telegraph network as early as 1855 (Das 1959, 109–47), China not until 1898 (Farnie 1969, 186–7). China in this period had a substantial trade deficit, made good only by remittances from migrants to other parts of Asia (Latham 1978a, 51–7). Even rice was imported in substantial quantities, and it has been usual to suggest that this was due to food shortages and crisis in the agricultural economy. But recent research has indicated that Chinese agriculture in this period was undergoing a profound transformation as farmers turned to commercial crops such as tea, sugar, tobacco, cotton and mulberry leaves for silkworm production (Liu 1989, 131–5; 1990, 61–6; Shi 1989, 170–74; 1990, 75–7). As they converted to these cash crops, farmers became better off and purchased rice, which was the most desirable basic foodstuff, like white bread in the West. The rice imports marked specialization and growing prosperity, not an economy unable to provide for itself (Latham 1994a, 23–4). Far from stagnating, the agricultural economy was striving to modernize, even if the statistical information is not adequate to plot it.

Of the other Asian countries, colonial Indonesia (Dutch East Indies) and independent Thailand (Siam) show positive growth rates. Circumstantial evidence suggests that this was true of British Burma, Ceylon (Sri Lanka), Malaya and also French Indo-China. There was considerable growth of exports from all these countries (Stover 1970, 46–9). But it is important to realize that these countries formed part of an interlocking market system, on which they were all interdependent.

The Dutch East Indies was the leading exporter, followed by Malaya, and then Ceylon. Whilst these can be categorized as colonial mining and plantation economies, they were all substantial importers of Asian foodstuffs, particularly rice, which was needed to feed immigrant workers. The Dutch East Indies began as a coffee exporter, but by the end of the period had substantially switched to sugar production, most of which was consumed in India, China and Japan (Kano 1986). Malaya was a producer of tin, contributing over 80 per cent of world production by the end of the century. Much of the value-added contribution of smelting was retained in the colony, for Singapore had the largest tin smelter in the world, producing blocks, slabs and bars. Another large smelter was installed in Penang in 1902. Malaya was also a major rubber producer, supplying world needs created by the motor car and the invention of the pneumatic tyre (Chiang 1978, 74, 92, 109–13). But the Dutch East Indies and Malaya were in food deficit, and relied heavily on imports of rice from Burma, Thailand and French Indo-China, who were specialist rice exporters.

Indeed, the dynamism of the export trade of the latter three countries in these years was due almost entirely to rice. Ceylon, a producer of tea and rubber, also depended on imported rice from Burma. An intercolonial and intra-Asian food distribution network had become established with Burma, Thailand and French Indo-China supplying rice to Malaya, the Dutch East Indies and Ceylon. The Dutch East Indies supplied sugar in return. The Philippines were also supplied with rice from French Indo-China (Latham and Neal 1983, 260–62). A dynamic and interdependent pattern of growth had been established.

The Depression years

After 1900 the pattern of dynamism which had been established continued, notwithstanding the disruption caused in Europe by the Great War.

In India no growth of per capita income is shown for 1900–29 (Table 6.2), which runs contrary to Mukherjee's contention that incomes grew modestly until the early 1920s when they levelled out (Mukherjee 1969, 61). This was partly because of the substantial population growth of these years, which rose by 32 million in 1921–31 and 51 million in 1931–41, to reach a total of 389 million (Davis 1951, 85). There was negative growth of -0.5 per cent in 1929–50, but this was affected by the population growth in the 1930s followed by wartime dislocation, and famine in the early 1940s associated with the disruption of Burma during the war. Burma was India's leading rice supplier. Over the period as a whole the development of her own modern cotton industry increasingly supplied the domestic market, and drove out British and other foreign imports (Sandberg 1974, 183). The number of mills rose from 271 in 1914 to 365 in 1935, mainly under Indian ownership. The industry was helped by tariffs after 1921. In 1914 factories produced about as much cloth as handloom weavers, and although handloom production increased, by the end of the 1930s factory production was more than two and a half times handloom output. The handloom weavers competed by using factory produced yarn, but despite increasing production their earnings fell to less than one-third of the previous level. Market forces drove them to the towns, where they became dependent on middlemen-employers in whose establishments they worked. It was not the British who wrecked the Indian handloom industry in the nineteenth century, but Indian factory production in the early twentieth century, and it marked an important progressive step in the economic development of India. Increasingly Indians also took control of the jute industry in Calcutta. There were 76 mills in 1918 and 110 in 1939 of which they owned more than half. In 1913 the Tata Iron and Steel Company made its first steel at Jamshedpur, and the Bengal Iron and Steel Company continued to produce 200 000 tons of pig iron a year, mostly for consumption by other Indian foundries. Protective tariffs were put in place in 1924, and raised again in 1927, but were actually lowered in the 1930s as international demand soared, Japan becoming the major purchaser of her exported pig iron. But a measure of the impact of the Depression upon the Indian economy is shown by the fact that total Indian consumption of steel, including imports, was still below the 1929 level in 1939. Another indictor of the Depression is coal production, mostly consumed domestically, which fell after 1930 and did not regain the pre-Depression level until 1937, when signs of recovery became evident. In agriculture massive land reclamation and irrigation schemes were put in place by the colonial government, but the area under cultivation showed little increase because of soil exhaustion elsewhere. Like China, India became increasingly an importer of rice, in her case mostly from Burma. Burma's capacity to increase her rice crop is crucial to understanding how India was able to feed her rapidly growing population in these years. Between 1931 and 1937 duties were raised to stop cheap Australian wheat flooding into India, and in 1932 tariffs excluded sugar from the Dutch East Indies. Nearly all agriculturalists felt the impact of the Depression but it was those dependent upon cash sales of their crops who were most affected. The more self-sufficient peasant fared somewhat better. The fact that there was no major decline in the consumption of cotton goods, kerosene, sugar and tea suggests that no undue hardship was occurring, and this is supported by the substantial increase in population (Anstey 1952, 490–576; Bhattacharyya 1972, 67–121; Blyn 1966, 94–163; Gadgil 1971, 207–48, 257–339; Thomas 1935, 470–81).

In China a growth of 0.4 per cent is indicated for the period 1900–29, followed by –1.3 per cent in 1929–50. Her growth was better than India's in 1900–29, but worse between 1929 and 1950, the regression in the latter period indicating the problems which China suffered in these years by way of floods, war and revolution. It is normal to characterize Chinese developments in these years as slow and marred by political warfare in the south between 1922 and 1927, and by the Japanese annexation of Manchuria in the north from 1932. Exports took only a small part of the country's production and the economy is often depicted as a vast peasant system in which there was little change in size or structure in these years. Yet there was industrialization in the cotton industry in Shanghai, domestic production replacing imports of cloth from abroad. Tariff autonomy in 1929 meant that duties could be substantially raised, and they were raised again in 1932 and 1934 (Sandberg 1974, 191–5). But mill cloth was only a small part of domestic cloth production, and even in 1936 handloom production was twice that of factory production. Perhaps more important, however, Chinese yarn from the mills of Tientsin, Tsingtao and Shanghai was used by the handloom weavers and replaced imported yarn from India. After the slow progress of the 1920s the Chinese economy experienced great difficulties due to the disastrous Yellow River floods of 1931, and the depression which affected Shanghai and the coastal provinces linked to the international economy (Allen and Donnithorne 1954, 175–81; Cheng 1956, 27–93, 186–256; Feuerwerker 1968, 1–47; King 1969, 85–6, 113–3; Kraus 1980, 3, 167). Yet Rawski's recent work indicates that it was in this period as a whole that modest sustained increases in output per head became a feature of Chinese economic life. These increases were linked to exports and the commercialization of agriculture (Rawski 1989, 344). Schran shows that those areas of China, such as Manchuria, which came under Japanese control showed more rapid advance. The same was true of Korea and Taiwan (Shran 1994).

Elsewhere in Asia there was progress and development up to about 1926 when export prices in many commodities began to fall. Overproduction of rubber (Bauer 1948, 4, 34–7, 56–9, 81, 99–100, 210–13) tin and tea led to output restriction schemes of limited success, and producers such as Ceylon and Malaya were badly affected (Snodgrass 1966, 34–71; Allen and Donnithorne 1957, 44 142–4, 152–61, 261–2; Lim 1967, 50–83, 133–46, 174–7). So too were the Dutch East Indies, who were hit by the collapse in the price of sugar, the major export crop (Allen and Donnithorne 1957, 34–6, 71–2, 84–5, 90–94, 99, 103–4, 120–26, 139–44; Furnivall 1944, 428–44). The Philippines, the other great Asian sugar producer, were cushioned from the collapse of the world sugar market by access to the American market due to colonial status, but were also affected when the US adopted measures in the 1930s to protect her interests in Cuba and her own domestic producers (Department of Overseas Trade 1935, 12–16). As the export earnings of these countries declined they found themselves short of foreign currency and were unable to purchase rice from abroad. They turned to rice self-sufficiency policies and adopted measures to exclude foreign rice. Their previous suppliers, Burma, Thailand and French Indo-China were in turn badly affected. The intra-Asian rice trade, one of the features of Asian dynamism up to this point, was a casualty. To make matters worse there was a glut in the rice market. There had been extension of cultivation in all the major suppliers, and in 1928 favourable climatic conditions gave rise to bumper crops which pushed prices down to disastrously low levels. Rice farmers and those that lent money to them were bankrupted. This coincided with a similar glut in the world wheat market, with similar consequences. The world glut in primary foodstuffs was a major underlying factor in the world Depression (Latham 1981, 176–8; 1986, 654–6, 663; 1988, 94–100).

The coming of the Depression to Asia in the 1930s marks a watershed in her economic development. The self-sufficiency policies that both colonial and sovereign countries alike were forced to adopt as their export earnings fell were an ominous harbinger for the future. These policies became all the more pronounced with the coming of the Pacific War, and were to be carried over into the postwar era.

Until recently it would have been argued that development in Asia up to the outbreak of the Pacific War was dependent upon the substantial capital flows from the West, which financed railways, transport facilities and general infrastructure (Woodruff 1966, 1982, 154–5, 1956–7). This made it possible to produce and move agricultural and mining commodities for export. These export earnings financed the borrowing which paid for the inflow of development material. But emphasis is now also placed on the simultaneous expansion of commercial agriculture in all Asian countries as peasants seized new opportunities created by access to wider markets at home and abroad. Much of this activity was not directed towards the West but to consumers within Asia. Attention has already been drawn to the intra-Asian rice market which had been established. But the purchasers of the products of Asia's emergent cotton industry and other manufacturing industries were also Asian. Thus positive interaction between agricultural advance and emergent industry, which typifies the process of industrialization, was taking place within a regional setting. The peasants who were supplying rice, tea and tobacco to the industrial workers in Bombay, Shanghai and Osaka were buying the cottons which the mills were producing (Sugihara 1986, 726). This internal Asian network transcended colonial boundaries and was the origin of modern Asian dynamism. The plantations and mines of the colonial powers were merely an implant on what was already a dynamic economic system. It was this internal dynamism which was to be so badly damaged in the years after the Pacific War.

The wasted years
The colonial period in Asia was brought to an end with the Pacific War. The Japanese Empire was the first to go, then came independence for the Philippines in 1946, and British India in 1947. The other British, French and Dutch possessions soon followed, leaving only the dynamic British Crown Colony of Hong Kong. It was now that the per capita GDP gap opened up between the Third World countries of Asia and Japan. The self-sufficiency policies carried over from the late colonial period contributed to this process.

India became independent in 1947, with Pakistan separating to go her own way. But it is in the period 1950–73 that the gap between her level of per capita income and that of Japan opens up. India's growth of per capita income in this period is given as 1.4 per cent, compared to 8.0 per cent for Japan. Between 1973 and 1990 the figure is 2.6 per cent, compared with 3.7 per cent for Japan. Whereas this was better than in any previous period, relatively it was a poor performance, and accounts for much of the disparity between Indian and Japanese levels of per capita income in 1990. It was better however than her neighbour Pakistan, with growth rates of 0.3 per cent and 2.9 per cent respectively for the periods 1950–73 and 1973–90, and

Bangladesh with –0.5 per cent and 1.7 per cent. It is fairly clear why India fared badly. She inherited from Britain a legacy of socialism. Although there was no policy of general nationalization, and private industry and private agriculture continued to exist, there was public ownership for all new basic industry, especially heavy industry. There was planned public investment, particularly in heavy industry, in manufacturing and in infrastructure. Gradually private industry was encompassed and reduced in size. Planning replaced market forces, and there were five-year plans on the Soviet model. But the economic performance of public-sector industries was disappointing and rates of return were low. Licensing of supplies and raw materials caused scarcities and there were shortages of power and transport. There were also problems caused by strikes and lockouts, poor management and inadequate technology. The whole system was weighed down under a mass of unnecessary bureaucracy and paperwork. Meanwhile the isolationist and self-sufficiency policies of the late colonial period were intensified, and links to the international economy were weakened. There were import controls, and currency control which restricted access to foreign currency, and hence the purchase of equipment vital for modernization. Investment from overseas was actively discouraged for fear of exploitation, and in consequence India rejected the flow of modern technological information and equipment which would have been embedded in these investment flows. The aim was autarkic development and import substitution through extensive domestic industrialization (Reynolds 1985, 304–17; Oshima 1987, 271–82). Only very recently have steps been taken to liberalize the economy and open it to investment from abroad.

China fared better if we are to believe the figures, with growth rates of per capita income of 3.5 per cent for 1950–73, and 6.3 per cent for 1973–90. But there are difficulties with the accuracy of the data and there was, for example, no modern census of the labour force until 1982 (Oshima 1987, 267–70). The *Financial Times* recently pointed out that according to official statistics, the growth rate of real GDP between 1978 and 1993 was 9 per cent per annum. However, if the reported growth rate is worked backwards from the World Bank's estimate for GDP per head of $470 in 1992, it becomes just $195 in 1980 (in 1992 dollars). This is less than the more reliable estimates of India's GDP per head in that year, which seems highly improbable. As the *Financial Times* commented, 'At least some of the associated increases in output could also be illusory, as turned out to be the case for the much vaunted growth of the former Soviet-bloc economies; (*Financial Times*, 4 November 1994, 15). Certainly the adoption of Stalinist policies brought problems, just as we now know they did for the Soviet Union itself. China was devastated during the war with Japan, and by the subsequent civil war. Much of industry was nationalized in 1949 and by the late 1950s the industrial sector was almost entirely socialist. The system was essentially Stalinist, with central planning, physical targets, allocation of raw materials and labour. The aim was self-sufficiency, with massive investment in heavy industry and the capital goods sector, often related to military demands. The Soviet Union provided equipment for some two hundred major projects, and provided engineering, managerial, and planning training and advice. Much of this activity was severely disrupted during the Great Leap Forward of 1958–60. Then came the Cultural Revolution of 1966, which encouraged challenge to managerial authority, and brought a two-year drop in industrial output. As for agriculture, in the 1950s land was pooled into cooperatives, then in the Great Leap Forward these were grouped into communes, with unrealistic objectives such as the idea of steel furnaces in every backyard. But the commune sector survived to become the main structure of the rural sector, although households were allowed individual vegetable plots for their own use, after their communal duties were fulfilled. Migration from the countryside to the cities was restricted. After 1977 and under Deng Xiaoping there was some reform and relaxation, with a more favourable attitude to foreign trade and foreign investment. There was borrowing from abroad for industrial projects such as fertilizer plants, and the purchase of items such as aircraft from the US. However, subsequently many plant-import contracts were cancelled. China joined the IMF and became eligible for World Bank loans. Special economic zones were established in Guangdong and Fujian provinces, to encourage inflows of capital and technology from abroad. But all this occurred after the progress of the economy had been impeded for years (Reynolds 1985, 277–92; Minami 1994, 5–14, 19–22; Oshima 1987, 271–86). Ominously the *Asian Wall Street Journal* has estimated that international banks had lent £3.27 billion to China in recent years for factory renovation and purchase of equipment. About half that sum remains outstanding, and £393 million is actually in default (*Daily Telegraph*, 12 December 1994, 12). Nonetheless, it is clear that if present policies are sustained and liberalization in general continues, with constant inflow of capital and technology, China's potential remains enormous (Overholt 1993).

What is to be said of the other Asian Third World countries? For the old colonial rice producers, probably the least said the better. Burma, now Myanmar, once one of the most dynamic parts of British India, has been reduced to isolation and poverty. Much the same can be said of the old French possessions, Vietnam, Laos and Cambodia. Pakistan was an agricultural country at independence, but has succeeded relatively well in achieving self-sufficiency and industralization, with the help of substantial foreign aid. Bangladesh, once East Pakistan, has fared less well, and remains one of the poorest countries, and cannot even feed herself in most years. Ceylon, now Sri Lanka, has continued her traditional exports of tea, rubber and coconut products. An extensive welfare programme adopted soon after independence proved costly, and absorbed funds which could have been used for investment in production. Substantial inflows of foreign consumer goods eroded the reserves accumulated during the war and in 1960 import controls were adopted. Subsequently foreign debts have grown ominously. There have been ethnic problems, and transition to industrialization has been slow. Nationalization of many key industries, including the tea plantations, resulted in inefficiency. In the 1980s attempts were made to cut the welfare programme, and denationalize industry, but there was resistance to these aims and a lack of buyers for the inefficient nationalized industries. The Dutch East Indies, now Indonesia, has seen political problems, and suffered under the isolationism of President Sukarno. He was subsequently replaced in 1966 by the military ruler General Suharto. Since then the market and private enterprise have been favoured, and there has been substantial growth. This however has been heavily supported by oil revenues.

The Philippines saw a relatively good rate of per capita income growth in 1950–73 and 2.4 per cent per annum. But between 1973 and 1990 it fell to only 1.0 per cent, making her one of the worst performers in Asia. She also had a high rate of population growth. Manufacturing interests which once were American and foreign-owned increasingly passed into domestic hands, but they were badly run and performed inadequately, and never developed substantial export markets. Agriculture in general stagnated although sugar and coconut products were leading export crops. The modest external deficit for many years was covered by US expenditure on military bases maintained there. However, she suffered a severe political and financial crisis in the early 1980s and a consequent check to her development, followed by persistently low growth. Thailand is the last of the great prewar rice exporters to remain active in the rice trade, although she has diversified into maize, fibre crops, cassava and rubber. Private enterprise has been encouraged, and the public sector kept to moderate proportions. She has received much foreign investment, which has been channelled into modernization and industrialization. Agriculture remains in private hands, and consequently commercial incentives to increase production remain. Malaysia is also one of the most successful countries, sustaining after independence the high growth of the colonial period. There was much damage during the war, and during the long communist insurgency which the British successfully suppressed before they left. She became independent in 1957, and the territories of East Malaysia were added in 1963. The economy is export-oriented, based on tin, rubber and palm oil. The balance of payments, as in the colonial period, has been strong. In the early 1980s Malaysia completed her transition to industrialization, with more than half the work force being engaged in the industrial sector, and full employment in general (Reynolds 1985, 135–65, 180–87, 350–67, 371–3; Oshima 1987, 203–34, 235–62).

Conclusion

What then are the conclusions to be drawn? First, the idea that there was stagnation in Asia can be firmly laid to rest. In the colonial period of the nineteenth and early twentieth centuries, there was substantial progress. The Depression of the 1930s checked this dynamism, but as the world moved back into growth after the Pacific War, many of the countries of Asia did not follow as fast as they might have done. Socialist self-sufficiency policies meant that India and China had unharnessed themselves from the surge of growth and modernization which took place. To a greater or lesser degree this was true of other countries. But those Asian countries which maintained their trade and financial links to the dynamic heart of the international economic system prospered and progressed, and continue to do so. Singapore, Hong Kong, Taiwan and South Korea are good examples (Oshima 1987, 161–73, 182–6; Reynolds 1985, 170–73, 176–80; Lee and Yamazawa 1990, xxiv–xxix). It remains to be seen whether the considerable potential for growth which is inherent in Asia will be unleashed in the new century, or whether negative domestic political agendas and policies will thwart this dynamism and continue to keep many of her countries in the Third World.

References

Allen, G.C. and Donnithorne, A. (1954), *Western Enterprise in Far Eastern Economic Development*, London: Allen & Unwin.

Allen, G.C. and Donnithorne, A. (1957), *Western Enterprise in Indonesia and Malaya*, London: Allen & Unwin.

Anstey, V. (1952), *The Economic Development of India*, 4th ed., London: Longmans, Green & Co.

Bauer, P.T. (1948), *The Rubber Industry. A Study in Competition and Monopoly*, London: Longmans, Green & Co.

Bhattacharyya, D. (1972), *A Concise History of the Indian Economy, 1750–1950*, Calcutta: Progressive Publishers.

Blyn, G. (1966), *Agricultural Trends in India, 1891–1947: Output, Availability, and Productivity*, Philadelphia: University of Pennsylvania Press.

Cheng, Y. (1956), *Foreign Trade and Industrial Development of China: An Historical and Integrated Analysis through 1948*, Washington, DC: Washington University Press.

Chiang, H.D. (1978), *A History of Straits Settlements Foreign Trade, 1870–1915*, Singapore: National Museum.

Das, M.N. (1959), *Studies in the Economic and Social Development of Modern India, 1848–56*, Calcutta: Mukhopadhyay.

Davis, K. (1951), *The Population of India and Pakistan*, Princeton: Princeton University Press.

Department of Overseas Trade (1935), *Economic Conditions in the Philippine Islands, 1933–34*, London: HMSO.

Farnie, D.A. (1969), *East and West of Suez: The Suez Canal in History*, Oxford: Clarendon Press.

Farnie, D.A. and Kawakatsu, H. (1994), 'China: A Microcosm of the World Market for Cotton Manufactures, 1868–1935?' in Latham and Kawakatsu (1994a).

Feuerwerker, A. (1968), *The Chinese Economy, 1912–1949*, Ann Arbor: Michigan University Press.

Feuerwerker, A. (1969), *The Chinese Economy c. 1870–1911* Ann Arbor: Michigan University Press.

Fischer, W., McInnis, R.M. and Schneider, J. (1986), *The Emergence of a World Economy 1500–1914*, Part II, Wiesbaden: Franz Steiner Verlag.

Furnivall, J.S. (1944), *Netherlands India: A Study of Plural Economy*, Cambridge: Cambridge University Press.

Gadgil, D.R. (1971), *The Industrial Evolution of India in Recent Times, 1860–1939*, Bombay: Oxford University Press.

Hayami, A. and Tsubouchi, Y. (eds) (1989), *Economic and Demographic Development in Rice Producing Societies: Some Aspects of Asian Economic History, 1500–1900*, Tokyo.

Hayami, A. and Tsubouchi, Y. (eds) (1990), *Economic and Demographic Development in Rice Producing Societies: Some Aspects of East Asian Economic History (1500–1900)*, Session B-3, Proceedings, Tenth International Economic History Congress, Leuven.

Kano, H. (1986), 'Javanese Sugar Industry in the 1920s: A Historical Case of "Dependent" Industrial Development', unpublished paper presented at Workshop 34 on 'Development Theory and Comparative Approaches to the Economic History of the Third World', Ninth International Economic History Congress, Bern, Switzerland, 24–29 August.

Kawakatsu, H. (1986), 'International Competition in Cotton Goods in the Late Nineteenth Century: Britain versus India and East Asia', in Fischer et al. (1986).

King, F.H.H. (1969), *A Concise Economic History of Modern China*, London: Pall Mall Press.

Kraus, R.A. (1980), *Cotton and Cotton Goods in China, 1918–1936*, New York: Garland Publishing Inc.

Latham, A.J.H. (1978a), 'Merchandise Trade Imbalances and Uneven Economic Development in India and China', *Journal of European Economic History*, 7.

Latham, A.J.H. (1978b), *The International Economy and the Undeveloped World*, London: Croom Helm.

Latham, A.J.H. (1981), *The Depression and the Developing World, 1914–1939*, London: Croom Helm.

Latham, A.J.H. (1986), 'The International Trade in Rice and Wheat since 1868. A Study in Market Integration', in Fischer et al. (1986).

Latham, A.J.H. (1988), 'From Competition to Constraint: The International Rice Trade in the Nineteenth and Twentieth Centuries', *Business and Economic History*, 17.

Latham, A.J.H. (1994a), '"Rice Moves to Areas where Incomes are Rising". A Re-interpretation of Asian Economic Development since 1800', in Latham and Kawakatsu (1994a).

Latham, A.J.H. and Kawakatsu, H. (eds) (1994a), *The Evolving Structure of the East Asian Economic System since 1700: A Comparative Analysis*, (Proceedings of the Eleventh International Economic History Congress), University Bocconi, Milan.

Latham, A.J.H. and Kawakatsu, H. (eds) (1994b), *Japanese Industrialisation and the Asian Economy*, London: Routledge.

Latham, A.J.H. and Neal, L. (1983), 'The International Market in Rice and Wheat, 1868–1914', *Economic History Review*, 36.

Lee, C.H. and Yamazawa, I. (1990), *The Economic Development of Japan and Korea: A Parallel with Lessons*, New York: Praeger.

Lewis, W.A. (1970), *Tropical Development, 1880–1913: Studies in Economic Progress*, London: Allen & Unwin.

Lim, C.-Y. (1967), *Economic Development of Modern Malaya*, Kuala Lumpur: Oxford University Press.

Liu, T. (1989, 1990), 'Rice Culture in South China, 1500–1900: Adjustment and Limitation in Historical Perspective' in Hayami and Tsubouchi (1989, 1990).

Maddison, A. (1989), *The World Economy in the 20th Century*, Paris: OECD.

Minami, R. (1994), *The Economic Development of China: A Comparison with the Japanese Experience*, Basingstoke and London: Macmillan.

Mukherjee, M. (1969), *National Income of India: Trends and Structure*, Calcutta: Statistical Publishing Society.

Oshima, H.T. (1987), *Economic Growth in Monsoon Asia: A Comparative Survey*, Tokyo: University of Tokyo Press.

Overholt, W.H. (1993), *China, The Next Economic Superpower*, London: Weidenfeld and Nicolson.

Railway Year Book (1916), London.

Rawski, T.G. (1989), *Economic Growth in Prewar China*, Berkeley: University of California Press.

Remer, C.F. (1933), *Foreign Investment in China*, New York: Macmillan.

Reynolds, L.G. (1985), *Economic Growth in the Third World, 1850–1980*, New Haven: Yale University Press.

Sandberg, L.G. (1974), *Lancashire in Decline: A Study in Entrepreneurship, Technology, and International Trade*, Columbus: Ohio State University Press.

Schran, P. (1994), 'Japan's East Asia Market, 1870–1940', in Latham and Kawakatsu (1994b).

Shi, Z. (1989, 1990), 'The Development and Underdevelopment of Agriculture During the Early Quing Period, (1644–1840)' in Hayami and Tsubouchi (1989, 1990).

Snodgrass, D.R. (1966), *Ceylon: An Export Economy in Transition*, Homewood, Ill.: Richard D. Irwin Inc.

Stover, C.S. (1970), 'Tropical Exports' in Lewis (1970).

Sugihara, K. (1986), 'Patterns of Asia's Integration into the World Economy, 1880–1913' in Fischer et al. (1986).

Thomas, P.J. (1935), 'India in the World Depression', *Economic Journal*, 45.

van der Eng. P. (1994), 'Assessing Economic Growth and Standards of Living in Asia, 1870–1990', in Latham and Kawakatsu (1994a).

Woodruff, W.M. (1966, 1982), *Impact of Western Man: A Study of Europe's Role in the World Economy*, New York: St Martin's Press.

/ 2 1 — 60
Turkey,
Malaysia,
India
O 19
F 31
F 14

7 Trade and exchange rate liberalization: the experience of Turkey, Malaysia and India*

Subrata Ghatak and Utku Utkulu

Introduction

The role of exchange rate distortions in economic development has received considerable prominence in the current economic literature (see Agarwala 1983; Lucas 1988; Krueger 1990; Bhagwati and Srinivasan 1983; Balassa 1989). The exchange rate is a major factor that affects the relation between domestic and foreign price. It can be used as a key instrument to promote export and economic growth and save valuable foreign exchange. However, in the early phase of economic development of less-developed countries (LDCs), the exchange rate did not play an important role in promoting economic growth. It was mainly used to tackle short-run balance-of-payments problems. Many LDCs in Asia and Africa regarded the exchange rate as a key weapon to promote import-substitution industrialization (ISI) policies. Typically, exchange rates were controlled to over-invoice the imports and under-invoice exports. Such a strategy resulted in the imposition of heavy taxes on exports and significant subsidies to imports of capital goods. Thus, direct government intervention emanating from fixing exchange rates or indirect state interference stemming from the imposition of tariffs and quotas on consumer goods, high rates of inflation in many LDCs, the existence of capital controls and the lack of a realistic realignment of the purchasing power parities, led to major distortions in the exchange rates. Sometimes these distortions were the result less of active policy decisions and more of rigid exchange rates in the face of far-reaching structural changes in the economic conditions (Agarwala 1983). The problem of distortions in exchange rates, fairly widespread in the 1950s and 1960s in LDCs, was aggravated in the early and late 1970s when rates of inflation accelerated mainly due to oil price shocks. In the early 1980s countries such as Mexico defaulted in their debt payments as they were under severe balance-of-payments crisis. The effect of this on the financial system of the US was very damaging, as it raised questions about the liquidity, confidence and credibility of such lending institutions for promoting economic growth. An influential study by the

*The authors are grateful for financial support for this study from the Leicester–Loughborough Universities joint research fund. They are also grateful to Professor D.H. Aldcroft for his helpful advice and comments. The usual disclaimer applies.

World Bank has confirmed the negative correlation between exchange rate distortions and export growth (World Bank 1987).

The main objective of this paper is to examine the impact of trade policy on the long-run growth of output in three developing countries in Asia, that is Turkey, India and Malaysia, which largely followed different strategies (e.g. inward-looking ISI policies via exchange rate distortions in the case of India and Turkey and an open, export-led growth (ELG) policy in the case of Malaysia) to promote physical and human capital accumulation and economic growth. In the next section, we shall describe a simple model of a black market in foreign exchange in LDCs to account for the exchange rate distortions. Then we shall develop a simple index of exchange rate distortion. We then report the results of our analysis about the nature of the long-run relationship between the improvement of the trade balance and the index of distortion in India, Malaysia and Turkey during the period 1955–91. The final section will draw some conclusions.

Black markets in LDCs and exchange rate distortions

During the 1950s and 1960s many LDCs imposed exchange controls to insulate the movements of the domestic output and employment from external shocks stemming from the international capital market. Many contend that such controls, along with the enormous level of effective protection and quantitative restrictions of imports to curb substantial balance-of-payments deficits, led to the emergence of the black market and substantial distortion of exchange rates. Others contend that the growth of such black markets (BMs) is closely linked to the developments of the financial markets in LDCs (Dornbusch et al. 1983). The other important determinant of the deviation of the equilibrium exchange rates could be changes in purchasing power parity, long-run competitiveness and interest rate differentials. Clearly, in this context, government intervention in the foreign exchange market played a crucial role in the formation of distortions of exchange rates. It is noteworthy that the dynamic specification of the exchange rate equation (actual or black market) has not been very satisfactory and most standard theories of exchange rate changes have not been vindicated in practice. Some argue that the exchange rates follow a random walk while others add a dragging anchor to its random movement (see Phylaktis 1991; Goodhart 1988). The strong rationality hypothesis, which considers the interest rate differential as a perfect proxy for all other lagged variables driving the exchange rate is, of course, one of the new theories which could be tested for LDCs.

Distortions in the exchange rates and the origin of black market (BM) rates: theory

The primary reasons for distortions in the exchange rates of LDCs are usually related to their persistent and large balance-of-payments deficits and substantial excess demand for foreign exchange. Such perennial excess demand is generally shown in chronic current account imbalances. More formally, the current account (*CA*) balance is equal to the net receipts from the rest of the world, i.e. national income at home (*Y*) minus national expenditure (*E*) which comprises consumption (*C*), investment (*I*), and government expenditures (*G*):

$$CA = Y - E = Y - (C + I + G)$$

Since national income can be saved (*S*), taxed (*T*), or consumed (*C*), we have:

$$CA = (S - I) + (T - G)$$

Thus, the *CA* balance is the sum of net savings and the government budget. With zero net transfers:

$$(S - I) + (T - G) = Y - E = CA = X - M$$

Hence, the CA worsens when budget deficits rise without being offset by a rise in private savings and remittances or a reduction in private investment/consumption. However, the *CA* deficit by itself is not a problem in LDCs which usually suffer from both the savings and the trade gap, i.e. $(I - S) > 0$ and imports (*M*) are greater than exports (*X*) or $(M - X) > 0$. The CA deficit becomes a problem when the ratio of deficit to gross domestic product (GDP) rises continuously, raising doubts about its sustainability given the constraints on future external borrowing and inflow of portfolio and direct investment in the face of a depletion of foreign exchange reserves.

Clearly, large *CA* deficits are sustainable for a long period by inflows of foreign investment and a high rate of output growth: witness the cases of South Korea in the 1960s and Thailand in the 1980s. On the other hand, such deficits are not sustainable in the event of a continuous depletion of foreign reserves and a rise in the debt–income ratio beyond a certain limit, say 50 per cent. To protect themselves against such serious debt problems and the probability of default leading to suspension of borrowing facilities in future, many LDCs indulge in significant overvaluation of currencies. Such overvaluations create deliberate distortions in the foreign exchange market to reduce import costs. Unfortunately, currency overvaluations penalize exports and do not help much to overcome long-term structural problems of the economy by expanding the tradeable sector.

Exchange rate distortions and the determination of the black market premium in the LDCs have been the subject of considerable investigation (see Dornbusch et al. 1983; Fishelson 1988; Blejer 1978; Culbertson 1975; Phylaktis 1991; Charemza and Ghatak 1990). Most empirical studies support the view that the official exchange rate, the official depreciation-adjusted interest rate differential, and foreign exchange restrictions are important determinants of the black market premium and distortions. However, in the Blejer model, the excess supply of money is first calculated and then used to explain the (nominal) black market exchange rate (BMR).

In the Dornbusch et al. (1983) model, the *BMR* is a function of the real official exchange rate, *e*, and the depreciation-adjusted interest differential, $i* + d* - i$ where $i*$ and i are the nominal interest rates on foreign and domestic currency respectively and $d*$ is the rate of depreciation of the official exchange rate. If the depreciation-adjusted interest differential is taken as a proxy for the expected profits differential between domestic savings and a black market transaction in foreign exchange, then $d*$ can be substituted for *d*, the depreciation of the domestic currency in the black market as the latter is a real surrogate for the expected devaluation of the official rate, particularly when many LDCs leave the official exchange rates constant for a long period of time rendering $i* + d* - i$ rather curious. Fishelson claims that such changes can be explained as follows:

$$PR = BMR/E - 1.0$$

where *PR*, *BMR* and *E* represent black market premium, nominal BM exchange rate and nominal official exchange rate respectively.

The differential rate of expected profits (*DE*) is then as follows:

$$DE = (1 + d)(1 + i*) - (1 + i) \text{ and } PR = a + bER + cDE + gPR\text{-}1$$

where *ER* and *PR*-1 are the real exchange rate in the country and the lagged dependent variable respectively.

The main result from Fishelson's study is that the expected profits from BM transactions drive the BM premium which are given negatively by the real official rate and positively by the expected profits from purchasing foreign exchange.

In the next section, we analyse the impact of trade policies on the export and economic growth of Malaysia, India and Turkey during the period 1950–90. It is important to bear in mind that while Malaysia generally followed an outward-looking ELG policy, India and Turkey pursued inward-looking ISI strategies.

Measuring trade liberalization[1]

The empirical definition of the concept of 'trade liberalization' is quite complex. The difficulty arises for both conceptual and practical reasons. Trade liberalization may embody a number of different aspects of policy reform. It may imply less intervention by governments in the traded goods sectors. Whether a less interventionist trade regime results in a less distorted, more open or outward-oriented economy will depend critically on the detailed characteristics of the pre-reform and post-reform trade and exchange regimes and their impacts on the pattern of incentives and production.

The above problems and the desire to capture a wide range of price distortions have encouraged attempts at the construction of composite indices of distortion (Agarwala 1983). Subjectivity is required to rank the distortions from different sources. The Agarwala results are cross-country in nature, and inappropriate for the present work. Efforts to replicate the approach for time-series work would be constrained by data availability, and would be open to inevitable criticisms concerning personal bias.

In the present work we prefer therefore to use information on the black market, exchange rate premium to capture the extent of distortions. The deviation between the black market rate and the official exchange rate, expressed as a proportion of the black market rate, seeks to capture the effects of trade and other interventions (e.g. capital market); the greater the deviation the more distorted the economy, with a reducing deviation being interpreted as increased liberalization.

Early work on trade regimes by Krueger (1978) and Bhagwati (1978), for example, emphasizes overall trade orientation, i.e. the degree to which the protective/incentives structure in a country is biased against exports (for a seminal work, see Bhagwati and Srinivasan 1983). This is the tradition followed also by the recent World Bank comparative study of trade liberalization episodes (Michaely et al. 1991), in which trade liberalization is viewed as a move towards neutrality. In that study the authors for each country were required to assess degree of liberalization on a subjective scale. (The scale ranges from 1 to 20, where 1 corresponds to the most restricted trade regime and 20 to free trade.) This subjectivity has been strongly criticized, particularly as a means of comparing liberalization episodes across countries (Edwards 1993; Greenaway 1993). Indeed it will be of some interest to compare the subjective dating and measures of the intensity of liberalization by the individual country authors of the Turkish study (Baysan and Blitzer 1991) with that indicated by the indices used in the present work. The present analysis focuses on openness and distortion indices.[2]

Country experiences[3]

Turkey: 1955–90

In the World Bank study on liberalizing foreign trade, Baysan and Blitzer (1991) focus on developments in the Turkish foreign trade sector between 1950 and 1984. They identify four dates over this period when marked attempts to reduce trade and other distortions were initiated, namely the years 1950, 1958, 1970 and 1980. In the first three cases the authors conclude that the liberalization was not sustained, and the reforms were not part of a planned programme to establish a liberal trade regime. Indeed, in none of these brief liberalizing episodes do Baysan and Blitzer assess the reforms to have been sufficient to merit the status of an 'outward-oriented' regime.[4] By contrast the 1980 liberalization is viewed as the start of a more fundamental and sustained liberalization: the index is set at 6 (within the restrictionist trade regime range) in 1980 and rises steadily to 14 (well into the 'outward-oriented' range) by 1985 (see Figure 7.1). The series of reforms included a near 50 per cent devaluation, an increase in direct export incentives, demand stabilization measures, and a declared intention to gradually liberalize the economy (i.e. dismantling the quantitative restrictions (QRs) and capital account liberalization). Besides the introduction of direct export incentives at the start of the episode, the Bank's view was that relatively little was achieved in terms of import policy until 1984. Some commodities were shifted from the more restrictive to the less restrictive list, and in 1981 some licensed imports were liberalized and the explicit import quota

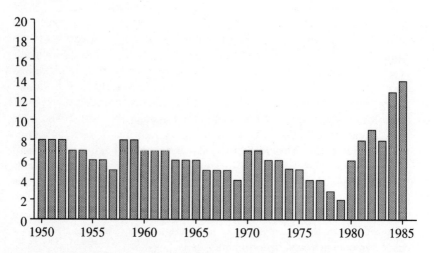

Source: Baysan and Blitzer (1991) and Michaely et al. (1991), esp. p. 289.

Figure 7.1   Trade liberalization index for Turkey (1950–85)

system was abolished. The system remained dominated by licensing and a protective tariff structure until the beginning of 1984, when about 60 per cent of previously licensed imports were liberalized. There were also changes in the administrative system: only goods explicitly listed as prohibited could not now be imported, where previously imports were banned if not explicitly listed as liberalized (for further details of the reforms see Aricanli and Rodrik 1990; Togan 1994; Uygur 1993).

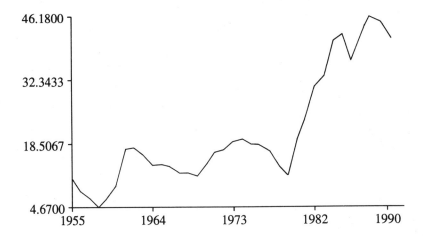

Figure 7.2   Openness measure [(exports + imports)/RGDP per capita]: Turkey

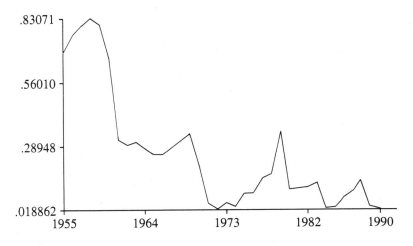

Figure 7.3   Exchange rate distortion index [ERDI=(BM-OF)/BM]: Turkey

Ghatak et al. (1995) show how the 'Baysan–Blitzer' (BB) index of liberalization for Turkey compares well with the indices of openness and distortion
used in their work. There is in fact a fairly close correlation (+0.7) between the
two indices (compare Figures 7.1 and 7.2). The liberalizations of 1950, 1958
and 1970 and the subsequent reversals are captured. The timing and scale of the
liberalization episode starting in 1980 is also dramatically represented by their
openness index. Besides, the exchange rate distortion index, ERDI (see Figure
7.3), also appears to pick up these two steps in the post-1980 liberalization: the
black market premium falls sharply between 1979 and 1980 and falls further
and sharply again between 1983 and 1984. Note also the re-emergence of the
premium in the 1985–88 period, a reversal which is not as evident from the
openness index. For the period as a whole (1955–90), however, two indices
correlate fairly closely (-0.69) while the distortion index also captures the 1958
and 1970 temporary liberalizations quite well. Other alternative measures for
trade liberalization such as real exports (Figure 7.4) and real imports (Figure
7.5) also capture the transitory nature of the earlier liberalizations, but record a
continuous liberalization after 1980. Taken together, the consistency between
various measures for trade liberalization and between these and the subjective
index provided by Baysan and Blitzer are reassuring. Since Ghatak et al.
(1995) also shows that the trade liberalization in Turkey affects economic
growth, the indices appear to be adequate measures of liberalization to capture
these growth effects. They examine the impact of trade liberalization on the
long-run economic development as measured by the real GDP in Turkey. Based
on the 'endogenous' growth theory, they employ bivariate and multivariate
cointegration analyses to test the long-run relationship among the relevant

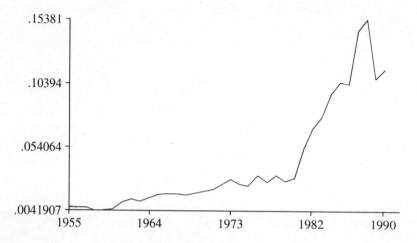

Figure 7.4   Real exports (in US$): Turkey

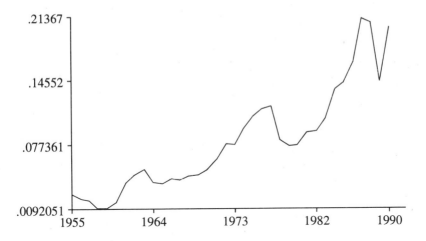

Figure 7.5   Real imports (in US$): Turkey

variables. Results for Turkey suggest a stable, joint long-run relationship among real GDP, a measure of trade liberalization and human and physical capital in accordance with the 'endogenous' growth theory.

Turkey is a typical lower middle-income country with a gross national product (GNP) per capita in 1990 of US$1 640. There is little doubt that the Turkish economy has achieved an impressive transformation from an inward-oriented economy based on import substitution to an outward-oriented one based on export promotion (for some key economic indicators, see Table 7.1) Turkey is one of the few countries that managed to maintain high GNP growth in real terms (about 5 per cent a year in the 1980s), after rescheduling its debts. The country has frequently been referred to as a 'success story' for other debtor countries to emulate (Arslan and van Wijnbergen 1993; Aricanli and Rodrik 1990). Riedel (1991), citing the Turkish stabilization programme implemented in the 1980s, argues that the outward orientation of trade can boost the export growth rates of LDCs. The most successful aspect of Turkish experience has probably been the considerable growth in exports during the 1980s (Table 7.1 and Figure 7.4). Exports (FOB) rose from US$2.9 to 11.7 billion between 1980 and 1988. The export composition changed in favour of manufactured goods and the export–import ratio improved (i.e. the share of manufactured goods in total exports rose from 36 to 77 per cent during the same period). The export boom was mainly in manufactured goods. In addition to the leading subsectors such as textiles and clothing, iron and steel, several other subsectors also enjoyed remarkable expansion. Along with the manufactured sectors, many service export industries such as tourism, transportation and contracting also increased their shares.

Table 7.1 The Turkish economy, 1965–91

| Mid–1990 population (million) | 56.1 |
| 1990 per capita GNP in US$ | 1,640 |

	Share of gross domestic product (from current price data)						Growth rate (%per year) (from constant price data)				
	1965	1973	1980	1989	1990	1991	1965–73	1973–80	1980–91	1990	1991
Gross domestic product	100.0	100.0	100.0	100.0	100.0	100.0	6.4	4.8	5.4	9.0	1.5
Net indirect taxes	9.8	10.1	5.3	9.7	11.0	15.5	..	..	..	..	..
Agriculture	30.9	24.8	21.4	15.1	16.1	..	2.5	4.5	3.0	11.8	0.2
Industry	22.4	23.1	28.6	32.0	29.6	25.7	7.9	5.5	5.3	5.8	2.9
of which manufacturing	14.4	15.6	20.0	22.8	20.9	..	9.5	4.1	7.2	8.0	..
Services	36.9	42.1	44.7	43.2	43.2	45.5	7.8	5.2	5.5	8.6	1.6
Resource balance	−1.4	−2.2	−7.8	−1.0	−4.8	..	..	..	..	..	..
Export of goods & NFS	6.3	8.8	6.4	22.3	18.6	..	9.6	−0.2	17.9	10.3	..
Imports of goods & NFS	7.7	11.0	14.2	23.3	23.4	..	10.8	−3.1	13.6	35.3	..
Total expenditures	101.4	102.2	107.8	101.0	104.8	97.8	6.8	4.0	5.2	14.8	..
Total consumption	86.5	83.2	85.9	78.3	81.7	76.1	6.0	4.2	5.6	14.5	..
Private consumption	74.2	70.7	73.4	66.7	67.6	60.1	6.1	3.8	5.9	14.8	..
General government	12.3	12.5	12.6	11.6	14.1	16.0	5.7	7.5	3.1	11.9	..
Gross domestic investment	14.9	19.0	21.9	22.7	23.1	21.7	9.7	3.1	3.8	16.0	..
Fixed investment	14.5	20.1	20.0	22.8	21.5	22.2	9.5	4.1	4.9	8.6	..
Changes in stocks	0.4	−1.0	1.9	−0.1	1.6	−0.6				..	..
Gross domestic saving	13.5	16.8	14.1	21.7	18.3	23.9	8.6	3.5	5.1	−9.3	..
Net factor income	0.4	−0.6	−2.0	−2.2	−1.8	−1.3	..	..	..	..	..
Net current transfers	0.0	0.0	3.8	4.0	3.1	..	..	..	..	..	..
Gross national saving	13.9	16.2	15.9	23.5	19.6	..	8.1	5.4	4.9	−9.7	..

In billions of LCUs
(at constant 1987 prices)

	1965	1973	1980	1989	1990	1991
Gross domestic product	17,450	29,017	39,687	61,258	66,791	69,417
Capacity to import	1,898	4,265	2,212	13,426	15,093	..
Terms of trade adjustment	742	1,646	-171	-1,435	-1,298	..
Gross domestic income	18,192	30,663	39,517	59,823	65,493	..
Gross national product	17,448	28,791	38,880	59,918	65,665	68,163
Gross national income	18,190	30,437	38,709	58,483	64,368	..

Inflation rate (% per year)

	1965–73	1973–80	1980–91	1990	1991
Gross domestic product	6.4	4.8	5.4	9.0	..
Capacity to import	9.5	-6.3	19.5	12.4	..
Terms of trade adjustment	..	..	..	..	..
Gross domestic income	6.5	4.1	5.5	9.5	..
Gross national product	6.3	4.6	5.5	9.6	..
Gross national income	6.4	3.9	5.5	10.1	..

Index (1987 = 100)

Price indices	1980	1986	1988	1989	1990	1991
Consumer prices (IFS 64)	10.6	72.0	175.4	286.3	459.0	..
Wholesale prices (IFS 63)	..	..	..	..	..	..
Implicit GDP deflator	10.9	72.4	166.7	273.9	423.6	663.8
Implicit expenditures defl.	11.0	72.3	166.1	280.4	427.3	..

Inflation rate (% per year)

	1965–73	1973–80	1980–91	1990	1991
Consumer prices (IFS 64)	8.2	35.8	45.1	60.3	..
Wholesale prices (IFS 63)					
Implicit GDP deflator	10.5	36.5	44.8	54.7	56.7
Implicit expenditures defl.	10.3	37.7	42.9	52.4	..

Growth rate (% per year)

Other indicators	1965–73	1973–80	1980–91
Population	2.6	2.1	2.3
Labour force	1.7	1.7	2.2
Gross national income p.c.	3.7	1.7	3.1
Private consumption p.c.	3.4	1.6	3.5
Import elasticity			
Imports (goods & NFS)/GDP	1.7	-0.6	2.5
Marginal savings rates			
Gross national saving	20.1	16.0	..
Gross domestic saving	21.8	6.3	37.0
ICOR (period averages)	..	7.2	..

Table 7.1 (cont.)

Share of labour force (%)

	1965	1973	1980	1990
Labour force	100.0	100.0	100.0	100.0
Agriculture	74.7	67.0	58.4	..
Industry	11.2	13.4	16.8	..
Services	14.2	19.6	24.8	..

	Volume index (1987 = 100)						Value at current prices (US$ million)					
	1980	1987	1988	1989	1990	1991	1980	1987	1988	1989	1990	1991
Merchandise exports												
X.OAGRI	..	..	..	..	..	..	1,541	1,497	2,004	1,796	2,074	..
X.MAN.TEXT	..	..	..	..	..	..	474	3,404	3,691	..	..	..
X.MET	70.4	100.0	98.9	107.2	109.4	131	191	272	377	413	332	..
X.FOOD.MEAT	30.2	100.0	87.0	96.1	..	..	356	337	330	273	..	..
Manufactures	11.1	100.0	103.6	98.4	..	..	1,047	8,065	8,944	9,086	10,281	..
Residual	..	..	..	..	..	..	-474	-3,404	-3,690	..	-1	..
Total exports fob	24.0	100.0	107.2	104.1	94.4	..	2,910	10,190	11,663	11,625	12,959	..
Merchandise imports												
Food	5.2	100.0	61.4	65.2	..	..	50	782	499	1,041	1,319	..
Fuel and energy	61.9	100.0	111.8	103.5	111.5	..	2,953	2,711	2,434	2,456	3,519	..
Other consumer goods	..	..	..	..	..	..	..	..	..	..	..	..
Other intermediate goods	..	..	..	..	..	..	..	7,219	7,870	8,409	12,200	..
Capital goods	43.4	100.0	..	93.5	..	..	1,435	3,450	3,537	3,886	5,264	..
Total imports cif	44.8	100.0	102.3	108.4	136.1	..	7,909	14,162	14,340	15,792	22,302	..

Index (1987 = 100)

	1980	1987	1988	1989	1990	1991
Merchandise terms of trade	119.0	100.0	106.8	109.6	134.7	..
Export price index	124.7	100.0	99.0	102.9	115.7	..
Import price index	95.5	100.0	107.9	106.5	116.4	..
Terms of trade						..

	Value at current prices (US$million)					
	1980	1987	1988	1989	1990	1991
Balance of payments						
Export of goods & NFS	3,621	13,842	17,105	17,612	20,167	22,052
Merchandise (fob)	2,910	10,322	11,929	11,780	13,026	13,672
Non-factor services	711	3,520	5,176	5,832	7,141	8,380
Imports of goods & NFS	8,082	15,246	15,631	18,464	25,374	24,384
Merchandise (fob)	7,513	13,551	13,706	15,999	22,580	20,998
Non-factor services	569	1,695	1,925	2,465	2,794	3,386
Resource balance	-4,461	-1,404	1,474	-852	-5,207	-2,332
Net factor income	-1,118	-1,792	-2,037	-1,745	-1,920	-2,495
(interest per DRS)	857	2,464	3,177	3,072	3,344	3,613
Net current transfers	2,153	2,066	1,827	3,135	3,349	2,854
(workers' remittances)	2,071	2,021	1,776	3,040	3,246	2,819
Curr. a/c bal. before off. transfers	-3,426	-1,130	1,264	538	-3,778	-1,973
Net official transfers	18	324	332	423	1,162	2,245
Curr. a/c bal. after off. transfers	-3,408	-806	1,596	961	-2,616	272
Long-term capital inflow	2,916	1,841	1,323	1,364	934	623
Direct investment	18	106	354	663	681	783
Net LT loans (DRS data)	1,880	1,716	3,456	1,087	1,178	24
Other LT inflow (net)	1,017	19	-2,487	-386	-925	-184
Total other items (net)	565	-455	-1,766	387	2,625	-2,094
Net short-term capital	-871	50	-2,281	-528	3,027	-3,020
Capital flows NEI	0	0	0	0	0	0
Errors and omissions	1,435	-505	515	915	-402	926
Changes in net reserves	-72	-580	-1,153	-2,712	-943	1,199
Net credit from the IMF	422	-315	-472	-251	-48	0
Other reserves changes	-494	-265	-682	-2,461	-895	1,199

Table 7.1 *(cont.)*

	Share of GDP (%)					
	1980	1987	1988	1989	1990	1991
Resource balance	-7.8	-2.1	2.1	-1.1	-4.8	-2.1
Interest payments	1.5	3.6	4.5	3.9	3.1	3.3
Current account balance	-6.0	-1.7	1.8	0.7	-3.5	-1.8

	1980	1987	1988	1989	1990	1991
Memorandum items						
Reserves excluding gold (US$m.)	1,077	1,776	2,344	4,780	6,050	5,144
Reserves including gold (US$m.)	3,298	3,631	3,912	6,298	7,626	6,616
Official X-rate (LCUs/US$)	76.04	857.21	1,422.35	2,121.68	2,608.64	..
GDP (millions of current US$)	56,919	68,013	70,887	79,074	108,447	110,460

	Share of GDP (%)						Growth rate (% per year)				
	1980	1987	1988	1989	1990	1991	1980–88	1988	1989	1990	1991
Government finance											
Current receipts	21.1	17.9	17.4	18.7	20.0	19.1	43.8	68.4	78.4	80.7	55.1
Current expenditures	20.6	17.8	17.7	19.7	20.6	24.3	45.3	71.9	84.8	76.6	91.7
Current budget balance	0.5	0.1	-0.3	-1.0	-0.6	-5.2	:	:	:	:	:
Capital receipts	:	:	:	:	:	:	:	:	:	:	:
Capital expenditures	4.3	4.5	3.5	4.5	4.1	4.1	46.1	34.9	:	:	:
Overall deficit	:	:	:	:	3.5	:	:	:	:	:	:
Official capital grants	:	:	:	:	:	0.4	:	:	:	:	:
External borrowing (net)	0.4	-0.5	0.2	-0.2	:	1.4	:	:	:	:	:
Domestic non-bank borrowing	-0.2	2.7	2.7	4.2	3.5	5.1	..	72.7	162.6	40.7	-34.8
Domestic bank financing	3.3	2.2	1.1	0.9	0.8	:	..	-16.1	36.5	55.9	938.8

	Net disbursement (US$ million)						Debt outstanding & disbursed (US$million)					
External capital flows, debt and debt burden ratios	1980	1987	1988	1989	1990	1991	1980	1987	1988	1989	1990	1991
Public & publicly guar. LT	1,834	1,560	3,433	923	918	-102	15,040	31,540	33,577	34,832	38,595	39,781

Official creditors	1,239	509	321	-478	147	-251	9,635	18,178	17,258	16,511	18,029	17,795
multilateral	410	655	579	64	262	-8	2,149	8,996	8,806	8,626	9,631	9,170
of which IBRD	267	471	360	-82	6	-215	1,158	6,290	6,130	5,869	6,272	6,169
of which IDA	-1	-4	-4	-5	-4	-4	189	170	166	162	157	154
Bilateral	828	-146	-259	-542	-115	-243	7,486	9,182	8,452	7,885	8,398	8,625
Private creditors	596	1,051	3,112	1,401	771	149	5,405	13,362	16,319	18,321	20,566	21,986
Suppliers	137	159	-14	-181	-209	-449	1,171	1,394	1,375	1,156	974	972
Financial markets	459	892	3,125	1,583	980	598	4,233	11,968	14,944	17,165	19,592	21,014
Private non-guaranteed	46	156	23	163	260	127	535	866	535	795	1,054	950
Total LT	1,880	1,716	3,456	1,087	1,178	24	15,575	32,406	34,112	35,627	39,649	40,731
IMF credit	485	-451	-431	-238	-49	0	1,054	770	299	48	0	0
Net short-term capital	-871	50	-2,281	-528	3,027	-3,020	2,490	7,623	6,417	5,745	9,500	9,600
Total, including IMF & net ST	1,494	1,315	743	320	4,155	-2,996	19,119	40,800	40,827	41,419	49,149	50,331

Ratio

	1980	1987	1988	1989	1990	1991
Bank and IDA ratios						
Share of total long-term DOD						
IBRD as % of total	7.43	19.41	17.97	16.47	15.82	15.14
IDA at % of total	1.22	0.52	0.49	0.45	0.40	0.38
IBRD+IDA as % of total	8.65	19.93	18.46	16.93	16.22	15.52
Share of LT debt service						
IBRD as % of total	12.12	15.70	15.91	15.74	17.33	14.49
IDA as % of total	0.23	0.10	0.08	0.09	0.08	0.06
IBRD+IDA as % of total	12.34	15.80	15.99	15.84	17.41	14.55
DOD-to-exports ratios						
Long-term debt/exports	271.19	195.95	172.88	162.55	157.31	155.71
IMF credit/exports	18.36	4.66	1.51	0.22	0.00	0.00
Short-term debt/exports	43.36	46.09	32.52	26.21	37.69	36.70
LT+IMF+ST DOD/exports	332.90	246.70	206.92	188.97	195.00	192.40

Table 7.1   (cont.)

DOD-to-GDP ratios						
Long-term debt/GDP	27.36	47.65	48.12	45.06	36.56	36.87
IMF credit/GDP	1.85	1.13	0.42	0.06	0.00	0.00
Short-term debt/GDP	4.37	11.21	9.05	7.27	8.76	8.69
LT-IMF+ST DOD/GDP	33.59	59.99	57.60	52.38	45.32	45.57
Debt service/exports						
Public & guaranteed LT	18.33	27.88	31.08	27.77	24.55	29.53
Private non-guaranteed LT	0.85	1.99	1.00	1.50	1.37	1.32
Total long-term debt service	19.19	29.87	32.08	29.27	25.92	30.85
IMF repurchases+serv. chgs	3.59	3.23	2.46	1.14	0.21	0.00
Interest only on ST debt	5.21	2.93	3.44	1.86	2.05	2.14
Total (LT+IMF+ST int.)	27.99	36.02	37.99	32.26	28.18	32.99

Although economic liberalization continued after 1986, the second half of the 1980s witnessed a sharp difference between domestic and external performance. On the domestic front, in 1987, strong pressures on the government for increased public spending led to a worsening of the budget deficit and high inflation. Expansionary fiscal policies in the period leading to the 1987 elections brought the budget deficit to about the same level as in 1980. While the deficit was reduced through cuts in public investment in 1988, the effort was not sustained, and in 1989, despite a sharp drop in output growth, inflation rose to about 70 per cent a year. High inflation is the main macroeconomic issue facing Turkey, and threatens the achievements of the 1980s. The fiscal deficit appears to be its chief cause. On the external front, the current account shifted into surplus in fiscal 1989, aided by growing revenues from tourism and worker remittances and continued export growth. Foreign direct investment also increased and Turkey was able to maintain its sources of external financing while repaying its external debt.

Malaysia: 1957–90

Since independence in 1957, Malaysia has followed a relatively open economy, generally driven by the market forces (see Figure 7.6). During the colonial period, the Malaysian economy was mainly supported by the tin and rubber industry. Between 1964 and 1984, along with increasing diversification, the real GDP grew by an impressive 6–8 per cent a year (see Figure 7.7) Malaysia went into recession during 1985–86 when commodity prices collapsed. Since 1987, manufactured exports have registered strong growth. In 1991, real GDP grew by 8.6 per cent (Table 7.2).

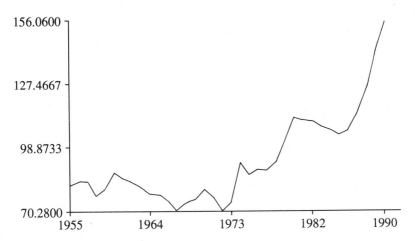

Figure 7.6   Openness measure: Malaysia

Table 7.2 The Malaysian economy, 1965–91

| Mid–1990 population (million) | 17.9 |
| 1990 per capita GNP in US$ | 2,320 |

	Share of gross domestic product (from current price data)						Growth rate (%per year) (from constant price data)				
	1965	1973	1980	1989	1990	1991	1965–73	1973–80	1980–91	1990	1991
Gross domestic product	100.0	100.0	100.0	100.0	100.0	100.0	6.7	7.5	5.6	9.8	8.6
Net indirect taxes	13.0	14.6	17.1	:	:	:	:	:	:	:	:
Agriculture	27.9	26.4	21.9	:	:	:	:	:	3.7	0.4	0.1
Industry	25.3	27.1	37.8	:	:	:	:	:	7.7	14.5	12.6
of which manufacturing	9.1	15.0	20.6	:	:	:	:	:	9.6	17.9	15.5
Services	46.8	46.6	40.3	:	:	:	:	:	4.6	9.9	8.3
Resource balance	4.3	5.5	2.5	5.0	-0.1	-5.5					
Export of goods & NFS	42.5	39.8	57.5	73.9	78.0	83.7	6.4	8.7	11.5	18.3	16.2
Imports of goods & NFS	38.2	34.3	55.0	68.9	78.1	89.1	4.4	11.3	9.2	27.0	22.2
Total expenditures	95.7	94.5	97.5	95.0	100.1	105.5	5.8	8.6	4.5	15.5	13.3
Total consumption	76.0	69.0	67.1	66.1	67.7	69.8	4.9	8.3	4.6	12.1	10.6
Private consumption	61.2	53.2	50.5	52.2	54.1	55.4	4.4	8.1	5.0	13.6	10.1
General government	14.7	15.8	16.5	14.0	13.6	14.4	6.9	8.8	3.3	6.5	12.8
Gross domestic investment	19.7	25.5	30.4	28.8	32.3	35.7	9.1	9.7	4.3	23.6	18.9
Fixed investment	17.1	23.9	31.1	29.6	32.7	35.6	11.3	10.2	4.2	22.0	17.2
Changes in stocks	2.6	1.7	-0.7	-0.8	-0.4	0.1	:	:	:	:	:
Gross domestic saving	24.0	31.0	32.9	33.9	32.3	30.2	7.4	10.6	6.4	5.4	1.1
Net factor income	-2.6	-3.3	-3.6	-5.8	-4.3	-4.0	:	:	:	:	:
Net current transfers	0.0	0.0	0.0	0.0	0.0	0.2	:	:	:	:	:
Gross national saving	21.4	26.8	29.1	28.0	28.0	26.4	7.0	10.8	6.3	10.6	2.1

In millions of LCUs (at constant 1987 prices)

	1965	1973	1980	1989	1990	1991	1965–73	1973–80	1980–91	1990	1991
									Inflation rate (% per year)		
Gross domestic product	20,251	35,273	58,193	94,306	103,556	112,410	6.7	7.5	5.6	9.8	8.6
Capacity to import	10,307	15,320	32,449	68,294	80,755	92,730	3.9	11.7	10.5	18.2	14.8
Terms of trade adjustment	1,053	–383	4,278	1,153	1,304	418					
Gross domestic income	21,304	34,890	62,471	95,460	104,860	112,828	5.6	9.0	5.2	9.8	7.6
Gross national product	19,535	33,920	56,109	88,836	99,080	107,925	6.6	7.4	5.5	11.5	8.9
Gross national income	20,587	33,537	60,387	89,990	100,384	108,344	5.4	9.0	5.1	11.6	7.9

Price indices

	1980	1986	1988	1989	1990	1991	1965–73	1973–80	1980–91	1990	1991
	Index (1987 = 100)										
Consumer prices (IFS 64)	78.4	99.1	102.0	104.8	107.6	112.2	2.1	5.4	2.6	2.6	4.4
Wholesale prices (IFS 63)											
Implicit GDP deflator	91.6	94.8	104.7	107.6	110.7	114.2	1.2	7.2	1.7	2.9	3.2
Implicit expenditures defl.	85.1	99.3	102.8	106.1	109.3	113.9	2.3	5.7	2.1	3.0	4.2

Other indicators

	1965–73	1973–80	1980–91
	Growth rate (% per year)		
Population	2.6	2.4	2.6
Labour force	3.2	3.7	2.8
Gross national income p.c.	2.8	6.5	2.4
Private consumption p.c.	1.8	5.6	2.3
Import elasticity			
Imports (goods & NFS)/GDP	0.7	1.5	1.6
Marginal savings rates			
Gross national saving	36.9	33.4	24.0
Gross domestic saving	42.1	35.3	26.6
ICOR (period averages)	..	3.6	5.0

Table 7.2 (cont.)

	Share of labour force (%)				Volume index (1987 = 100)						Value at current prices (US$ million)						Index (1987 = 100)					
	1965	1973	1980	1990	1980	1987	1988	1989	1990	1991	1980	1987	1988	1989	1990	1991	1980	1987	1988	1989	1990	1991
Labour force	100.0	100.0	100.0	100.0																		
Agriculture	58.6	49.9	41.6	..																		
Industry	13.0	15.8	19.1	..																		
Services	28.5	34.3	39.3	..																		
Merchandise exports																						
X.FUEL					62.4	100.0	110.4	118.4	122.8	128.1	3,082	2,496	2,335	2,910	3,932	3,706						
X.OAGRI.RUBBER					94.1	100.0	99.4	91.8	81.6	78.3	2,121	1,554	2,007	1,458	1,119	1,079						
X.TIM					65.9	100.0	89.6	92.1	88.8	84.0	1,202	1,696	1,530	1,608	1,494	1,435						
X.FOOD.FAT					52.4	100.0	101.8	121.4	138.7	134.7	1,155	1,301	1,729	1,728	1,626	1,797						
Manufactures					34.3	100.0	127.0	161.1	194.8	..	3,601	8,110	10,253	13,510	17,429	20,576						
Residual					91.4	100.0	106.1	118.7	148.4	..	1,780	2,792	3,247	3,824	3,356	5,672						
Total exports fob					56.5	100.0	113.2	135.9	157.8	180.3	12,941	17,949	21,101	25,038	28,956	34,264						
Merchandise imports																						
Food					71.4	100.0	112.2	120.8	130.9	..	1,225	1,253	1,545	1,702	1,694	1,867						
Fuel and energy					426.2	100.0	83.9	53.6	58.4	..	2,116	1,455	1,579	1,995	2,366	2,561						
Other consumer goods					117.8	100.0	133.7	160.2	193.7	..	552	983	1,381	1,103	1,666	1,958						
Other intermediate goods					83.7	100.0	117.3	143.8	161.8	..												
Capital goods					99.6	100.0	131.2	195.0	235.2	..	4,183	5,715	7,392	10,772	14,734	19,595						
Total imports cif					95.9	100.0	122.8	158.0	184.1	230.7	10,773	12,674	16,532	22,467	29,251	36,680						
Merchandise terms of trade																						
Export price index																	127.6	100.0	103.9	102.6	102.2	105.9
Import price index																	88.6	100.0	106.2	112.2	125.4	125.4
Terms of trade																	144.0	100.0	97.8	91.5	81.5	84.4

140

	Value at current prices (US$million)					
	1980	1987	1988	1989	1990	1991
Balance of payments						
Exports of goods & NFS	14,098	20,149	23,359	27,680	33,011	39,053
Merchandise (fob)	12,868	17,754	20,852	24,667	28,956	34,264
Non-factor services	1,229	2,396	2,507	3,013	4,055	4,789
Imports of goods & NFS	13,489	15,688	19,759	25,793	32,930	41,605
Merchandise (fob)	10,462	11,918	15,306	20,754	27,032	35,023
Non-factor services	3,026	3,770	4,453	5,039	5,897	6,583
Resource balance	609	4,461	3,600	1,886	81	-2,552
Net factor income	-873	-1,963	-1,941	-2,179	-1,831	-1,862
(interest per DRS)	589	1,720	1,718	1,440	1,398	1,630
Net current transfers	0	69	70	-17	16	116
(workers' remittances)	..	..	..	..	..	0
Curr. a/c bal. before off. transfers	-307	2,567	1,729	-309	-1,733	-4,298
Net official transfers	23	69	81	97	61	0
Curr. a/c bal. after off. transfers	-285	2,636	1,810	-212	-1,672	-4,298
Long-term capital inflow	1,021	-548	-1,224	848	2,588	3,358
Direct investment	934	423	719	1,668	2,902	3,164
Net LT loans (DRS data)	1,111	-624	-1,802	-730	-226	166
Other LT inflow (net)	-1,025	-347	-142	-90	-88	28
Total other items (net)	-268	-969	-1,016	594	1,037	1,291
Net short-term capital	414	-989	-1,113	696	606	1,036
Capital flows NEI	0	0	0	0	0	0
Errors and omissions	-682	20	97	-101	431	255
Changes in net reserves	-468	-1,119	430	-1,230	-1,953	-351
Net credit from the IMF	..	..	..	..	..	..
Other reserves changes	-468	-1,119	430	-1,230	-1,953	-351

Table 7.2 (cont.)

Share of GDP (%)

	1980	1987	1988	1989	1990	1991
Resource balance	2.5	14.1	10.4	5.0	0.2	-5.5
Interest payments	2.4	5.4	5.0	3.8	3.3	3.5
Current account balance	-1.3	8.1	5.0	-0.8	-4.1	-9.2

Memorandum items

	1980	1987	1988	1989	1990	1991
Reserves excluding gold (US$m.)	4,387	7,435	6,527	7,783	9,754	..
Reserves including gold (US$m.)	5,755	8,573	7,491	8,733	10,659	..
Official X-rate (LCUs/US$)	2.18	2.52	2.62	2.71	2.70	2.75
GDP (millions of current US$)	24,488	31,602	34,696	37,457	42,373	46,672

Government finance

	Share of GDP (%)						Growth rate (% per year)				
	1980	1987	1988	1989	1990	1991	1980–88	1988	1989	1990	1991
Current receipts	26.1	22.8	24.2	24.9	25.3	26.2	4.6	21.1	15.0	14.7	15.9
Current expenditures	22.9	25.4	24.0	24.5	23.2	24.0	6.1	8.1	13.8	7.1	15.9
Current budget balance	3.2	-2.6	0.2	0.4	2.1	2.2	..	..	..	..	..
Capital receipts	..	..	..	..	..	..	..	..	..	..	..
Capital expenditures	..	..	..	..	..	..	..	..	..	..	..
Overall deficit	..	..	..	..	-6.9	-6.9	..	..	..	..	..
Official capital grants	0.6	..	..	..	..	0.2	..	..	..	..	..
External borrowing (net)	..	-3.1	-3.4	-1.0	-0.8	..	11.5	-18.7	-9.8	-3.4	-3.3
Domestic non-bank borrowing	4.3	10.8	7.7	6.2	5.3	4.6	..	..	..	..	..
Domestic bank financing	..	..	..	..	..	..	..	..	..	..	..

External capital flows, debt and debt burden ratios

	Net disbursement (US$ million)						Debt outstanding & disbursed (US$million)					
	1980	1987	1988	1989	1990	1991	1980	1987	1988	1989	1990	1991
Public & publicly guar. LT	889	-269	-1,532	-813	-441	6	4,008	19,247	17,101	15,516	16,107	16,145

The following reproduces a rotated two-panel debt table. The first six data columns are Debt Outstanding and Disbursed (DOD); the next six are Net flows. Years are 1980, 1987, 1988, 1989, 1990, 1991.

	DOD 1980	DOD 1987	DOD 1988	DOD 1989	DOD 1990	DOD 1991	Net flow 1980	Net flow 1987	Net flow 1988	Net flow 1989	Net flow 1990	Net flow 1991
Official creditors	1,444	4,472	4,230	3,703	4,532	4,339	133	-100	-73	-210	354	235
multilateral	745	1,576	1,472	1,461	1,812	1,798	85	15	-4	20	57	120
of which IBRD	504	1,116	998	983	1,103	1,207	54	-7	-17	15	41	24
of which IDA	0	0	0	0	0	0	0	0	0	0	0	0
Bilateral	699	2,897	2,758	2,242	2,720	2,542	48	-116	-70	-230	297	116
Private creditors	2,564	14,774	12,872	11,813	11,575	11,806	756	-169	-1,458	-604	-796	-230
Suppliers	195	791	561	325	285	199	113	-73	-211	-195	-60	-194
Financial markets	2,369	13,984	12,311	11,488	11,290	11,607	643	-96	-1,248	-409	-735	-35
Private non-guaranteed	1,248	2,610	2,340	1,377	1,489	1,515	223	-355	-270	83	215	160
Total LT	5,256	21,857	19,441	16,893	17,596	17,661	1,111	-624	-1,802	-730	-226	166
IMF credit	0	0	0	0	0	0	0	0	0	0	0	0
Net short-term capital	1,355	2,345	1,595	2,273	1,906	2,076	414	-989	-1,113	696	606	1,036
Total, including IMF & net ST	6,611	24,202	21,036	19,166	19,502	19,737	1,526	-1,613	-2,914	-35	379	1,203

Ratio

	1980	1987	1988	1989	1990	1991
Bank and IDA ratios						
Share of total long-term DOD						
IBRD as % of total	9.60	5.10	5.13	5.82	6.27	6.83
IDA as % of total	0.00	0.00	0.00	0.00	0.00	0.00
IBRD+IDA as % of total	9.60	5.10	5.13	5.82	6.27	6.83
Share of LT debt service						
IBRD as % of total	9.57	4.70	4.18	4.77	6.39	6.28
IDA as % of total	0.00	0.00	0.00	0.00	0.00	0.00
IBRD+IDA as % of total	9.57	4.70	4.18	4.77	6.39	6.28
DOD-to-exports ratios						
Long-term debt/exports	35.43	104.16	79.52	58.55	50.47	43.33
IMF credit/exports	0.00	0.00	0.00	0.00	0.00	0.00
Short-term debt/exports	9.13	11.18	6.52	7.88	5.47	5.09
LT+IMF+ST DOD/exports	44.56	115.34	86.04	66.43	55.94	48.42

Table 7.2 (cont.)

DOD-to-GDP ratios						
Long-term debt/GDP	21.46	69.16	56.03	45.10	41.53	37.84
IMF credit/GDP	0.00	0.00	0.00	0.00	0.00	0.00
Short-term debt/GDP	5.53	7.42	4.60	6.07	4.50	4.45
LT+IMF+ST DOD/GDP	27.00	76.58	60.63	51.17	46.02	42.29
Debt service/exports						
Public & guaranteed LT	2.54	14.65	17.80	12.96	9.59	8.03
Private non-guaranteed LT	2.07	5.64	4.76	2.36	1.65	1.65
Total long-term debt service	4.60	20.29	22.56	15.32	11.24	9.68
IMF repurchases+serv. chgs	0.00	0.00	0.00	0.00	0.00	0.00
Interest only on ST debt	1.69	0.91	0.71	0.69	0.48	0.55
Total (LT+IMF+ST int.)	6.30	21.20	23.27	16.01	11.73	10.23

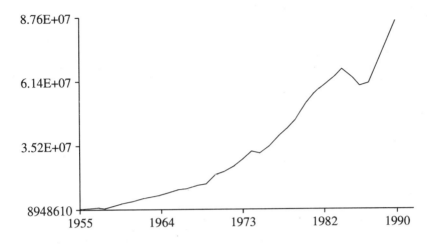

Figure 7.7   Real GDP (in US$): Malaysia

Although the Malaysian economy mainly relies on market forces, the government plays an important role in the economy, both as a producer and a regulator. Malaysia also encourages foreign investment in the export sector. Indeed, the American and Japanese multinationals dominate a substantial section of the manufacturing sector. To create a favourable macroeonomic environment, the government has so far followed a prudent fiscal policy, with a surplus in the operating account and a small deficit in the capital budget, funded mainly by bond sales. Recently, the government has been pre-paying foreign debt. National savings as a percentage of GDP reached 30 per cent in 1991. Similarly, the use of monetary policy has so far been targeted to achieve price stability by controlling monetary aggregates, the rate of interest, reserve requirements and, sometimes, open market operations. A tight control of the public-sector deficit as a proportion of GDP helped the creation of a macroeconomic environment within which commerce and industry flourished considerably (Table 7.2).

As regards exchange rate policy, Malaysia has so far followed an open foreign exchange regime as reflected in low rates of distortions between the black market and the official exchange rate (see Figure 7.8).[5] Occasionally, the Central Bank intervenes in the market to smooth the fluctuations of the Malaysian ringgit against, say, the US dollar. The long-run stability of the ringgit in the international currency market reflects its real underlying value rather than direct interventions to stimulate exports. Foreign payments (remittances) are freely permitted. Most prices (excepting those for fuel, rice, sugar, flour, public utility goods and tobacco) are market-determined. In comparison with most LDCs, Malaysia has experienced a fairly stable rate of

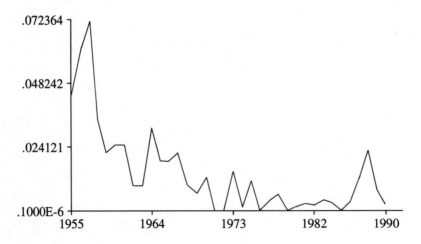

Figure 7.8   Exchange rate distortion index: Malaysia

inflation. Between 1980 and 1991, manufacturing exports registered strong growth among all the export categories (see Table 7.2). Both the short- and long-term debt–GDP ratios declined substantially between 1987 and 1991. Average tariffs account for only 15 per cent of prices on a trade-weighted basis. However, in the agricultural sector, there are important tariff and non-tariff barriers to encourage domestic production.

Malaysia is on the verge of becoming an upper middle-income country with a GNP per capita in 1990 of US$2 320. There have been three main determinants in Malaysia's economic development: remarkable attention and priority have been given to agriculture, resulting in high productivity gains; manufacturing growth has been rapid, at about 12 per cent a year over the last two decades, initially led by domestically oriented subsectors, but more recently led by export-oriented industries; and the economy has been kept very open[6] (World Bank 1992, 327). Exports reached 74 per cent of GNP in 1989, while imports, stimulated by high growth, have risen to 70 per cent of GNP. The increasing export orientation of the economy has been accompanied by a transition from an initial dependence on rubber and tin to a broadly diversified range of products including palm oil, logs, petroleum and gas, cocoa, and manufactured goods (see Table 7.2).

Ghatak et al. (1994) comprehensively test the export-led growth hypothesis for Malaysia for the period 1955–90, using cointegration and causality testing based on Hsiao's synthesis of the Granger test and Akaike's minimum final prediction error criterion. Their results provide a robust support for the export-led growth (ELG) hypothesis: aggregate exports tend to raise real GDP and *non-export* GDP in terms of Granger causality (see Granger 1988).

This relationship is found to be driven by manufactured rather than by traditional exports.

India: 1950–90

India has a population of 850 million and one of the lowest per capita GNPs in the world. In 1990 it stood at US$360. Nearly 70 per cent of the labour force is employed in agriculture, accounting for one-third of the GDP (US Department of State 1992). From its independence in 1947 until the late 1970s, India's economic policies were dominated by self-sufficiency, import substitution, and state control of basic infrastructure and manufacturing industries. While this approach led to rapid expansion of India's industrial base, productivity growth was repressed by lack of foreign and domestic competition. During this period, GNP growth rates seldom exceeded 3.5 per cent.

A consensus began to build in the late 1970s, and especially after 1984, that India would have to liberalize her economy to reduce poverty rapidly, create adequate resources for social programmes, and modernize its infrastructure and manufacturing sector (World Bank 1992, 262). In the late 1980s, especially, successive governments relaxed some restrictions on trade and investment, while at the same time boosting domestic demand through debt-financed deficit spending. India's private sector reacted well to the opportunities opened up under the new policies. GDP growth accelerated to over 5 per cent during the 1980s and there was a marked increase in exports of manufactures (see Table 7.3). Various measures of trade liberalization confirm the increasing openness of the Indian economy, especially in the second half of the 1980s (see Figures 7.9–11).

However, macroeconomic imbalances became a serious problem. The budget deficit rose steadily from 6.4 per cent of GDP in fiscal 1981 to over 9 per cent in fiscal 1991, while the current account deficit rose from 1.7 per cent to 3 per cent of GDP (see Table 7.3). In 1991, the government's domestic debt had risen to 56 per cent of GDP. India's external debt also rose from US$20 billion in 1981 to US$70 billion in 1991, while the debt–service ratio increased from 10 per cent to 29 per cent. The government that came to power in June 1991 inherited an economy in crisis. However, in less than a year, the new government had overcome the immediate balance-of-payments problems and reduced macroeconomic imbalances, and initiated a major transformation of India's development strategy. Radical industrial, trade and financial policy changes beginning in 1991 have made remarkable progress in starting to liberalize what was one of the most closed and regulated economies in the world (Ghatak 1993).

Table 7.3   The Indian economy, 1965–91

Mid–1990 population (million)	849.5
1990 per capita GNP in US$	360

	Share of gross domestic product (from current price data)						Growth rate (% per year) (from constant price data)				
	1965	1973	1980	1989	1990	1991	1965–73	1973–80	1980–91	1990	1991
Gross domestic product	100.0	100.0	100.0	100.0	100.0	100.0	3.7	3.8	5.6	5.5	2.2
Net indirect taxes	8.0	8.1	10.0	10.9	10.8	10.4	..	..	..	..	..
Agriculture	40.6	42.8	34.3	28.2	28.9	28.3	3.3	1.8	3.2	4.2	0.0
Industry	20.2	19.9	23.3	25.2	24.6	23.9	3.9	5.2	6.3	6.7	–0.
of which manufacturing	14.3	14.3	15.9	16.4	16.2	15.6	4.3	4.9	6.7	7.3	–1.5
Services	31.3	29.2	32.4	35.7	35.8	37.4	4.1	4.9	6.8	5.9	7.0
Resource balance	–2.0	–0.5	–3.6	–2.5	–2.4	–0.8					
Export of goods & NFS	3.6	4.3	6.5	7.7	7.7	8.9	2.8	6.7	6.0	3.8	–0.4
Imports of goods & NFS	5.6	4.8	10.1	10.3	10.1	9.8	1.8	7.9	5.0	1.8	–9.3
Total expenditures	102.0	100.5	103.6	102.5	102.4	100.8	3.6	3.9	5.5	5.3	1.4
Total consumption	87.0	83.5	82.6	76.7	53.4	79.8	3.6	3.8	5.8	5.7	3.8
Private consumption	78.2	75.2	73.0	65.0	41.3	68.0	3.4	3.6	5.5	5.3	4.5
General government	8.8	8.3	9.6	11.8	12.1	11.8	5.7	5.7	7.7	8.4	–0.4
Gross domestic investment	17.0	18.3	20.9	23.2	22.8	21.0	3.6	4.2	4.7	3.9	–6.8
Fixed investment	15.8	14.6	19.3	21.0	20.1	18.9	2.5	5.7	4.9	2.8	–4.7
Changes in stocks	1.1	3.6	1.6	2.1	2.8	2.1	..	..	..	..	..
Gross domestic saving	14.9	17.7	17.4	20.6	20.4	20.2	5.2	3.0	5.2	4.4	–0.8
Net factor income	–0.5	–0.3	0.2	–1.2	–1.3	–1.5					
Net current transfers	0.0	0.2	1.7	0.8	0.7	1.0	..	..	..	..	..
Gross national saving	14.4	17.6	19.2	20.2	19.8	19.5	5.6	4.4	4.3	3.4	0.5

In billions of LCUs (at constant 1987 prices)

	1965	1973	1980	1989	1990	1991	1965–73	1973–80	1980–91	1990	1991
							Growth rate (% per year)				
Gross domestic product	1,391	1,814	2,337	3,877	4,091	4,182	3.7	3.8	5.6	5.5	2.2
Capacity to import	67	119	137	256	263	287	6.8	4.1	7.0	2.8	9.1
Terms of trade adjustment	-10	19	-19	-6	-9	16				..	..
Gross domestic income	1,381	1,833	2,318	3,871	4,082	4,198	4.0	3.7	5.7	5.5	2.8
Gross national product	1,378	1,805	2,344	3,836	4,046	4,132	3.8	3.9	5.5	5.5	2.1
Gross national income	1,369	1,824	2,325	3,830	4,037	4,149	4.0	3.8	5.5	5.4	2.8

Price indices — Index (1987 = 100)

	1980	1986	1988	1989	1990	1991	1965–73	1973–80	1980–91	1990	1991
							Inflation rate (% per year)				
Consumer prices (IFS 64)	54.2	91.9	109.4	116.1	126.5	145.2	5.9	5.3	8.6	9.0	–
Wholesale prices (IFS 63)	62.9	94.3	108.6	..	128.1	146.1	6.6	7.0	6.7		13.4
Implicit GDP deflator	58.2	92.1	108.2	116.2	129.4	145.8	6.2	6.8	8.2	11.4	12.8
Implicit expenditures defl.	58.9	91.5	108.2	116.8	130.2		6.1	7.1	8.2	11.5	11.9

Other indicators

	1965–73	1973–80	1980–91
	Growth rate (% per year)		
Population	2.3	2.3	2.1
Labour force	1.6	1.7	2.0
Gross national income p.c.	1.6	1.4	3.3
Private consumption p.c.	1.0	1.3	3.3
Import elasticity			
Imports (goods & NFS)/GDP	0.5	2.1	0.9
Marginal savings rates			
Gross national saving	27.7	24.9	20.6
Gross domestic saving	26.6	15.9	23.6
ICOR (period averages)	–	6.1	4.1

Table 7.3 (cont.)

	Share of labour force (%)				Volume index (1987 = 100)						Value at current prices (US$ million)						Index (1987 = 100)					
	1965	1973	1980	1990	1980	1987	1988	1989	1990	1991	1980	1987	1988	1989	1990	1991	1980	1987	1988	1989	1990	1991
Labour force	100.0	100.0	100.0	100.0																		
Agriculture	72.9	71.1	69.7	..																		
Industry	11.9	12.8	13.2	..																		
Services	15.1	16.1	17.0	..																		
Merchandise exports								..	..					..	..							
BEV.TEA					116.2	100.0	98.1	106.0	113.7	119.4	539	457	414	543	599	537						
MET.FE					79.2	100.0	116.5	126.0	118.9	126.1	384	419	464	557	585	645						
BEV.COFFEE					101.5	100.0	92.9	129.6	103.7	76.7	271	203	193	206	141	101						
Manufactures					60.4	100.0	117.3	136.6	135.2	131.4	5,067	9,013	11,105	13,185	14,383	13,795						
Residual					91.3	100.0	93.7	104.6	146.5	157.5	2,071	2,552	2,087	2,360	2,777	2,923						
Total exports fob					70.2	100.0	111.5	128.7	135.1	134.4	8,332	12,644	14,262	16,850	18,485	18,002						
Merchandise imports																						
Food					78.8	100.0	115.1	50.6	52.1	22.4	1,348	1,292	1,203	714	713	303						
Fuel and energy					111.9	100.0	113.2	122.2	139.0	157.3	6,669	3,148	2,938	3,766	5,967	5,158						
Other consumer goods					11.5	100.0	145.3	118.8	114.6	80.9	371	3,139	4,575	3,962	4,015	2,590						
Other intermediate goods					81.9	100.0	136.4	147.6	145.9	132.8	5,197	7,502	10,967	11,783	11,440	10,558						
Capital goods					58.7	100.0	71.7	83.3	79.4	37.4	2,307	4,732	3,657	4,189	4,292	2,058						
Total imports cif					75.1	100.0	117.5	116.3	119.3	105.2	15,892	19,812	23,339	24,414	26,427	20,667						
Merchandise terms of trade																						
Export price index																	93.9	100.0	101.2	103.6	108.2	105.9
Import price index																	106.9	100.0	100.2	106.0	111.8	99.2
Terms of trade																	87.9	100.0	100.9	97.7	96.7	106.8

150

Value at current prices (US$million)

	1980	1987	1988	1989	1990	1991
Balance of payments						
Export of goods & NFS	11,281	16,215	18,218	20,913	22,685	21,950
Merchandise (fob)	8,332	12,644	14,262	16,850	18,485	18,000
Non-factor services	2,949	3,571	3,956	4,063	4,200	3,950
Imports of goods & NFS	17,408	22,839	26,564	27,752	29,807	23,990
Merchandise (fob)	15,892	19,812	23,339	24,414	26,430	20,670
Non-factor services	1,516	3,027	3,225	3,338	3,377	3,320
Resource balance	-6,127	-6,624	-8,346	-6,839	-7,122	-2,040
Net factor income	356	-2,471	-2,985	-3,305	-3,741	-3,650
(interest per DRS)	642	2,728	3,148	3,504	3,936	4,379
Net current transfers	2,860	2,698	2,654	2,256	2,000	2,685
(workers' remittances)	2,786	2,724	2,225	2,186	1,947	2,020
Curr. a/c bal. before off. transfers	-2,911	-6,397	-8,677	-7,888	-8,863	-3,005
Net official transfers	643	410	406	500	480	450
Curr. a/c bal. after off. transfers	-2,268	-5,987	-8,271	-7,388	-8,383	-2,555
Long-term capital inflow	2,110	7,940	9,950	9,270	5,650	4,050
Direct investment	10	180	290	350	110	200
Net LT loans (DRS data)	1,424	3,776	4,364	4,230	2,925	4,425
Other LT inflow (net)	676	3,984	5,296	4,690	2,615	-575
Total other items (net)	-1,202	-1,213	-1,899	-1,722	-247	875
Net short-term capital	0	220	250	920	220	-1,010
Capital flows NEI	0	0	0	0	0	0
Errors and omissions	-1,202	-1,433	-2,149	-2,642	-467	1,885
Changes in net reserves	1,360	-740	220	-160	2,980	-2,370
Net credit from the IMF	1,010	-1,080	-1,210	-1,010	1,210	780
Other reserves changes	350	340	1,430	850	1,770	-3,150

Table 7.3 (cont.)

	Share of GDP (%)					
	1980	1987	1988	1989	1990	1991
Resource balance	-3.6	-2.6	-3.1	-2.5	-2.4	-0.8
Interest payments	0.4	1.1	1.2	1.3	1.3	1.8
Current account balance	-1.7	-2.5	-3.2	-2.9	-3.0	-1.2

	1980	1987	1988	1989	1990	1991
Memorandum items						
Reserves excluding gold (US$m.)	6,858	6,391	4,959	4,108	2,338	5,491
Reserves including gold (US$m.)	11,924	11,449	9,246	11,610	5,637	7,616
Official X-rate (LCUs/US$)	7.86	12.96	13.92	16.23	17.50	24.86
GDP (millions of current US$)	172,308	256,527	272,839	270,420	295,023	249,082

	Share of GDP (%)						Growth rate (% per year)				
	1980	1987	1988	1989	1990	1991	1980–88	1988	1989	1990	1991
Government finance											
Current receipts	8.9	11.3	11.3	11.3	11.9	12.3	17.7	18.1	14.9	10.0	34.2
Current expenditures	8.9	12.6	12.7	13.2	14.6	14.0	19.5	19.6	18.2	18.1	24.1
Current budget balance	..	-1.3	-1.5	-1.8	-2.7	-1.7	..	..	..	..	..
Capital receipts	..	..	..	..	..	..					
Capital expenditures	6.4	6.8	6.4	6.6	6.2	3.7	15.0	10.8	17.8	3.7	-26.3
Overall deficit	6.4	8.1	7.8	8.4	8.9	6.5	..	..	..	..	..
Official capital grants	..	..	..	..	..	..	..	..	..	..	..
External borrowing (net)	1.0	0.9	0.6	0.6	0.8	1.2	..	..	..	..	..
Domestic non-bank borrowing	1.7	3.7	4.1	3.7	2.9	1.7	29.4	30.9	4.3	-9.2	-60.9
Domestic bank financing	3.7	3.2	2.8	4.1	5.2	3.6		6.0	66.2	38.1	-14.7

	Net disbursement (US$ million)						Debt outstanding & disbursed (US$million)					
	1980	1987	1988	1989	1990	1991	1980	1987	1988	1989	1990	1991
External capital flows, debt and debt burden ratios												
Public & publicly guar. LT	1,569	5,710	7,119	6,654	4,326	4,764	18,372	46,662	50,706	56,567	60,976	64,652
Official creditors	934	2,489	2,633	2,505	2,261	2,889	16,315	30,003	30,842	33,328	36,003	38,893

Multilateral	23,725	21,669	19,664	18,061	16,588	6,070	2,056	1,631	1,639	2,228	1,761	777
of which IBRD	8,465	7,685	6,615	5,590	4,661	827	925	724	1,094	1,414	865	103
of which IDA	14,145	13,334	12,521	12,019	11,615	5,142	810	648	468	675	848	637
Bilateral	15,167	14,334	13,664	12,781	13,415	10,245	833	647	867	404	728	158
Private creditors	25,759	24,972	23,240	19,864	16,659	2,056	1,875	2,065	4,149	4,486	3,221	635
Suppliers	1,860	726	682	632	715	118	1,134	43	48	−80	−93	−37
Financial markets	23,899	24,246	22,558	19,232	15,944	1,939	741	2,022	4,101	4,566	3,314	672
Private non-guaranteed	1,230	1,488	1,551	1,473	1,652	336	−258	−104	−82	−104	59	194
Total LT	65,882	62,464	58,119	52,179	48,315	18,708	4,506	4,222	6,572	7,015	5,769	1,763
IMF credit	4,908	2,623	1,566	2,573	4,023	977	−459	1,214	−1,008	−1,210	−1,082	1,013
Net short-term capital	3,899	4,908	4,689	3,772	3,519	926	−1,009	219	917	253	220	0
Total, including IMF & net ST	73,189	69,995	64,374	58,524	55,856	20,610	4,278	5,655	6,485	6,057	4,909	2,777

Ratio

	1980	1987	1988	1989	1990	1991
Bank and IDA ratios						
Share of total long-term DOD						
IBRD as % of total	4.42	9.65	10.71	11.38	12.30	12.85
IDA at % of total	27.49	24.04	23.03	21.54	21.35	21.47
IBRD+IDA as % of total	31.91	33.69	33.75	32.93	33.65	34.32
Share of LT debt service						
IBRD as % of total	10.64	19.83	16.97	17.98	18.82	18.54
IDA as % of total	3.87	4.09	3.91	3.79	3.58	4.16
IBRD+IDA as % of total	14.51	23.92	20.88	21.77	22.40	22.70
DOD-to-exports ratios						
Long-term debt/exports	123.48	249.24	250.38	247.38	2.52	2.71
IMF credit/exports	6.45	20.75	12.35	6.67	0.11	0.14
Short-term debt/exports	6.11	18.15	18.10	19.96	0.20	0.16
LT+IMF+ST DOD/exports	136.04	288.14	280.82	274.00	2.82	3.01

Table 7.3 *(cont.)*

DOD-to-GDP ratios						
Long-term debt/GDP	10.86	18.83	19.12	21.49	0.21	0.27
IMF credit/GDP	0.57	1.57	0.94	0.58	0.01	0.01
Short-term debt/GDP	0.54	1.37	1.38	1.73	0.02	0.02
LT-IMF+ST DOD/GDP	11.96	21.77	21.45	23.81	0.24	0.30
Debt service/exports						
Public & guaranteed LT	7.70	18.76	20.01	19.14	0.22	0.22
Private non-guaranteed LT	0.80	2.25	1.95	1.96	0.02	0.02
Total long-term debt service	8.50	21.02	21.96	21.10	0.24	0.24
IMF repurchases+serv. chgs	0.09	7.11	6.93	5.07	0.03	0.03
Interest only on ST debt	0.70	1.29	1.38	1.26	0.02	0.01
Total (LT+IMF+ST int.)	9.29	29.42	30.27	27.44	0.28	0.28

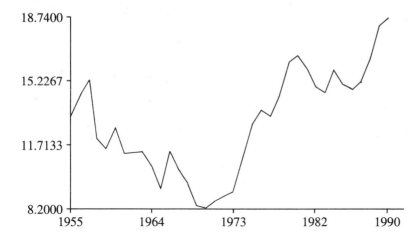

Figure 7.9   Openness measure [(exports+imports)/RGDP per capita]: India

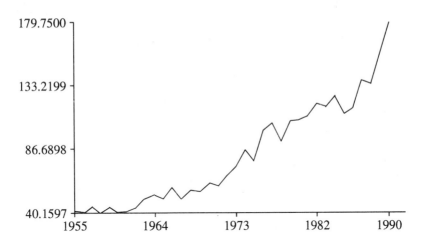

Figure 7.10   Real exports (in US$): India

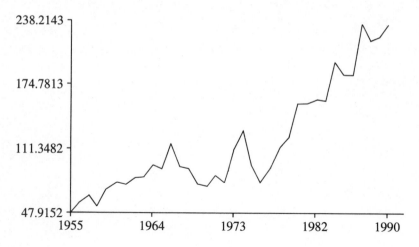

Figure 7.11   Real imports (in US$): India

Evidence from estimated correlation matrix and cointegration analysis
Table 7.4 reports the results of the estimated correlation matrix on the correlation between various trade liberalization measures and real GDP for Turkey, Malaysia and India.[7] The results refer to a 'strong' positive correlation between real GDP (RGDP) and various measures of trade liberalization such as openness measure (OPEN), real exports (REX), real imports (RIM) and real exchange rates (RER). A negative (expectedly) correlation is observed in the case of real GDP (RGDP) and the exchange rate distortion index (ERDI). Overall, we have preliminary and indicative evidence for all three countries that the underlying relationship between trade liberalization and real GDP is quite 'strong', as shown by the high correlation coefficients estimated. How-

*Table 7.4   Estimated correlation matrix of variables: correlation between
real GDP and measures of 'trade liberalization' for Turkey,
Malaysia and India*

	RGDP	OPEN	REX	RIM	ERDI	RER
Turkey						
RGDP	1.00	0.87	0.88	0.95	−0.72	0.75
Malaysia						
RGDP	1.00	0.90	0.98	0.95	−0.55	0.68
India						
RGDP	1.00	0.70	0.97	0.95	0.41	0.80

ever, these results are only indicative and do *not necessarily* imply a causal and/or 'genuine' long-run relationship between trade liberalization and output. To be more conclusive and to make sure that we do not deal with a spurious relationship, we need to apply cointegration analysis.[8]

The application of the integration and cointegration analyses[9] to the annual data suggests that all the variables (i.e. log of real GDP (LRGDP); log of various trade liberalization measures such as openness measure (LOPEN), real exports (LREX), real imports (LRIM), real exchange rates (LRER) and exchange rate distortion index (LERDI); log of physical and human capital measures (LK and LH respectively)) for Turkey, Malaysia and India are all non-stationary in levels, but stationary in first differences (relevant figures available on request). The augmented Dickey–Fuller (ADF) test results for unit roots confirm that all variables are integrated of order one in levels but integrated of order zero (i.e. stationary) in first differences.[10]

The empirical evidence establishes the long-run complementary effects of the physical and human capital accumulation on the output growth for Turkey and Malaysia. For India, in the cointegrating regression, the long-run complementary effects of physical and human capital accumulation on the output are rather weak. We believe this is due to a 'multicollinearity' problem.

Conclusions

The following conclusions can be drawn on the basis of our case studies for Turkey, Malaysia and India. First, the three countries under investigation, our multivariate cointegration analyses and the error-correction models accord well with the hypothesized role of trade policy in the 'new' growth theory: that is, trade policy can affect both the short- and the long-run output growth rate. In the long run, the effect on output growth rate is jointly determined by increasing physical and human capital accumulation.

Second, our analyses indicate that real export growth also causes *non-export* real GDP growth for Malaysia. The Malaysian evidence highlights the relative importance of non-traditional exports in total exports.

Third, the Indian evidence particularly supports the positive joint effect of *imports*, physical capital accumulation and real exchange rates on the long-run output growth. However, the trade liberalization in India in the conventional sense, i.e. export promotion via elimination of exchange rate distortions, reduction of tariffs and quotas and many other bureaucratic interventions, has only recently begun. Hence further research is necessary to draw firm conclusions.

Notes

1. This section draws on Ghatak et al. (1995).
2. There is, in any case, some overlap between the alternative indices, and the indices used here may also capture the effects of trade regime bias.
3. For various measures of trade liberalization used in the present work, and also for their definitions and data sources, see the Appendix.
4. The range 10–20 of their trade liberalization index is reserved for 'outward-oriented' trade regimes. The highest value given by the authors in these periods is 8.
5. For the definition of our exchange rate distortion index (ERDI), see the Appendix.
6. This point is strongly confirmed by various measures of trade liberalization for Malaysia. See relevant figures in the Appendix.
7. For definitions and data sources of the variables used, see the Appendix.
8. Since our multivariate cointegration results for Turkey and Malaysia draw on Ghatak et al. (1994a, 1994b), the readers are referred to these sources for more information and details.
9. For more information on the integration and cointegration analyses, see Engle and Granger (1987), Charemza and Deadman (1992).
10. Econometric computations in this study have been carried out by Microfit 3.0 version – see Pesaran and Pesaran (1991).

References

Agarwala, R. (1983), 'Price distortions and growth in developing countries', *World Bank Staff Working Paper*, no. 515, Washington, DC: World Bank.

Aricanli, T. and Rodrik, D. (eds) (1990), *The Political Economy of Turkey: Debt Adjustment and Sustainability*, London: Macmillan.

Arslan, I. and Van Wijnbergen, S. (1993), 'Export Incentives, Exchange Rate Policy and Export Growth in Turkey', *Review of Economics and Statistics*, 75.

Balassa, B. (1989), 'Outward Orientation', in H. Chenery and T.N. Srinivasan (eds), *Handbook of Development Economics, Vol. II*, Amsterdam: North-Holland.

Baysan, T. and Blitzer, C. (1991), 'Turkey', in D. Papageorgiou, M. Michaely and A.M. Choksi (eds), *Liberalising Foreign Trade: New Zealand, Spain and Turkey: Vol. 6*, A World Bank Study, Cambridge: Basil Blackwell.

Bhagwati, J. (1978), *Anatomy and Consequences of Exchange Control Regimes*, Cambridge: Ballinger for NBER.

Bhagwati, J. and Srinivasan, T.N. (1983), *Lectures on International Trade*, Cambridge, Mass.: MIT Press.

Blejer, M. (1978), 'Exchange Rate Restrictions and Monetary Approach to Exchange Rates', in J.A. Frenkel and H.S. Johnson (eds), *The Economics of Exchange Rates*, Reading: Addison-Wesley.

Charemza, W.W. and Deadman, D.F. (1992), *New Directions in Econometric Practice*, Aldershot: Edward Elgar.

Charemza, W.W. and Ghatak, S. (1990), 'Demand for Money in a Dual-currency Quantity-constrained Economy: Hungary and Poland, 1956–1985', *Economic Journal*, 100.

Culbertson, W.P. (1975), 'Purchasing Power Parity and Black-Market Exchange Rates', *Economic Inquiry*, 13.

Dornbusch, R., Dantas, D.V. et al. (1983), 'The black market for dollars in Brazil', *Quarterly Journal of Economics*, 98.

Edwards, S. (1992), 'Trade Orientation, Distortions and Growth in Developing Countries', *Journal of Development Economics*, 39.

Edwards, S. (1993), 'Openness, Trade Liberalization, and Growth in Developing Countries', *Journal of Economic Literature*, 31.

Engle, R.F. and Granger, C.W.J. (1987), 'Cointegration and Error-Correction: Representation, Estimation, and Testing', *Econometrica*, 55.

Fishelson, G. (1988), 'The Black Market for Foreign Exchange', *Economics Letters*, 27.

Ghatak, S. (1993), 'Exchange Rate Liberalisation and Recent Trade Performance', *Oxford Analytica*, May.

Ghatak, S., Milner, C. and Utkulu, U. (1994), *Exports, Export Composition and Growth: Cointegration and Causality Evidence for Malaysia*, Discussion Papers in Economics, No. 94/17, Department of Economics, University of Leicester.

Ghatak, S., Milner, C. and Utkulu, U. (1995), *Trade Liberalisation and Endogenous Growth: Some Evidence for Turkey*, *Economics of Planning*, 28.

Ghatak, S. and Utkulu, U. (1993), *Trade Orientation and Economic Growth: The Turkish Evidence, 1955–1990: A Cointegration Analysis*, Discussion Papers in Economics, no. 93/11, Department of Economics, University of Leicester.

Ghatak, S., and Utkulu, U. (1994), 'Exchange Rate Distortions and Real Exports in Turkey: A Cointegration and Error-correction Analysis: 1955–1990', Mimeo, Department of Economics, University of Leicester.

Goodhart, C. (1988), 'The Foreign Exchange Market: A Random Walk with a Dragging Anchor', *Economica*, 55.

Granger, C.W.J. (1988), 'Some Recent Developments in a Concept of Causality', *Journal of Econometrics*, 39.

Greenaway, D. (1993), 'Liberalising Foreign Trade through Rose Tinted Glasses', *Economic Journal*, 103.

Kamin, S.B. (1993), 'Devaluation, Exchange Controls, and Black Markets for Exchange Rates in Developing Countries', *Journal of Development Economics*, 40.

Krueger, A. (1978), *Liberalization Attempts and Consequences*, New York: Ballinger.

Krueger, A. (1990), 'Comparative Advantage and Development Policy Twenty Years Later', in A. Krueger (ed.), *Perspectives on Trade and Development*, Hemel Hempstead: Wheatsheaf.

Lucas, R. (1988), 'On the Mechanics of Economic Development', *Journal of Monetary Economics*, 22.

Michaely, M., Papageorgiou, D. and Choksi, A.M. (eds) (1991), *Liberalising Foreign Trade: Lessons of Experience in the Developing World: Vol. 7*, A Research Project of the World Bank, Cambridge, Mass., Basil Blackwell.

Pesaran, M.H. and Pesaran, B. (1991), *Microfit: An Interactive Econometric Software Package (User Manual)*, Oxford: Oxford University Press.

Phylaktis, K. (1991), 'The Black Market for Dollars in Chile, Mimeo, City University Business School.

Riedel, J. (1991), 'Strategy Wars: The State of Debate on Trade and Industrialisation in Developing Countries', in A. Koekkoek and L.B.M. Mennes (eds), *International Trade and Global Development: Essays in Honour of Jagdish Bhagwati*, London: Routledge.

Summers, R. and Heston, A. (1991), 'The Penn World Table (Mark5): An Expanded Set of International Comparisons, 1950–1988', *Quarterly Journal of Economics*, 106.

Togan, S. (ed.) (1994), *Foreign Trade Regime and Trade Liberalisation in Turkey During 1980s*, Aldershot: Avebury.

US Department of State (1992), *Country Reports on Economic Policy and Trade Practices*, St Louis: Department of State.

Uygur, E. (1993), 'Trade Policies and Economic Performance in Turkey in the 1980s', in M.R. Agosin and D. Tussie (eds), *Trade and Growth: New Dilemmas in Trade Policy*, New York: St Martin's Press.

World Bank (1987), *World Development Report*, Washington, DC: World Bank.

World Bank (1992), *Trends in Developing Economies*, Yearbook, New York: World Bank.

Statistical appendix

Data sources

The data used in this study are annual for the period 1955–90 and are taken from the following sources:

1.   International Monetary Fund (IMF), International Financial Statistics, Yearbooks (various issues).
2.   World Bank, World Tables, Yearbook (various issues).
3.   State Planning Organization (SPO), Turkey.
4.   State Institute of Statistics (SIS), Turkey.
5.   Cowitt, P.P., World Currency Yearbook (previously known as Pick's Currency Yearbook), various issues, International Currency Analysis, Brooklyn.
6.   Penn-World data developed by Summers and Heston (1991).

Definitions of the variables

RGDP: Real GDP expressed in US dollars (source 6).

RNGDP: Non-export real GDP (sources 1 and 2).

REX: Real exports expressed in US dollars (sources 1, 2 and 3).

REXm, REXf and REXp: Refer to the real exports for manufactured, fuel and primary products respectively (sources 1 and 2).

ERDI: Exchange rate distortion index of Turkey constructed on the basis of the formula ERDI=(BM\$-OF\$)/MB\$ where BM\$ (source 5) and OF\$ (source 1) represent annual average black market and official exchange rates both expressed in domestic currency per US dollar. The same definition of ERDI is also used by Ghatak and Utkulu (1993, 1994). The ERDI, here, is like the black market premium used by others as it measures the difference between the BM\$ and OF\$ as a proportion of BM\$ (see Fishelson 1988, Kamin 1993, Edwards 1992). Note that, in LDCs, BM\$-OF\$ is generally observed to be positive.

RIM: Real imports expressed in US dollars (sources 1, 2 and 3).

OPEN: Openness index (source 6) defined as OPEN=[(exports+imports)/real GDP per capita] expressed in US dollars.

RER: Real exchange rates defined as RER=(OF*WPIUS)/CPI where OF,WPIUS and CPI represent official nominal exchange rate expressed in domestic currency per US dollar (source 1), wholesale price index of the US (source 1) and consumer price index of the country under consideration (source 1).

H: Measure of human capital (source 4) proxied by secondary school enrolment rates: [number of students enrolled at secondary schools/total population (000)].

K: Measure of physical capital (source 6) proxied by real gross domestic investment (private and public) as percentage of real GDP per capita.

8 The role of technology in the creation of rich and poor nations: underdevelopment in a Schumpeterian system

Erik S. Reinert

Introduction[1]

There is a growing awareness of the role of technology in creating economic growth. A large research programme by the OECD–TEP (Technology and Economy) – recently brought this issue, and the underlying evolutionary theory of economic growth, into focus. However, the insights of Schumpeterian or evolutionary economics have so far not been used to study the problems of underdevelopment, only to study the growth problems of the industrialized nations. This paper is, as far as this writer is aware, the first attempt to use Schumpeterian analysis of technological change to explain poverty and underdevelopment. 'Schumpeterian poverty' indeed sounds like a contradiction in terms.

The aim of this paper is to show that the dynamics of Schumpeterian economics, in addition to explaining the creation of wealth, also implicitly contain the elements of a theory of relative poverty. It attempts to explain the role of technological change in the creation of what is labelled 'Schumpeterian underdevelopment'. It is argued that the German tradition of economics, of which Schumpeter is a part, has always encompassed the necessary elements of a theory of *uneven* growth. List, Marx and Schumpeter have all emphasized different aspects of this uneven growth. To all of them, technological change was at the core of their theories. This contrasts sharply with the Anglo-Saxon tradition, where technological change has been neglected. As a consequence of this, particularly since the 1890s, Anglo-Saxon economics has produced theories of growth and trade which imply *even* growth, a converging distribution of world activity and income (factor-prize equalization).

The organization of the paper is as follows. The next section contrasts Anglo-Saxon and German economic traditions from the point of view of theories of *uneven* growth vs theories of *even* growth. Then the question of the relationship between technological change and underdevelopment is raised, and two key mechanisms which create uneven distribution of the gains from technological change are identified. These are: the consequences of the extremely uneven advance of the 'technological frontier'; and classical and collusive spreads of technological gains. The next section shows how these mechanisms work to create three cases of 'Schumpeterian underdevelopment' in the Caribbean. The following section claims that the aspects of technological change identified earlier may create conflicting interests between the two parts that every individual plays in economic life, that of producer and that of consumer. It is claimed that these are identical only under the assumptions of neoclassical economics and in special cases of what is labelled *symmetrical* trade. Finally, the policy conclusions of these findings are discussed. It is shown how the conflicting interests of man-the-consumer and man-the-producer, produced by classical and collusive spreads of technical change, were central to the creation of US industrial policy in the early nineteenth century.

Anglo-Saxon vs German economics: theories of *even* vs theories of *uneven* growth

Friedrich List, Karl Marx and Joseph Alois Schumpeter are the German economists who have had major influence on economic policy outside the German-speaking area. The theories of Marx and Schumpeter are deeply rooted in the traditions of the German historical school of economics, and although Friedrich List antedates what is generally seen as the starting point of the older historical school, his approach is clearly that of a 'proto-historical school'. The roots of this line of thought go back to the times of the cameralists, at least as far back as Wilhelm von Hornick (1684).[2] All three authors – List, Marx and Schumpeter – share an essentially very similar dynamic view of economic development. This is especially evident when their theories are contrasted with the Anglo-Saxon economic tradition, that which provides the foundation for our present world economic order. The German tradition produces theories of *uneven* growth; Anglo-Saxon neoclassical economics tends to produce theories of *even* growth. This is particularly true when neoclassical economics is translated into international economic policy, and the finer points of the theory are lost. In terms of economic policy, a key difference between these two bodies of thought is that whereas in Anglo-Saxon economic theory the location of production in space is not an issue, this location is often crucial to economic wealth in German economic policy. Anglo-Saxon economics is primarily a theory of *exchange*, whereas German economic theory to a much larger extent involves *production*. In German theory, differences in circumstances of production translate into differences in wealth.

Before Adam Smith many English theories of growth were also theories of uneven growth. I have argued elsewhere (Reinert 1994) that the mercantilist view was that economic growth was *activity-specific*, that it took place in some economic activities and not in others. It should also be noted that in the nineteenth-century US the economic theories which served as guidance for economic policy (as opposed to what was often taught at 'ivy league' universities) were 'German-type' theories. Friedrich List's prolonged stay in the US in the 1820s clearly provided a cross-fertilization of German theories and US Hamiltonian thoughts on the matter of economic policy. Similarly, in Japan, the economic theories adopted after the Meiji restoration were specifically based on German *national*ökonomische theories, openly rejecting the *cosmo*political aspects of English economic theory.

The similarities between Marx and Schumpeter are readily admitted by Schumpeter, most clearly so in the foreword to the Japanese version of the *Theorie der wirtschaftlichen Entwicklung* (Schumpeter 1912; 1934). Schumpeter explains here how he was looking for 'a source of energy within the economic system, that would of itself disrupt any equilibrium that might be attained ...It was not clear to me at the outset...that the idea and the aim are exactly the same as the idea and the aim which underlie the teachings of Karl Marx'. The similarities in the two systems are, Schumpeter says, 'obliterated by a very wide difference in general outlook'. Clemence (1951) translates and reproduces the Japanese foreword. Many authors, starting in the late 1940s, have compared Marx and Schumpeter. A bibliography of 'Works on Schumpeter' lists 77 works – of a total of 1916 entries – treating both Marx and Schumpeter (Augello 1990).[3]

In spite of their similarities, the 'wide difference in general outlook' between the two economists has continued with their modern disciples. A special division of labour of Schumpeter's *creative destruction* has taken place between Schumpeterians and Marxists: the Schumpeterians explain the *creative* part, e.g. the growth of the English cotton textile industry, whereas the Marxists concentrate on the *destructive* part: the bones of the Bengali weavers, the previous suppliers of the same product to the English and Indian markets, 'whitening the plains of India'. Schumpeterians produce theories of *development*; Marxists produce theories of *underdevelopment*. Both these sets of theories, however, intrinsically contain the elements of the opposite view. Marxian economics (as distinguished from Marxist economics) produces a dynamic theory of development, albeit uneven, where the 'bourgeoisie cannot exist without constantly revolutionising the instruments of production'. Rosenberg (1976, 126–38) comments on Marx's view of technology, where the uneven distribution of wealth is kept up by, among other factors, the imperfect competition produced by constant innovations.

A similar picture of Schumpeter's *dynamic income inequalities* can be found in his *Theory of Economic Development*: Schumpeter recognizes that 'the upper strata of society are like hotels which are always full of people, but people who are forever changing.' (Schumpeter 1912; 1934, 156).[4] As opposed to Marx, Schumpeter's interest in the fate of the groups not living in this upper-class hotel, however, is very limited. The key factor which unites Marx and Schumpeter – and distinguishes both these approaches from Anglo-Saxon economic theory – is that theirs is essentially a theory of *uneven* growth. For this reason, in any 'German-type' theoretical approach, problems of income distribution are implicit in the system, whereas this type of problem is non-existent at the paradigm level in Anglo-Saxon economics.

If we compare the world of today with the world in which Marx wrote, two important developments have taken place, especially since the Second World War. These developments have changed the geographical setting of distributional problems, from being essentially *national* to being *international* problems: first, successful mechanisms for income redistribution in most industrialized countries have alleviated national problems of income distribution; and second, 'globalization' has substituted the present international division of labour for the previous national one, also in manufacturing goods. In this way the distributional conflicts have been moved more and more from the national (between 'classes') to the international arena (between nations). National problems of income distribution, in the sense of poverty alleviation, have to a large extent been solved in many industrial countries, particularly in some European countries and in Japan. The enormous costs involved in this redistribution within the industrial nations are rarely debated, least of all on a theoretical level.

Since Adam Smith, Anglo-Saxon economics has been *cosmo*political. In English classical theory distributional issues were not a core issue – but, as Lionel Robbins (1952) has shown, in practical economic policy distributional issues were indeed considered on the national level. In neoclassical theory, national and international distributive issues have been assumed away through the inclusion of simplifying assumptions. Over time these simplifications crystallized into the two key assumptions of neoclassical economics: perfect information and the absence of increasing returns. It is the inclusion of these two assumptions – both counterfactual – which has created the blind spot of neoclassical economics: the inability to account for the extremely different levels of development between the nations of the world. With the assumptions of perfect information and constant returns to scale in place, any theory of economic growth automatically becomes a theory of *even* growth. These assumptions seem to remove the reasons for a Smithian 'division of labour': differences in human knowledge and fixed costs in specialized machinery. Perfect information seems difficult to reconcile with a notion of 'human capital'. Constant returns to scale seems difficult to reconcile with the existence of fixed costs, which create varying degrees of 'minimum efficient size'. These two assumptions – implicit or explicit – turned English economics into a *cosmo*political school of economics. As a reaction to this, nineteenth-century German economics became *National*ökonomie and *Voks*wirtschaft –

terms which stick to this very day both in Germany and in Scandinavia. Here, less restrictive assumptions were made.

What Marx and Schumpeter have in common are strong roots in the German historical school of economics. These roots are not clear to the observer of today, for at least two reasons. First of all the German historical tradition is hardly known outside the German-speaking world; very few works have been translated. Exceptions are Roscher (1882) and Sombart (Backhaus 1995). Second, the followers of both Schumpeter and Marx have, for different reasons, consciously and/or unconsciously cultivated the originality of their leading man. In the communist bloc Marx's doctrine was cultivated as being the product of what in another religion is called an 'immaculate conception': Marx could not be seen as having borrowed from despicable bourgeois economists. The fact is that Marx borrowed heavily from the founder of the German historical school, Wilhelm Roscher (1854).

Together with Charles Babbage (1832) and Andrew Ure (1835), both of whom he quotes several times, Roscher was probably the first economist to understand fully the economics of technological change and mass production: 'He [Roscher] created the image of large-scale industry whose essential feature is increasing returns or decreasing costs' (Streissler 1994, 1). Roscher also specifically pointed to the existence of increasing returns in research. Whereas Babbage and Ure wrote specialized treaties on the economics of large-scale industry, Roscher incorporated these insights into a holistic economic theory. Roscher's work was to be the standard textbook for a generation of Germans, appearing in 26 editions. Marx differed from the rest of the German school by subscribing to Ricardo's labour theory of value, which to Roscher and to the German historical tradition was un-German and 'typically English'. The importance given to economies of scale in German economics goes back before Roscher to previous works by Hufeland (1807) and Hermann (1832). Roscher also refers several times to Serra (1613), whose treatise was the first to associate national welfare with increasing returns, and national poverty with the lack of it.

Schumpeter's originality in the Anglo-Saxon environment was clearly to a large extent also a product of the ignorance, outside Germany, of the traditions on which he built. Most Schumpeterians, especially non-Germans, would probably be surprised by a recent German book that describes Schumpeter's *Capitalism, Socialism and Democracy* (Schumpeter 1942) as essentially a reworking of a German debate which had taken place decades earlier, where, the author carefully points out, Schumpeter neither refers to the debate itself, nor to its protagonist Werner Sombart (Appel 1992).[5]

All of this is in sharp contrast to the Anglo-Saxon tradition. Adam Smith provided the great insight of the importance of 'division of labour', but he failed to see its organizational implications. He assumed markets would continue to function as perfectly as the agricultural markets of his time. On the other hand, he specifically states that the lack of progress of agriculture at the time of his writing was probably due to the 'lack of scope for the division of labour'. Adam Smith goes half-way to seeing the connection between 'lack of division of labour' and perfect competition, but not all the way. The differences in organization of production have been left out in neoclassical theory, as has any follow-up of the consequences of various degrees of 'division of labour'. Neoclassical economics is essentially a theory of the exchange of goods already produced, taking no account of the diversity of conditions of production and their influence on pricing behaviour. Neoclassical theory is, it seems, one which cannot accommodate the existence of fixed costs, since these create increasing returns. We are, seemingly, still victims of Adam Smith's inability to see the necessary organizational consequences of his key insight into the importance of division of labour. The division of labour will create firms organized around the combining of tasks into which the manufacturing, assembly and sale of a final product have been divided. The fixed costs invested in machinery and equipment will by definition create a minimum efficient size, increasing returns, barriers to entry and imperfect competition. The understanding of this is traditionally part of German economics but, since the early 1890s, definitely not of the paradigm of Anglo-Saxon economics. Rosenberg (1994, 24–46), referring to Charles Babbage, has an interesting discussion of 'division of labour' in the history of economics.

For this reason, a most significant long-term pattern of economic policy emerges: 'German-type' theories of uneven growth dominated the take-off stage of all industrialized countries, including England from the late 1400s up until the late 1800s. The economic policies of these nations have gradually changed to 'English-type' theories as they, one by one, reached the 'technological frontier'. At that point increasing returns in industrial activities turn from being a barrier to growth (for nations not engaged in such activities) into a mechanism where international trade is beneficial to both trading partners. In the early stages, increasing returns create a barrier to development and an obstacle, but as the economy industrializes they become an important ally. As a consequence of this, to a poor country with an economy based on natural resources, free trade was seen as a poverty trap (due to the existence of diminishing returns and perfect competition). To a nation engaged in increasing return activities, the existence of these factors becomes yet another reason for free trade. The earliest treatment of this is probably that found in Charles King (1721, I, 3). In a successful strategy, increasing returns must be part of economic growth theory in the early take-off stage. Therefore a 'German-type' theory has always been present at an early stage in all industrialized countries. Once a nation is established in a virtuous circle of increasing return activities and dynamic imperfect competition, leaving increasing returns out of economic theory is not harmful on a short-term basis. Consequently, the successful former laggard countries all convert to Anglo-Saxon-type theories – especially with respect to international trade – without any short-term damage.

In Anglo-Saxon economics all economic activities are 'alike': they are all equally suited to promote national welfare. In German economic theory some economic activities are 'better' than others: those exhibiting dynamic imperfect competition produced by 'historical increasing returns'. Engaging in these 'better' activities is a necessary requirement if a country is to 'catch up' with the leading nations of the world.

'German' economic theory has been the basis of the economic policies of the 'laggards', including England when it was one. Anglo-Saxon economics has been the theory of the 'leaders' – the theory embarked upon when 'German' theory has brought a nation into international leadership. For this reason, all rich countries have attempted to export 'Anglo-Saxon' ideas, whereas they themselves have stuck to 'German' ideas. The policy of the US in imposing free trade on Japan and Latin America, while still engaged in extremely heavy-handed protection of national industry at home, is but one example. Today's *managed free trade* is an attempt to achieve the same thing: the advantages of 'German' theories for home use combined with Anglo-Saxon for the rest of the world.

The basic difference between a rich and a poor nation in the world of today is that whereas *all* rich nations – except some small city states – have been through a long stage of 'German' economic policy, in most cases lasting at least one hundred years; it is difficult to find a poor nation which has been through this stage. The key feature of this 'German' economic policy is the combination of competition *and* protection of manufactures. The thinking of the times is well reflected in the title of Whatley (1774): *Principles of Trade. Fredom* [sic] *and Protection are its best Suport* [sic]*: Industry, the only Means to render Manufactures cheap.* This second edition incorporates laudatory notes by Benjamin Franklin on the subject.

Technological change and Schumpeterian underdevelopment

As stated in the previous section, in German economic theory, some economic activities are 'better' than others, in the sense that they produce dynamic technical change and increasing returns. English economic theory tended to neglect these factors and, for this reason, for the purposes of economic growth, all economic activities became 'alike'. This was a necessary condition for equilibrium. Increasing returns were, however, still important in the first edition, but not in the later, of Alfred Marshall's *Principles*. Marshall, consequently, is able to give us a formula for an excellent industrial policy: 'A tax ...on the production of goods which obey the Law of Diminishing Return, and devoting the tax to a bounty on the production of those goods with regard to which the Law of Increasing Returns acts sharply' (Marshall 1890, 452). This insight had to be sacrificed in later editions, since the existence of increasing returns was incompatible with equilibrium. What in Marshall's early writings starts out as a 'Law' (with a capital 'L') of increasing returns, is reduced to being a 'tendency' in subsequent editions, later to disappear from mainstream theory altogether with John Hicks. Today, new trade theory and new neoclassical growth theory are about to rediscover the impact of increasing (but not diminishing) returns. An excellent survey of these models is found in Verspagen (1992); see also Romer (1994). Today's policy conclusions from new trade theory and new growth theory are no different from Marshall's in 1890, Roscher's in the 1850s, or Serra's in 1613.

Schumpeter's dynamic system, with the role of 'historical increasing returns', retains the characteristics of other authors of the German school, and therefore of a system which produces uneven growth. My notion of Schumpeterian underdevelopment relates to two aspects of technological change, discussed below. Both of these mechanisms are based on the existence of increasing and diminishing returns, imperfect information, barriers to entry, and resulting imperfect competition.

The uneven advances of the 'technological frontier'

It is often visualized that technological knowledge moves forward in the form of a technological 'frontier' of knowledge. The word 'frontier' conveys a notion of a fairly orderly and even progress, where a borderline is being pushed ahead, somewhat reminiscent of the 'frontier' being pushed from the east to the west coast in US history. I feel our understanding of wealth and poverty is hampered by this vision of an orderly 'frontier'. The historical pattern of technological change looks more like a scatter diagram than an orderly frontier. Technical change happens very fast in some areas, dragging with them others, but in some areas the 'frontier' hardly moves at all for centuries. At any particular time both the search for new technologies, and technological change itself, are – in Nathan Rosenberg's word – 'focused' (Rosenberg 1976, Ch. 6) on specific areas of technological problems and opportunities. In the stone age, technical change was concentrated in the stone implements industry, in the bronze age in bronze implements, and in the machine age in the activities which were being mechanized. Even today, two hundred years into the machine age, some activities are still not mechanized – cutting hair, picking strawberries or sewing baseballs.

'If improvements in all the arts were to take place *at the same rate*, they would obviously have no effect to alter the exchangeable value of things', said US economist Henry Vethake (1844, 95). In a system with perfect information and constant returns to scale, the sequence of technological change makes no difference to the distribution of wealth. Vethake's insight has been almost completely neglected in neoclassical economic theory. A paper by Robert Lucas (1988) provides an exception. In this paper Lucas presents a formal model in which learning takes place at different rates in different sectors of the economy. As to the practical consequences of uneven learning, Lucas provides an unusually candid remark from a formal economist: 'The consequences for human welfare involved in questions like these are simply staggering: Once one starts to think about them, it is hard to think about anything else'.

The two ways in which the benefits from technical change spread
Under perfect competition, the advances from technical change will spread in the economy in the form of lowered prices to the end user. In (Reinert 1994) I argue that this is the assumption made already by both Adam Smith and David Ricardo. In the same paper – contrary to the assumptions of both of classical and neoclassical economics – I propose that in order to capture the mechanisms of national wealth and poverty, it is necessary to understand how the benefits from technological change can be distributed in one of two ways: one which creates wealth and one which merely preserves the *status quo*:

- *To the customers* buying the product in the form of lowered prices and/ or better quality. I call this the *classical* form of distribution of the gains from technological change, because Adam Smith and David Ricardo both state that this will be the effect of technical improvements. This mechanism will operate when conditions of production and markets are similar to those assumed in neoclassical theory.
- *To the owners and workers* in the producing firm, and later to the *government* of the producing country in the form of higher taxable income. I call this the *collusive* form of distribution of the gains from technical change, because the forces of the producing country (capital, labour and government) in practice – although not as a conspiracy – 'collude' to appropriate these gains. This mechanism will operate if the technical change is accompanied by the creation of barriers to entry, where increasing returns are a key mechanism.

A typical example of the *collusive* form is Henry Ford's decision to increase the wages of his workers from an average of $2.34 for a nine-hour day to $5 for an eight-hour day in January 1914 (Raff 1988, 387). A typical example of a *classical* distribution would be the employment of bar code readers in supermarkets. This technological improvement would not show up as higher wages to the store staff. Harvard's Zwi Griliches uses this case to show what I call 'invisible economic growth', those cost-cuts and quality improvements which never show up in any statistics (*Business Week* 1994).

Most technical changes contain an element of both *classical* and *collusive* distribution of the benefits from technical change. What we measure as economic growth is largely the collusive mode. Collusive technical change is accompanied by the creation of higher barriers to entry, more imperfect competition, and it normally affects the minimum efficient size of an operation. The effects of classical technical change 'fall through' the producing organization without changing the structure of the firm or the industry, and are visible mainly as lower prices of the end product. This classical technical change does not affect the bargaining power of labour. Classical technical change takes place under conditions that do not strongly violate the neoclassical assumptions of perfect competition, and is most frequently found in agriculture and in the traditional service sector. Typically an invention initially creates a temporary monopoly which allows for a collusive spread of benefits, but as the technique in question becomes commonplace, its benefits will spread more and more as lower prices, not as higher wages and profits. Table 8.1 illustrates the characteristics of classical and collusive spread of technical change.

In a typical industrialized country 70 per cent of GNP is accounted for by factor payments to labour in the form of wages. What we measure historically as growth in GNP is to a large extent the impact of technical change on monetary wages. Classical technological change tends to leave fewer traces. When, as in the last decade, an increasing percentage of GNP growth takes place in the service sector – following Petty's Law – the classical-type spread of technical change becomes more dominant in the economy. Because of the decentralized nature of service production (the classical definition is that a service product must be produced where it is consumed), economies of *scope* in multisite operations are more of a success factor in the service industry than traditional economies of *scale*, typical of a Fordist-type factory. This, combined with the use of technology to *replace* and not to *enhance* labour skills in the traditional service sector, allows for a classical rather than a collusive spread of the benefits of technical change in this sector. An important part of the explanation of the 'Solow paradox' – that computers are visible everywhere except in government statistics – clearly lies in the combination of the huge measurement problems in the service sector combined with the classical spread of technological change in this area.

The two phenomena – the classical spread of technological gains and the measurement problems – are closely intertwined. A considerable portion of the lower growth in what we measure as GNP in most industrialized countries over the last decade is most likely the result of increasing employment in the traditional service sector which produces 'invisible growth' (lowered transaction costs in grocery purchases due to checkout scanners, etc.). How-

Table 8.1   Characteristics of the two modes of diffusion of productivity improvements

Characteristics of mode	The collusive mode	The classical mode
Divisibility of investments	Indivisible, comes in *chunks*	Divisible
Degree of perfect information	imperfect (e.g. patents, internal R&D)	Perfect (competitive market for technology itself)
Source of technology from user company point of view	Internal, or external in *big chunks* = high degree of economies of scale	External
Barriers to entry	Increase	No change
Industry structure	Increases concentration	Neutral
Economies of scale	Increase	No change
Market shares	Very important	Unimportant
How benefits spread		
GNP as measured	Highly visible	Tends not to appear ('Solow paradoxes')
Profit level	Increases stakes: possibility for larger profits or losses	No change
Monetary wages	Increase	No change
Real wages (nationally)	Increase	Increase
Price level	No change	Decreases
Terms of trade	No change	Turns *against* industry experiencing technological progress
Examples of innovations in the two groups	New pharmaceuticals, mainframe computer production, automotive paint production	Electricity, telephones, sewing machines, use of PCs, dispersion paint production, containers
Where found	Mainly in industry, in recent products and processes	In primary and tertiary industries, *use* of new basic technologies, mature industry

ever, the subject of this paper is not the measurement problems of GNP caused by technical change, but the effects of technical change on income distribution among nations.

In the collective bargaining process, the collusive mode is traditionally seen as being 'fair'. If a company improves its labour productivity, part of the benefits of this should go to labour *in that firm*. The phenomena which I describe as the classical and collusive modes of distributing the proceeds from technical change were thoroughly discussed in a 'comprehensive series of investigations of the relation of the distribution of income to economic progress' by the Brookings Institution (Bell 1940, 3). These investigations led to the publishing of a series of books between 1935 and 1940 (Bell 1940; Moulton 1935; Nourse and Drury 1938), several of which directly address the way benefits from technological change spread in the economy. In the framework of the Brookings Institution, my classical spread is called 'distributing income through price reductions' and the collusive spread is called 'distributing income through raising money wages'. In general, the Brookings studies find that, although the classical way of distributing gains from technological progress is the preferred one from the point of view of society as a whole, the imperfectly competitive markets for goods and labour in industry make this impossible to achieve. These studies point, however, to the serious problems of income distribution caused (within the US) by the collusive spread of the benefits from technical change in industry and the classical spread in agriculture. In a paragraph entitled 'The conflict between wage earners and farmers' Moulton (1935, 124–5) has the following comments as to the national income distribution resulting from collusive spread of gains. We ask the reader also to study the paragraph substituting for the US farmers a Third World nation producing raw materials or mature industrial products under conditions of near-perfect competition:

> In considering the price-reduction method [our classical mode] as an alternative to wage increases [our collusive mode] attention should also be called to a broad social consequence of the latter that has apparently seldom been recognized. The disparities in the income and purchasing power of the industrial and agricultural populations resulting from the wage increasing method create a basic maladjustment between two great divisions of our economic life and imposes a serious barrier to economic progress. It is apparent that there would be a growing disparity in the economic position of the agricultural and industrial populations even if prices of industrial products showed no tendency to rise as wages rose:[6] the income of the urban population would be increasing while that of the agricultural population would be stationary. In practice there is, however, a tendency for industrial prices to rise somewhat as wages are increased, and the consequence is that the purchasing power of the farm tends to be actually reduced. The consequent inability of the agricultural population to buy ever increasing quantities of industrial products limits the scale on which industrial establishments can operate.

The struggle to obtain higher living standards through the medium of higher money wages has been the cause of a long and deep-seated conflict between the agricultural and urban population. The people of the cities have fought for higher wages even though it has meant somewhat higher prices for industrial products. The farmers have long fought for lower prices on the commodities they have to buy. The struggle underlies the so-called granger movement of the seventies; it explains the traditional opposition of the agricultural South to high protective tariffs; and it lies at the basis of farmer opposition to trusts, monopolies, and combinations in all their forms.

These paragraphs describe the problems of income distribution between two groups within the same nation who both produce at what was then the *technological frontier*: both the US farmers and the US industrial population were the most productive in the world. Yet, one group got rich and the other group stayed poor. At about the same time another American author tried to explain the same phenomenon from a leftist point of view in a book called *Why Farmers are Poor* (Rochester 1940). I would argue that the reason for this poverty *of the world's most efficient farmers on the world's probably most fertile soil* is as follows.

The productivity increases of the farmers are taken out in the form of lowered prices, in the classical way, whereas the productivity increases of their trading partners producing industrial goods are taken out collusively, in the form of higher wages. In a neoclassical world of perfect information and no economies of scale, this would of course not be a problem, because the individual farmers would all produce the tractors and all the other industrial implements in their own backyard without any loss of efficiency compared to industrial production. In real life, however, the farmers were facing high barriers to entry – the 'perfect information and constant returns to scale option' is of course non-existent. The farmers of the US in the 1930s suffered from 'Schumpeterian underdevelopment'.

If we now place these two groups in two different countries, an industrial country and an agricultural country, and open for trade, we would have achieved a much bigger gap in the standard of living than the one which so much worried the Brookings Institution in the late 1930s. Placing the two groups of producers in two different countries would have eliminated important distributive mechanisms that existed within the US. Migration of surplus labour from the farms to the industrial districts as farming demanded less labour and more capital was an important distributive mechanism, as was the pressure from alternative employment in the cities on farm wages. The government tax base was much larger in the cities and in industrial areas, so infrastructure, schools, and other government services in the farming areas were clearly heavily subsidized by the industrial districts. Last but not least, the farmers, in spite of their steadily declining numbers, did have political power. Moulton mentions the granger movement which started just after the Civil War, whose activities served as the basis for later legislation affecting income distribution within the US: for example, railroad and public utility regulations, antitrust laws and measures establishing a postal savings bank and parcel post on government hands. Our basic point is that had the industrial population and the agrarian population in the US been living in two different nations, we would have found a deeply impoverished agricultural nation and an extremely wealthy industrial nation. Both would have been the world's most efficient, but one would still have suffered from Schumpeterian underdevelopment.

This is but one example. Using other examples from the Caribbean later in the paper, I shall argue that wealth is not caused by relative efficiency but by *imperfect competition*. From the point of view both of an individual and of a nation, the choice of economic activity is much more important than the degree of efficiency. There is, for nations as well as for individuals, an optimization process available.

Over time, labour mobility inside the industrialized nations tends to contribute to a more equitable division of industry rent *within* nations. Typically, the government sector – a gigantic redistributive machinery – represents more than 50 per cent of GNP in an industrial nation. Within the EU, similar transfer mechanisms are at work, particularly in the agricultural sector. Typical of these redistributive measures are that they are carried out as a matter of political necessity, and that, in spite of the huge numbers involved, no one ever asks *why* the maldistribution occurs in the first place. Joan Robinson was correct in pointing out that neoclassical economics does not have any theory of uneven distribution of wealth, but what is so surprising is the apparent lack of articulated demand for such a theory.

Three cases of Schumpeterian underdevelopment in the Caribbean

The case of serious maldistribution of income in the US between the agricultural and industrial sectors – both the world's most efficient at the time – demonstrates that being wealthy is not so much a matter of being efficient, it is more *what one chooses to be efficient in*. Schumpeterian underdevelopment happens if a nation chooses to be efficient *in the wrong sector*. This mechanism works similarly with individuals: the most efficient dishwasher in the country has a much lower income than the most efficient lawyer.

There are two mechanisms which come together to cause this: the uneven advance of the phenomenon which by a misnomer is called the *technological frontier*, and the *collusive* vs *classical* spread of the benefits from technical change. These mechanisms are able to operate because of what Schumpeter called 'historical increasing returns' – the fact that the technological change that we measure as economic growth has been accompanied by higher fixed costs creating greater economies of scale. This 'visible' (as opposed to the often invisible growth in the traditional service sector) technological change consequently operates under very imperfect competition protected by two important sets of barriers to entry: scale-based and knowledge-based, which interact and cumulate in creating Myrdalian vicious circles.

One important feature of neoclassical economies is that, under its standard assumptions, all economic activities become 'alike'. In neoclassical economics, a faster technological change in one industry than in another is neutralized by instant adjustment, provided by 'perfect information', 'perfect foresight', and 'constant returns to scale'. In real life the existence of huge differences in knowledge and information, 'bounded vision' and huge increasing returns to scale combine to chain nations to the trajectories they have historically embarked upon, or in the case of the Caribbean, those they *have been* embarked upon. In the following examples we shall observe how, in the case of three Caribbean islands, Schumpeterian underdevelopment occurs. In all three cases the choice of economic activity, rather than the efficiency, determines wealth or poverty.

Cuban counterpoint of tobacco and sugar

In 1940 the foremost Cuban social scientist in this century, Fernando Ortìz, published a book (Ortìz 1940) with a fascinating account of how Cuban society and history have been shaped in very different ways by tobacco and sugar, 'two gigantic plants, two members of the vegetable kingdom which both flourish in Cuba and are both perfectly adapted, climatically and ecologically, to the country. The territory of Cuba has in its different zones the best land for the cultivation of both plants. And the same happens in the combinations of the climate with the chemistry of the soil' (Ortìz 1947, 7).

From an economic point of view, Cuba clearly has an absolute advantage in the production of both crops. But to Cuba, one crop – tobacco – produced wealth; the other – sugar – poverty. The counterpoint between tobacco and sugar is a parallel to the uneven wealth creation we witnessed in a previous paragraph, between the industrial and agricultural sectors in the US. Both in the US and Cuban cases we are studying *the most advanced production in the world*, both in the activities which produced wealth and the activities which produced poverty. The difference here is that we are studying two agricultural products which are both being transformed into an industrial product. We must, then, go beyond the standard categorizations of agriculture as being 'bad' and industry as being 'good', to find the mechanisms at work.

In Cuban society tobacco was the hero, sugar the villain. Tobacco – predominantly grown on the western part of the island – created a middle class, a free bourgeoisie. Sugar – grown on the rest of the island – created two classes of people: masters and slaves. The cultivation and picking of tobacco created a demand for specialized skills: tobacco leaves were harvested individually, and the market price of the product depended on the skill of the picker. Tobacco bred skills, individuality and modest wealth. 'Sugar was an anonymous industry, the mass labor of slaves or gangs of hired workmen, under the supervision of capital's overseers' (Ortìz 1947, 65). Where tobacco required skill, care and judgement, sugar only required brute force in cutting the cane. Tobacco was individuality and division of labour; sugar was bulk and commodity. Tobacco carries its origins with it as a brand name, 'sugar comes to the world without a last name, like a slave.' Tobacco is stable prices; sugar is wildly fluctuating prices. A skilled tobacco selector can distinguish 70 or 80 different shades of tobacco, but all saccharose is the same. Timing is crucial in the harvesting of tobacco; for the cutting of cane timing is not important. Tobacco is delicately cut leaf by leaf with a small sharp knife, making sure that the rest of the plant survives. The sugar plant is brutally slashed with a big machete. Working with sugar is a trade; working with tobacco an art.

As a result of this, Ortìz says, the tobacco worker is not only wealthier than the destitute sugar workers; 'he is better mannered and more intelligent'. Tobacco is wealth and intelligence; sugar is poverty and ignorance. Sugar is foreign capital; tobacco is predominantly national capital. 'In the history of Cuba sugar represents Spanish absolutism; tobacco, the native liberators. Sugar has always stood for foreign intervention'. 'Sugar has always preferred slave labour; tobacco free men. Sugar brought in Negroes by force; tobacco encouraged the voluntary immigration of white men.'

Differences in barriers to entry are clearly a key factor producing the differences in production and marketing which created the Cuban counterpoint. Cuban tobacco was one of the few cases of brand name products from the Third World. Cuba had an absolute advantage in the world in both products, but one brought wealth and the other poverty. This is a parallel case to the Brooking Institution study from the US in the 1930s, which showed a US 'counterpoint' similar to the Cuban: the US had both the world's most efficient farmers and the world's most efficient industry. But the farmers stayed poor and the industrial workers got rich. Both in the US and in Cuba world level efficiency led to wealth for those who specialized in one product, and poverty to those who specialized in another. We are facing cases of *classical* spread of the gains from technological change in the case of the US farmer and the Cuban sugar workers, and *collusive* spread in the case of US industry and Cuban tobacco production. It is also worth noting that in spite of a much larger technological change in sugar refining than in cigar making, the cigar makers were consistently wealthier than their sugar-producing colleagues. From the point of view of the nation involved, imperfect competition and no technical change is infinitely better than technical change and perfect competition. Farming in the US and sugar in Cuba led to Schumpeterian under-development; industry and tobacco did not.

Fifty years after the original publication of *Cuban Counterpoint*, a Cuban author in exile dedicated his book *La Isla que se repite* (*The Island which Repeats itself*) to its author, Fernando Ortìz (Benìtez Rojo 1989). The title of the book says it all: in spite of a change in political paradigm, the qualities inherent in sugar production – not only in Cuba but anywhere – continue to shape Cuba and determine its economic faith.

Two years ago two US political scientists and Latin-Americanists published a study of the political and economic structure of two Caribbean islands: the Dominican Republic and Jamaica (Hillman and D'Agostino 1992). In spite of the extremely different historical and administrative backgrounds of the two islands, one coming from the Spanish tradition and one from the English, the authors found both nations had very similar political and economic structures and the same set of problems. Again, their conclusion is, without referring to Ortìz, that the fate of both islands is shaped by the economic forces of sugar production. No matter what your past, producing the same thing will make you alike.

Many modern studies point to the extreme poverty of the world's most efficient sugar producers. The titles indicate the social concerns which prompted their publication: *The Hunger Crop. Poverty and the Sugar Industry* (Coote 1987) and *Bitter Sugar* (Lemoine 1985). The policies of the industrialized countries subsidizing their own inefficient sugar production – beet sugar in Europe and cane sugar in the US – plus the increased competition from corn-based sweeteners just add to the desolation of this 'lock-in effect'. Some years ago, *The Economist* dedicated a cover story – 'Enslaved by Subsidies' – to the sugar policies of the industrialized nations, calling it 'a case study in taxing the rich to ruin the poor' (*The Economist* 1985).

Haiti – economic counterpoint in baseballs and golf balls
Today the unchallenged position at the bottom of the sugar hierarchy is held by the Haitian seasonal workers in the sugar fields of the Dominican Republic (Lemoine 1985). But the Republic of Haiti also dominates the world market for a manufactured product: baseballs, produced mainly for the US market, provide a classic case of Schumpeterian underdevelopment.

Economists make sense of the enormous variations of industries by placing them in groups according to a standard industrial classification. Even seemingly homogeneous groups, however, may contain enormous diversity in the economic conditions individual products create in the country of production. The world's most efficient golfball producers are located in industrialized countries and make a normal industrial wage of 9 dollars per hour. The world's most efficient baseball producers are in Haiti, working 10 hours per day for an hourly wage of 30 US cents. The wage ratio between the two groups of workers, both in the same industry and both being the most efficient in the world, is about 30 to 1.

Why is there no factor price equalization with the industry producing balls for various sports? The technological explanation is: the machine age has not yet reached the production of baseballs; they have to be hand-sewn, even in the US. The currents of creative destruction have not yet penetrated this little industry. The baseball-producing industry is a relic from an otherwise extinct technoeconomic paradigm, to use the terms of Perez and Freeman.

As in sugar production, the characteristics of the product 'baseballs' themselves contain the elements of poverty and underdevelopment. No new skills are developed because there is no *demand* for new skills. No learning-by-doing takes place in Haiti, because there is no learning taking place in baseball production *anywhere*. The Haitians are not working with capital and with machines, because not even all the capital of the US has managed to mechanize baseball production. The mercantilists told us that economic growth was *activity-specific* – it happened in some industries and not in others. And they were right.

When Haiti sells baseballs to the US and buys golfballs back, one hour of labour in the US is exchanged for 30 hours of labour in Haiti. This in spite of the fact that US baseball sewers are *not* more efficient than the Haitians. These are the 'unequal exchange' effects of Schumpeterian underdevelopment.

The Dominican Republic and technological change in pyjama production

The Dominican Republic scores considerably higher in terms of GNP per capita than Haiti. As we have seen, the Dominican Republic can afford to import labour which is even cheaper than her own for the *zafra* – the sugar harvest. Over the last decade more than 400 000 new manufacturing jobs have come to the Dominican Republic. Most people expected economic growth and higher wages to result from manufacturing. After all, wasn't the wealth of the US built on manufacturing?

Much to the surprise of everybody, the 400 000 manufacturing jobs did not increase welfare to any measurable extent. The explanation lies in the way the market mechanisms of Schumpeterian underdevelopment assign production processes with and without technical change. The Dominican Republic produces garments, made from imported fabrics. Pyjamas bought in the US fifteen years ago would have a label reading: 'Fabric made in the US, cut and assembled in the Dominican Republic.' About ten years ago, the labels were changed. They now read: 'Fabric made *and cut* in the US, assembled in the Dominican Republic'. What had happened?

It was at this time that a new technology – laser cutting – hit the garment industry. As a result, the labour content in the operation fell dramatically, and the cost of labour was no longer a strategic factor in the cost of the final product. The cutting operation was therefore taken back to the US when the new technology appeared.

As long as the frontier of technological change moves forward extremely unevenly in a world with imperfect competition, free trade will lead to Schumpeterian underdevelopment in parts of the world economy. Production processes with no technological development, with no creative destruction, will, by the logic of the market, be farmed out to the poor nations. In some cases, where a huge closed market absorbs one small and relatively poor nation, this 'farming out' of products with less technical change may have beneficial effects to both trading partners. The inclusion of small and relatively poor Portugal in the EU can prove beneficial to all, just as the import of a few Third World citizens to wash dishes in the First World can be to the benefit of all parties.[7] However, the number of poor compared to the number of rich in the world today makes this 'absorption', this attempt to make the poor nations rich, not a viable strategy. The extremely high costs faced by West Germany in absorbing the relatively rich and much smaller East Germany testify to this.

The circular flow and the two economic roles of man
If the world is a stage where each must play his part, we are all – in an economic sense – playing two different roles: that of the producer and that of the consumer. On the one hand, we produce goods (man the producer), and on the other hand we consume goods (man the consumer) which are exchanged for the ones we produce. What counts as GNP is limited to production where these roles are *separated*, where the producer is not the consumer. The economics profession has abdicated from the study of situations where the roles of producer and consumer of a good are played by the same person. These cases of household economies have been left to economic anthropology. It is the *exchange*, and not the production, which is at the very heart of modern economics.

A special feature of neoclassical economics is the perfect harmony of interest between these two roles of man (or woman). This is one aspect of what Lionel Robbins (1952) refers to as the *Harmonielehre* resulting from the assumptions of economic theory. Man the producer never has any conflict of interests with his other self – man the consumer. Individual human beings, during their life span, face a similar situation as that of society as a whole. But individuals have possibilities to optimize their strategies, a path which today is difficult for a nation. For the individual, who consciously or unconsciously selects a profession, the two roles of consumer and producer imply trade-offs. The individual can embark on a path which optimizes his income. One can easily imagine man the consumer rejecting the suggestions of his producer self that present consumption has to be reduced in order to attend law school. A reasoned discussion between man the consumer and man the producer, both inhabiting the same individual, may lead to the conclusion that the individual in question would be better off quitting the job as a dishwasher and going to law school, i.e. foregoing consumption now for more prestige and consumption in the future. Among thousands of different professions, individuals are able to *optimize* their situation. Normally this optimization carries with it a trade-off between present and future income. The optimization between professions is clearly recognized also by economists, on a practical level or in the guise of 'human capital'. Certainly no economists, not even traditional trade theorists, tell their children to stick to the job washing dishes because 'factor-price equalization is just around the corner – the time when people washing dishes will make the same amount of money as lawyers. Indeed, it would be easy to produce a convincing Ricardian-style argument for the would-be lawyer, that the world would be richer if he stuck to washing dishes and did not try to become a lawyer.

Why does this optimization option apply to individuals and not to nations? We all agree that our children should rather become lawyers than wash dishes in a restaurant. Why is it conceptually impossible for an economist to extend this argument to apply to a nation specializing in dishwashing trading with a nation of lawyers? Why is a certain path obviously an optimizing path to an individual, but not to a collection of individuals like a region or nation? Why do economists make opposite recommendations to one individual than to a group of individuals facing the same options? Why would we never dream of recommending to nations whose part in the international division of labour is similar to washing dishes that they can optimize by changing into a different profession?

The answer is relatively simple: neoclassical theory has abstracted from – assumed as not existing – all the characteristics which distinguish the job of washing dishes from the job of being a lawyer. Under conditions of perfect competition and perfect information with constant returns to scale, lawyers and dishwashers would make the same salaries. Under these conditions all individuals in an economy would have the same salaries; no trade-offs and no optimizations would be possible.

Individual wage differences as well as differences in industry profitability are caused by a package of factors which carry the collective label 'barriers to entry' – fixed costs and increasing returns, imperfect competition, speed of technological change, and many others which are listed in Figure 8.1. The quality index represents a continuum from perfect competition to monopoly, on which any economic activity conceptually can be plotted. The score on this index reflects the degree to which an activity can support a high wage for the individual and a high standard of living for the nation exporting this good.

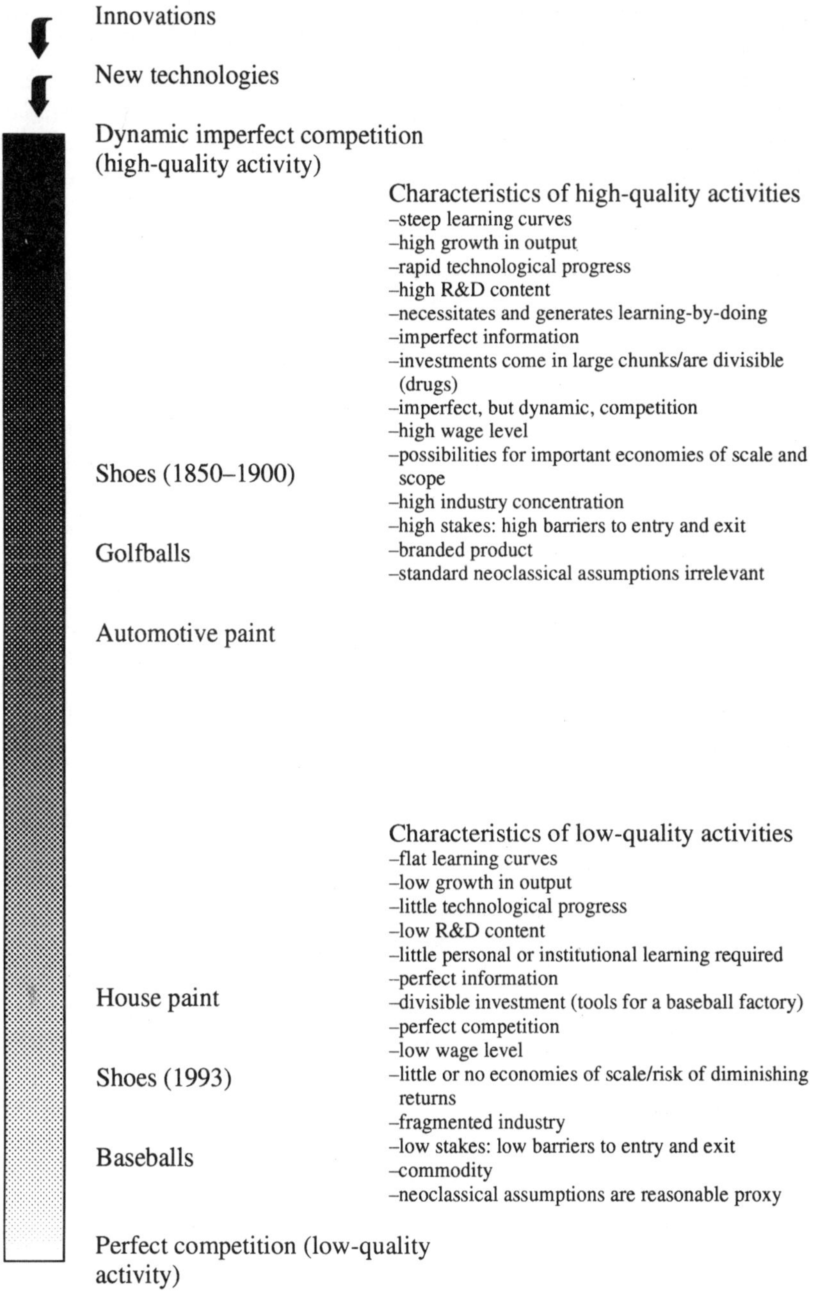

Innovations

New technologies

Dynamic imperfect competition
(high-quality activity)

Characteristics of high-quality activities
–steep learning curves
–high growth in output
–rapid technological progress
–high R&D content
–necessitates and generates learning-by-doing
–imperfect information
–investments come in large chunks/are divisible
  (drugs)
–imperfect, but dynamic, competition
–high wage level
–possibilities for important economies of scale and
  scope
–high industry concentration
–high stakes: high barriers to entry and exit
–branded product
–standard neoclassical assumptions irrelevant

Shoes (1850–1900)

Golfballs

Automotive paint

Characteristics of low-quality activities
–flat learning curves
–low growth in output
–little technological progress
–low R&D content
–little personal or institutional learning required
–perfect information
–divisible investment (tools for a baseball factory)
–perfect competition
–low wage level
–little or no economies of scale/risk of diminishing
  returns
–fragmented industry
–low stakes: low barriers to entry and exit
–commodity
–neoclassical assumptions are reasonable proxy

House paint

Shoes (1993)

Baseballs

Perfect competition (low-quality
activity)

Figure 8.1   The quality index of economic activities

In other words, the score of the quality index shows the degree of 'industry rent' available to the individual or to the nation. Schumpeter's 'historical increasing returns' – the interplay of scale and technological change over time – are an important factor creating high-quality activities.[8] Schumpeterian underdevelopment is the result of a specialization, within the international division of labour, in activities with a low score on the quality index of economic activities.

The national strategies under mercantilism and cameralism shared the view of economic growth being *activity-specific*: it took place in some economic activities and not in others (Reinert 1994). In order to get rich, a nation had to engage in the activities which gave the nation *productive powers* or *nationale Produktivkraft*, the equivalent of today's 'competitiveness', as discussed in Reinert (1995). This was the core of English economic policy from the late 1400s and in the economic policies of France (starting in the 1600s), Germany (from its cameralist past and with the Zollverein in the 1830s), the US (starting in 1820), and Japan (after the Meiji Restoration). In practical terms this meant engaging in the economic activities which at any point in time were in the process of being mechanized, through bounties, subsidies and protection. By singling out the activities which at any point in time were in the process of being mechanized, this 'mercantilist' trade policy developed a 'national innovation system'. Seen from a slightly different angle, the slope of the national learning curves were maximized. The scale effects and the barriers to entry created in these activities secured the creation of 'industry rent', which produced the gap in standards of living between the European countries and their colonies. The exceptions were formed by the 'white' colonies – those which in the early UN statistics were grouped under the heading 'areas of recent settlement'. These nations followed the former strategies of the metropolis countries, protecting and supporting local industry even from that of the mother country.

The Ricardian trade theory excludes all the factors which cause 'industry rent'. Our personal 'gut feelings' when we give our children or others advice on what profession to seek takes the industry rents in our own economies into account. When we analyse the relationship between nations, this tacit knowledge is automatically blocked off, and we return to Ricardo and a world where all the factors creating uneven wealth within a nation are assumed not to exist. But why are Ricardo and Samuelson able to convince us that a nation of dishwashers will be equally rich as a nation of lawyers when we intuitively know that each individual lawyer will be much richer than each individual person making a living washing dishes?

In a world where the division of labour causes different degrees of imperfect competition, scale effects and – in general – a different market value on different types of knowledge, an uneven income distribution is bound to be found. It is not the existence of increasing returns and barriers to entry *per se* that causes this maldistribution, but the fact that different economic activities embody these characteristics to varying degrees. Relative wealth and poverty are created by the asymmetry between different degrees of imperfect competition, not by imperfect competition in and of itself. In the very hypothetical case that all activities had the same degree of imperfect information and increasing returns, we could still have an even income distribution. On the quality index this would correspond to persons or nations trading in professions with the same score on the quality index – the case of the lawyer going to the doctor. This case was specifically recognized in the most important work on 'national strategy' in eighteenth-century England, when Charles King explicitly lists among 'good trade' the exchange of manufactured goods for other manufactured goods (King 1721). Paul Krugman's conversion from free-trade scepticism after he rediscovered increasing returns – and consequently an important mechanism of uneven development – in the late 1970s (Krugman 1979; 1981) to virtually advocating free trade across the board today (Krugman 1994) seems to be based on this 'special case': when nations trade at the same degree of increasing returns – or at the same degree of imperfect information for that matter – the existence of increasing returns and imperfect information is correctly seen as an additional argument for free trade. This is, however, only a special case – e.g. that of Germany and France trading large cars, or that of the lawyer visiting the doctor: both benefit mutually from the specialization of the other (essentially from the saving of fixed costs and from having better information), and income distribution is not affected. This case – lawyers and doctors exchanging services in activities with the same score on the quality index – we shall refer to as *symmetrical* trade. However, if two nations previously under autarky, both consisting of lawyers and people washing dishes, suddenly open up for trade so that one country specializes in legal matters and the other specializes in washing dishes, we have the case of an *asymmetrical* specialization which will have serious effects on income distribution: one nation will be much richer than before and one will be much poorer. This, in a very simplified form, is what has caused the GNP per capita in Eastern Europe to fall between 30 and 50 per cent in three years. This is what Friedrich List saw happening in France after the fall of Napoleon, and what converted him from being a free trader to being a promoter of industrialization and of the somewhat vague concept of *nationaler Produktivkraft*, normally as ill-defined as the concept of 'competitiveness' today.

The nation at the losing end of this deal, the nation specializing in the activity with no 'historical increasing returns' and no 'industry rent', will be poor. Adam Smith's 'division of labour' is free of distributional effects on income only when all the economic activities created by the division of tasks are 'alike', when they have the same degree of scale effects, imperfect information, barriers to entry, etc. The spectrum of economic activities which surrounds us is clearly extremely divergent in terms of these characteristics, and consequently an increasing division of labour also opens up for increasing divergence of income levels, both inside nations and between nations.

Conclusion: Schumpeterian underdevelopment – policy conclusions past and present

The rediscovery of the effects of increasing returns in new trade theory and new growth theory are made without any reference to the economic thinking and to economic policies of past centuries. The new theories open up for an understanding of uneven growth, but they are hardly translated to practical policy, least of all in the policies of the First World towards the Third World, which is where they would have had the most impact. The editor of the Papers and Proceedings of the 1993 Annual Meeting of the American Economic Association appropriately heads the section on new trade theory: 'Free Trade: A Loss of (Theoretical) Nerve?' (*American Economic Review* 1993, iv).

One basic reason for this is the unwillingness to test the theoretical models in economics with observable economic facts. The practical relevance of a theoretical economic model is hardly ever tested with actual observations of how the world economy operates. Paul Krugman's 1981 paper, quoted in the previous section, actually contains a relevant description of how international trade creates wealth on one side and poverty on the other. Without knowing it, Krugman rediscovered and mathematized the principal nineteenth-century argument for protection of industry which made his own country rich. This is only one of Krugman's models. Another earlier model is in 'a clever paper on interstellar trade, where goods are transported from one stellar system to another at speeds close to that of light; the resulting relativistic correction to time entails different interest rates in different frames of reference' (Dixit 1993, 173). One of these theories is very important to human welfare; the other is not. As long as verification in the real world is not part of economic modelling – and cleverness and not relevance tends to be a main criterion for success – both these theories are part of what essentially is a purely theoretical intellectual game. On one level, there is nothing wrong with this. Playing simulation games, like chess, is perfectly legitimate. Problems arise only if the general public, in particular those responsible for the economic policy of the Third World, are led to believe that there is any direct relationship between economic modelling and what goes on in the world economy.

Here the laments of Colin Clark, in the foreword to his book *The Conditions of Economic Progress* (Clark 1940, vii–viii) are even more valid now than at the time of his writing:

I have left the academic world with nothing but regard for the intellectual integrity and public spirit of my former colleagues in the ... Universities; but with dismay at their continued preference for the theoretical rather than the scientific approach to economic problems. Not one in a hundred – least of all those who are most anxious to proclaim the scientific nature of Economics – seem to understand what constitutes the scientific approach, namely, the careful systematisation of all observed facts, the framing of hypotheses from these facts, prediction of fresh conclusions on the basis of these hypotheses, and the testing of these conclusions against further observed facts. It would be laughable, were it not tragic, to watch the stream of books and articles, attempting to solve the exceptionally complex problems of present-day economics by theoretical arguments, often without a single reference to the observed facts of the situation. ...The hard scientific discipline has yet to be learned, that all theories must be constantly tested and re-tested against observed facts, and those which prove wrong ruthlessly rejected.

The observed or 'stylized' facts are that an increasing international division of labour is accompanied by an increasing gap in income between poor and wealthy nations, with little movement between the two groups. The same effect is also found within the EU: larger markets require more redistribution. Every year the European Union increases the amount of money flowing through its enormous redistributional machinery, which adds to the redistribution which already absorbs around 50 per cent of GNP – the government sector – in the industrialized nations. Another key stylized fact is that economic welfare seems to be much less a product of the *efficiency* of a nation in its specialization, but much more the product of the *choice* of economic activity. The cases where nations are efficient in their production compared to world 'best practice', but are still poor, I have labelled as cases of Schumpeterian underdevelopment.

The policy implications which slowly emerge from new neoclassical growth theory and new trade theory are in principle not different from those of Serra, Roscher, or the early Marshall, authors writing from 1613 to 1890. These new theories rediscover the essence of mercantilist industrial policy: in a world inhabited by economic activities with different potentials for raising national income, there are optimizing paths. These insights are being used in the industrial policies of the First World, but they are absent from the policy of the First World towards the Second (previously communist) and the Third World, which is where they would have the most effect.

In any country, a mediocre lawyer has a much higher income than the most efficient dishwasher in a restaurant. For a person washing dishes, studying to become a lawyer is an optimizing path, one which will maximize future income compared to a do nothing (*laissez-faire*) option: 'My comparative advantage in society, due to my low wages, is to wash dishes.' A similar situation faces nations stuck in Schumpeterian underdevelopment. Haiti could, instead of exchanging 30 hours of labour producing baseballs for export for one hour of US labour in imported golfballs, optimize national welfare by producing golfballs less efficiently than the US. Even if the US managed to stay ten times as efficient as Haiti producing golfballs, the Haitian would, in terms of balls at today's prices, still be three times as rich under autarky in golfballs than under specialization and free trade. Under autarky in sporting balls, Haiti could improve its position compared to free trade. How would Haiti get the capital? Presumably the same way our law student will: taking up a loan and paying it back from his future 'industry rent'.

In any system with differing degrees of increasing returns and a mixed pattern of collusive and classical distribution of gains from technical progress, some nations will be better off under autarky than under free trade. This is the basic reason why most of the German historical economists, including the dean of the historical school, Werner Sombart, were fundamentally critical of free trade between nations at different levels of development. The Haitian example, far from being a far-fetched theoretical argument, was at the core of the optimizing path embarked upon by the US in the 1820s: the American system of industrial protection, which in a period of less than 100 years made the US into the world's powerhouse.

The economist who, next to Alexander Hamilton, was the spiritual father of the North American protection of industry, Daniel Raymond, compared the situation of individuals to that of nations: 'If an individual can do this, so may a nation' (Raymond 1820, 115). The core of Raymond's argument was one of optimization: the increased prices paid in the US for industrial products under protection would be more than compensated by the increase in wages, since industrial workers everywhere had so much higher wages than farm labour.[9] In the case of the nineteenth-century US economy, the trade-off between man the consumer and man the producer led to the conclusion that, there and then, free trade was a suboptimal option. Both the Second (former communist) World and the Third present many cases of Schumpeterian underdevelopment where there are similar optimizing paths to be explored. Exploiting these requires more 'theoretical nerve' from economists, and a conscious move into what Colin Clark would have called 'factual and scientific investigations' to complement the theoretical ones which dominate today.

Notes

1. This paper draws heavily on a paper presented at the 5th Conference of the Joseph Alois Schumpeter Society in August 1994, in Münster, Germany. Helpful comments provided by Keith Smith and the editor of this volume are gratefully acknowledged. The usual disclaimer applies.
2. Von Hornick's important work appeared in sixteen editions between 1684 and 1784, all in German. This was considerably more than the most famous English economists at the time. Mun's *England's Treasure* from 1664 reached eight editions in English and six in translations, Child's *Brief Observations* of 1690 reached ten editions in English and two transla-

tions. For a study of economic policy making under the 'proto-historical' school after Hornick, see Tribe (1988).

3. The largest numbers of publications comparing Marx and Schumpeter have appeared in Italian books and journals, a total of 23. The second most frequent nation is Japan.

4. This part is not found in the 1912 German edition.

5. 'Ohne auf Sombart und die allgemeine Literatur der zwanziger und dreissiger Jahre hinzuweisen, bot Schumpeter (in *Kapitalismus, Sozialismus und Demokratie*) im wesentlichen nur dass, was bereits Jahrzehnte zuvor in den deutschen Diskussionen über die "Zukunft der Kapitalismus" geschrieben und gesagt worden war, wobei er freilich die gesellschaftlich konservativen Folgerungen, die bei Sombart in der Forderung nach Reagrarisierung und Autarkie gipfelten, nicht übernahm' (Appel 1992, 260).

6. This statement should be compared with the terms-of-trade debate following the Prebisch–Singer argument in the early 1950s. Moulton shows a mechanism where one group grows rich and the other poor with terms of trade unchanged. My collusive spread and Moulton's argument reflect the views of Singer rather than Prebisch: see Singer's 1949 paper 'The Distribution of Gains between Investing and Borrowing Countries', reproduced in Singer (1964).

7. During 1994, the Tamil refugees in Switzerland, who were threatened with expulsion, proved to have only one political ally: the association of restaurant owners who depend on them for dishwashing.

8. The 'quality index' can be seen as an attempt to explain Robert Reich's 'high-quality jobs' and 'low-quality jobs'. A nation specializing in 'low-quality jobs' – like Haiti – will suffer from Schumpeterian underdevelopment.

9. This wage difference is well documented in Clark (1940), where he finds, e.g. that in Norway agricultural wages were only 8 per cent of industrial wages (presumably leaving out the value of room and board).

References

American Economic Review, 83 (2), May 1993.

Appel, M. (1992), *Werner Sombart. Theoretiker und Historiker des modernen Kapitalismus*, Marburg: Metropolis.

Augello, M.M. (1990), *Joseph Alois Schumpeter. A Reference Guide*, Berlin: Springer-Verlag.

Babbage, C. (1832), *On the Economy of Machinery and Manufactures*, London: Charles Knight.

Backhaus, J. (1995), *Werner Sombart (1863–1941): Social Scientist*, 3 vols, Marburg: Metropolis.

Bell, S. (1940), *Productivity, Wages, and National Income*, Washington, DC: The Brookings Institution.

Benítez Rojo, A. (1989), *La isla que se repite*, Hanover, New Hampshire: Ediciones del Norte.

Business Week (1994), 'America's New Growth Economy', 16 May.

Clark, C. (1940), *The Conditions of Economic Progress*, London: Macmillan.

Clemence, R.V. (1951), *Essays of J.A. Schumpeter*, Cambridge, Mass.: Addison-Wesley.

Coote, B. (1987), *The Hunger Crop. Poverty and the Sugar Industry*, Oxford: Oxfam.

Dixit, A. (1993), 'In Honor of Paul Krugman: Winner of the John Bates Clark Medal', *Journal of Economic Perspectives*, 7.

Hermann, F.B.W. (1832), *Staatswirtschaftliche Untersuchungen*, Munich: A. Weber.

Hillman, R.S. and D'Agostino, T.J. (1992), *Distant Neighbours in the Caribbean. The Dominican Republic and Jamaica in Comparative Perspective*, New York: Praeger.

Hufeland, G. (1807), *Neue Grundlegung der Staatswirthschaftskunst, durch Prüfung und Berichtigung ihrer Hauptbegriffe von Gut, Werth, Preis, Geld und Volksvermögen mit ununterbrochener Rücksicht auf die bisherigen Systeme*, Giessen and Wetlar: Tasche & Müller.

King, C. (1721), *The British Merchant or Commerce Preserv'd*, 3 vols, London: John Darby.

Krugman, P. (1979), 'Increasing Returns, Monopolistic Competition, and International Trade', *Journal of International Economics*, 9.

Krugman, P. (1981), 'Trade, Accumulation, and Uneven Development', *Journal of Development Economics*, 8.

Krugman, P. (1994), *Peddling Prosperity. Economic Sense and Nonsense in the Age of Diminished Expectations*, New York: Norton.

Lemoine, M. (1985), *Bitter Sugar*, London: Zed Books.

Lucas, R. (1988), 'On the Mechanisms of Economic Development'. *Journal of Monetary Economics*, 22.

Marshall, A. (1890), *Principles of Economics*, London: Macmillan.

Moulton, H.G. (1935), *Income and Economic Progress*, Washington, DC: The Brookings Institution.

Nourse, E. and Drury, H. (1938), *Industrial Price Policies and Economic Progress*, Washington, DC: The Brookings Institution.

Ortiz, F. (1940), *Contrapunteo Cubano del Tabaco y el Azúcar*, Havana: Jesus Montero. Second edition: Caracas: Biblioteca Ayacucho, 1978. English translation by H. de Onìs (1947), *Cuban Counterpoint. Tobacco and Sugar*, New York: Alfred A. Knopf, with an introduction by Bronoslaw Malinowski.

Raff, D.M.R. (1988), 'Wage Determination Theory and the Five-Dollar Day at Ford', *The Journal of Economic History*, 43.

Raymond, D. (1820), *Thoughts on Political Economy*, Baltimore: Fielding Lucas.

Reinert, E.S. (1994), 'Catching-up from way behind: a third world view perspective on first world history', in J. Fagerberg et al. (eds), *The Dynamics of Technology, Trade and Growth*, Aldershot: Edward Elgar.

Reinert, E.S. (1995), 'Competitiveness and its Predecessors – a 500 year Cross-national Perspective', in *Economic Dynamics and Structural Change*, March.

Robbins, L. (1952), *The Theory of Economic Policy in English Classical Political Economy*, London: Macmillan.

Rochester, A. (1940), *Why Farmers are Poor. The Agricultural Crisis in the United States*, New York: International Publishers.

Romer, P.M. (1994), 'The Origins of Endogenous Growth', *Journal of Economic Perspectives*, 8.

Roscher, W. (1854), *Die Grundlagen der Nationalökonomie*, Stuttgart: Cotta.

Roscher, W. (1882), *Principles of Political Economy*, Chicago: Callaghan & Co.

Rosenberg, N. (1976), *Perspectives of Technology*, Cambridge: Cambridge University Press.

Rosenberg, N. (1994), *Exploring the Black Box. Technology, economics, and history*, Cambridge: Cambridge University Press.

Schumpeter, J.A. (1934), *The Theory of Economic Development*, Cambridge, Mass.: Harvard University Press. Original German edition: *Theorie der wirtschaftlichen Entwicklung*, Berlin: Duncker & Humblot, 1912.

Schumpeter, J.A. (1942), *Capital, Socialism, and Democracy*, New York: Harper.

Serra, A. (1613), *Breve trattato delle cause che possono far abbondare li regni d'oro e argento dove non sono miniere*, Napoli: Lazzaro Scoriggio.

Singer, H. (1949), 'The Distribution of Gains between Investing and Borrowing Countries', reproduced in Singer (1964).

Singer, H. (1964), *International Development. Growth and Change*, New York: McGraw-Hill.

Streissler, E.W. (1994), 'Increasing Returns and the Prospects of Small-scale Enterprise', paper presented at the Sixth Annual Heilbronn Symposium in Economics and the Social Sciences, 'Wilhelm Roscher (1817–1894). A Centenary Reappraisal', June 1994.

The Economist (1985), 'Enslaved by Subsidies', 10 August.

Tribe, K. (1988), *Governing Economy. The Reformation of German Economic Discourse 1750–1840*, Cambridge: Cambridge University Press.

Ure, A. (1835), *The Philosophy of Manufactures, or, an exposition of the scientific, moral, and commercial economy of the factory system of Great Britain*, London: Charles Knight.

Verspagen, B. (1992), 'Endogenous Innovation in Neo-classical Growth Models: A Survey', *Journal of Macroeconomics*, 14.

Vethake, H. (1844), *Principles of Political Economy*, 2nd edn, Philadelphia: J.W. Moore.

von Hornick, W. (1684), *Österreich über alles wann es nur will*, Nürnberg: n.p.

Whatley, G. (1774), *Principles of trade. Fredom and protection are its best suport. Industry, the only means to render manufactures cheap*, London: Brotherton and Sewell.

9   Capital markets in a divided world

Ross E. Catterall

The nature of capital markets

The purpose of this chapter is to analyse the relationship between aspects of
the development of financial markets and the process of economic development. The means by which capital is provided to foster economic expansion
is an under-researched area, as is the impact that capital markets have on the
growth process. Greatest attention has been focused on the issue of capital
exports from more advanced nations, rather than the extent to which domestic
financial markets have developed and in what ways they have been able to
provide support for the growth process. It is not uncommon to learn about the
contributions to output that notable investment projects have made and the
technical nature of the processes involved, without learning even in general
terms how finance for the project was organized and provided. However, it is
not the purpose here to provide a detailed analysis of the role of capital
markets in financing projects in the various areas discussed. Attention in this
paper is centred on identifying the factors that were critical in leading to
flourishing domestic financial institutions and markets, which were able to
underpin economic activity rather than purely finance government debt or
inflation.

The chapter does not adhere to the rigid (and rather obsolete) traditional
distinction between capital markets and money markets. According to this
distinction, the 'capital market' refers to any market in long-term financial
investments (such as shares and bonds) which represent corporate capital and
government debt, whereas the 'money market' is the market in which banks
and other financial intermediaries provide short-term financial facilities and
trade in short-term financial investments such as bills and commercial paper.
Not only does such a distinction particularly reflect the way in which transactions have taken place in London financial markets, it also fails to recognize
the broadening scope of the activities of individual financial service providers, which has been particularly evident during the 1980s. Thus the term
'capital market' as used in this paper implies a broader range of activities
than is traditionally the case. It is taken to mean a market, or more probably a
group of interrelated markets, in which capital in its financial or monetary
form is lent and borrowed (or 'raised') on varying terms, and for varying
periods. This includes both very short-term facilities as well as capital normally regarded as permanent, such as equities. The term 'capital market' is

189

used interchangeably with 'financial market' although the latter is perhaps strictly a broader term – encompassing foreign exchange and derivative markets.

The main focus of this chapter is on the period since 1960 and it is thematic in its approach, rather than chronological. The themes discussed relate to the role of capital markets and associated financial intermediaries in mobilizing savings for productive purposes, meeting the financial requirements of expanding economic activities, reducing transaction costs for both surplus and deficit units, and providing liquidity for the existing stock of financial assets. In part the discussion highlights the marked disparities and imperfections that developing countries have in their financial markets compared to the developed world. These disparities have often been the result of monetary, fiscal and regulatory policies which have distorted seriously the nascent capital market. They also reflect issues such as the ability of the economy to generate savings, and the prevailing cultural attitudes towards banks, other financial intermediaries, and the securities markets. However, it is clear that the less developed world is not alone in experiencing capital market imperfection and disparity.

The globalization of financial markets

During the 1980s, financial and capital markets in the developed world began a phase of rapid change and development, which was intimately interrelated with governmental actions to reduce the regulation of financial service providers. The trend was to a globalization of financial services, in which investors were attracted to international capital issues and financial intermediaries adopted a much more global approach in lending and borrowing. There were marked changes of attitude by both the financial service providers and their customers. To many expanding enterprises seeking to merge and acquire other enterprises a high degree of leverage (gearing) became acceptable (at least until the onset of significantly higher interest rates and recession in the later part of the decade). Financial institutions were prepared to lend liberally (usually on a syndicated basis) and the financial engineers they employed began to create increasingly exotic credit instruments and derivative products. There was considerable activity in the traditional stock and bond markets as they became arenas for corporate control, often across national boundaries.

In Europe the progress of global expansion was driven on by the progress towards the single market and its integral component, the single market in financial services. The aim was to create an integrated financial area to complement that provision of an internal market in financial services. The key features of this integrated financial area were:

- Freedom of establishment (e.g. by a financial service provider setting up a branch or local office) in any other member state on the same terms as apply to a resident of that member state.
- Unrestricted freedom to supply financial services across borders within the Community. This necessitates the removal of exchange controls (Dixon 1993, 51).

Underlying the aims of freedom of establishment and free movement of services in the financial sector was an aim of establishing a European capital market by proceeding to complete liberalization of capital movements between member states. This would enable residents of any member state to have access to the financial markets of other member states and to all the financial products available there, without the hindrance of restrictions on capital transfers, exchange controls or fiscal discrimination. Thus a European capital market would help to break down market imperfections. It might, for example, create new forms of security or new forms of intermediation, compared to what was already available in member states. The absence of exchange controls would not only permit intra-Community financial flows, but it would also increase the degree of integration with international capital markets. Overall more competition in the financial services sector would act as a spur to efficiency, a wider range of products, better terms for clients and the ability for European financial service providers to compete more effectively with their North American counterparts. Moreover, many European domestic financial markets had a postwar history of detailed regulation. Not only would a freer environment allow more effective competition with US intermediaries and markets. It would also enable the bulk of Europe to compete more aggressively with the City of London – a dominant force in the provision of international capital.

Although the EC did not attain all the planned features of the single market in financial services by 1 January 1993 when the single market itself came into operation, considerable progress towards the goal was made by that date. The EC's financial markets were converging with the 'megatrend' driven on by the US and the UK to liberalize and deregulate global capital collection and provision. This 'megatrend' was facilitated by the information technology revolution, offering the promise of instantaneous transference of funds between financial centres, and by the drive to remove the plethora of regulations (including exchange controls) affecting capital movements and intermediary activities.

Deregulation and globalization – the twin themes influencing the capital markets of the developed world in the 1980s, brought enormous optimism about the sustained growth of the sector. Although this optimism was dented by the ongoing debt crisis affecting the less developed world and the global stock market crash of 1987, neither of these two events extinguished the underlying belief in the continued expansion of the opportunities that the financial services sector could provide for its clients, and hence its own profits growth. However the LDC debt crisis did significantly affect the direction of global expansion.

A significant factor in cross-border capital market expansion was the ending of exchange controls by the UK in 1979 (largely because of the build-up of North Sea oil revenues). This resulted in UK institutional investors searching out rewarding investment opportunities in overseas markets. Although UK professional investors led the way, the Swiss banks also followed, especially favouring US stock purchases for their clients. By the mid-1980s US pension funds had become actively involved in foreign security investment, as had the Japanese (although their equity purchases were heavily concentrated in US stocks). Finally, the bandwagon was joined by British, continental European and US retail investors (Baring 1994).

Despite the rapid growth of investment in non-domestic markets, the focus of the new global investors remained narrow. Foreign capital typically favoured the security which the large liquid stock markets of the US, the UK, Japan, Germany, France, the Netherlands and Switzerland provided. Moreover, investors typically bought 'blue-chip' shares – those of the largest and most prestigious companies quoted on each market. Less developed equity and bond markets were not favoured, given the ongoing debt problems experienced by the LDCs. The debt problems experienced by countries such as Mexico, Nigeria, Brazil, Argentina and Peru made investors wary of the risks involved in security investment in emerging financial markets, and focused stock and bond attention on the markets of the developed world (Valdez 1993; Tucker et al. 1991).

The trend towards globalization of financial markets as a whole suggests that these markets are being levered apart in the developed and underdeveloped world, just as incomes have been. The markets, which have historically been far from homogeneous (Goldsmith 1969 and 1985), became less so during the 1980s. Financial markets became increasingly divided. For the Third World formal markets were either non-existent, or their development was patchy and incomplete, with little or no competition allowed within a highly regulated institutional environment. By contrast the developed countries' markets offered liquidity, sophistication in the range of services offered and breadth and depth of investment outlets for both institutional and private investors. They were also characterized by growing aggressive competition to do business between financial institutions operating in an increasingly deregulated environment. The whole expansion process was driven on by deregulation, innovation and financial engineering, and new technology. The traditional distinction between money and capital markets became increasingly irrelevant in the developed world during the 1980s, where financial markets increasingly became tripartite in nature:

- The markets for securities (or the exchange markets) where financial instruments with debt and/or equity characteristics are initially sold or exchanged in secondary market transactions to provide liquidity and manage investment portfolios. These activities include trades in what are traditionally regarded as both money market and capital market securities.
- The markets for financial services (or product markets) where financial firms assist customers to borrow, invest, fund expansion outside the usual bond and equity market channels, make payments and manage risk. Institutions in this market include commercial banks, pensions funds, mutual funds, insurance companies, securities firms, venture capitalists and investment banks. They provide a link between the markets for securities and the markets for derivative instruments.
- The markets for derivative financial instruments (or risk management markets) which trade in financial assets 'derived' from other financial assets (e.g. an option to buy a bond, where the option is the derivative and the bond is the underlying financial asset). These markets are used by companies and investors to transfer the risk of changing interest rates and security prices to other financial market participants (Scott 1991).

In the developed economies – especially in North America and Europe – these financial market developments have gone hand in hand with the attempt by financial service providers to become 'one-stop-shops' offering to corporate clients the whole gamut of ever-changing financial service provision. The emphasis has shifted away from traditional distinctions between lending and security activity and more towards the 'universal banking' approach common in Germany and Switzerland. Moreover, regulatory reform has tended to break down traditional lines of demarcation, facilitating this development (Kim 1993).

The levering apart of financial markets which occurred during the 1980s was partly the result of international investor disinterest in the emerging markets during the decade, but also the existence of what has come to be known as 'financial repression', or excessive regulation (MacKinnon 1973). This repression resulted from the desire of LDC governments to control the allocation of credit within the economy and to have a capital market which was a conduit for financing government debt. For example, in 1986, 70 per cent of new lending by the national banks in Pakistan was directed by the government, and in India about one-half of bank assets had to be held in government bonds or other required reserves (Pomfret 1992, 137).

The form of financial repression differs from country to country, but typically includes interest ceilings and preferential interest rates for certain borrowers, reserve requirements forcing banks to hold government debt, strict exchange controls which discourage inflows of capital from elsewhere, and special taxes on financial transactions as a source of additional government revenue. The results of these policies are that savings with formal financial intermediaries are discouraged, especially where inflation reduces the real interest rate received to a negative value; government expenditure may be inadequately controlled as the banks are a ready source of further funds; some corporate borrowers may extend themselves too far because of low preferential interest rates and they may also favour inappropriately capital-intensive technology; and black markets for loanable funds are likely to develop outside official channels of financial intermediation. In circumstances such as these, financial markets could not be expected to develop in the same ways as those in the advanced nations, unless financial reform was forthcoming. Financial market expansion was taking place in the LDCs in the 1980s, but the emphasis was on the development of stock markets, where strongly rising share prices were a propulsive factor.

Although many unique elements are involved, there are common trends in a number of semi-industrial LDCs. First, government policy forced mainly non-preferred LDC corporations to seek long-term finance from the stock market (Pagano 1993). Second, because of interest rate ceilings, in countries where the household savings ratio was high, particularly Asia, savers were forced to look for other opportunities for investment. These included both the stock market and unofficial outlets. It is not clear whether the overall savings ratio was raised as a result, or whether savings were being switched from one instrument of savings to another (Singh 1994, 134). However, share ownership and stock market participation by the general public (rather than financial institutions) increased markedly during the 1980s in many countries (sometimes encouraged by governments seeking a means of privatizing state monopolies). Third, although the renewed rise of global investing after 1979 was mainly concentrated on mature stock markets, some of the new global enthusiasm of advanced country investors did spill over into emerging markets. The combined effect of rising domestic and international demand for shares issued by companies in LDCs was a strong rise in share prices in emerging markets.

This rise in share prices during the 1980s dramatically reduced the cost of capital raised from equity issues. In 1980 in the case of Korea, the average price/earnings ratio was about 3 and the cost of raising capital through a share issue was thus about 33 per cent. But by 1989 the average price/earnings ratio was 14, implying the cost of equity capital had fallen to 7.1 per cent (Amsden and Euh 1990). The actual cost of equity capital was as low as

Table 9.1 *Asian stock market growth*

| | Total market capitalization | | | | Market concentration 1991 (1) | P/E ratio Q1, 1992 | Yield % (2) | Market returns % (3) |
| | 1986 | | 1991 | | | | | |
	US$bn	% GDP	US$bn	% GDP				
Indonesia	1	1.0	16	14.8	51.0	13.5	N/A	N/A
Korea	14	13.2	111	39.2	30.9	12.8	34.3	24.8
Philippines	N/A	N/A	10	22.2	56.3	19.6	39.2	34.2
Taipei China	15	19.4	11	61.0	53.9	43.2	46.5	41.5
Hong Kong	40	155.0	119	163.0	45.0	11.9	16.9	50.0
Malaysia	15	54.1	56	118.5	28.0	14.5	19.0	48.0
Singapore	28	157.7	45	112.5	35.0	17.2	20.4	40.2
Japan	1,781	89.7	2,904	86.4	17.1	36.5	19.7	42.6

Notes:
1. Capitalization of ten largest firms as % of total.
2. Estimated annual dividend yield.
3. Estimated annual increase in security values, January 1986–September 1991.

Source: Andersen (1993).

3 per cent after taking taxation into account, and this compares with a figure of 12.5 per cent for preferential loans from the commercial banks (Euh and Barker 1990). Given these cost differentials, many LDC corporations resorted to equity financing during the 1980s. This is a surprising situation given that many large corporations in LDCs are family controlled, and therefore assumed to be reluctant to issue equity to the market for fear of losing control (Singh 1994, 131). Despite this, Singh reports that over 6 000 companies were listed on Indian stock markets in 1990 compared with a little over 2 000 in the UK, about 650 in Germany and less than 250 in Italy. Although India is well ahead of other LDCs in terms of equity listings, most leading emerging markets show significant increases in the number of companies listed and market capitalization as a proportion of GDP during the 1980s. Table 9.1 shows some of the dimensions of Asian stock market growth.

Although LDC corporations were active users of domestic equity markets during the 1980s, these opportunities applied only to the largest concerns, and for small and medium-sized companies severe financing difficulties existed. If they were borrowers from the banking system, they faced significantly higher debt costs than their larger counterparts, and many financially repressive economic regimes had allowed little development of a formal system of financial intermediation for smaller companies. Thus smaller business units in the LDCs were caught in the 1980s equivalent of the 'Macmillan gap' (Cmd. 3897 1931, 404). Denied any access to funds from the official banking system, the smallest borrowers were forced into grey and black markets of high interest-rate money lenders, urban pawnbrokers and loan sharks. Unofficial, informal and unregulated credit markets perform an important role in filling the gap of the official market, but it is scarcely the best way of creating and sustaining entrepreneurs, to combine a high-cost black market for funds with an overregulated banking sector and a partial development of official financial markets. The recognition that this was a suboptimal situation acted as a spur to many LDCs to follow the developed world's process of deregulation and financial reform. This was also seen as the path to financial maturity.

In summary, the following themes dominated international financial markets during the 1980s:

- For the developed economies the 1980s were a 'tumultuous decade' in which 'the speed with which financial institutions and markets were transformed ... was incalculable and the transformations themselves were nothing short of staggering' (Geisst 1993, 127). New product markets and activities abounded with multifaceted involvement from financial institutions trading on a global basis.
- Much of the tumult generated by financial market development during

the 1980s was the result of deregulation, which was intimately interrelated with the EC's single market in financial services. By comparison, financial markets in the less developed world were controlled, directed and financially repressed, and lacked the broad range of borrowing and lending services and instruments that had been created in the developed world.

- Despite the fact that deregulation, technology and the sheer optimism of the financial services sector drove on financial markets in the advanced countries, in one area there was significant growth in the LDCs. This was the growth of domestic equity markets partly as a result of the regulation and inefficiency of the rest of the financial sector.

- Equity market growth in the LDCs was an important feature of the 1980s for these countries, at least as far as the largest companies were concerned. It made new share issues possible, which were by and large used to increase the net assets of the core business, rather than engage in merger and acquisition activity (Singh 1994).

- By contrast, in the developed world the expansion of financial intermediation and financial markets on a broad front made money 'relatively easy to come by' and 'mergers and acquisitions dominated the financial markets until the market collapse of October 1987' (Geisst 1993, 128). Much of the activity of the markets until that time was frothy rather than substantial in nature, and whilst it contributed to the profitability of the financial services sector, there is a question mark over its role in creating new enterprises.

- Overall, developed and underdeveloped financial markets were being levered apart by the process of deregulation, which created a range of activities unknown in the underdeveloped world, where traditional stock markets were developing rapidly, but little else was to change until late in the decade. By that time many LDC governments wished to copy the financial reforms and deregulation of the developed countries. As a result of the curious situation which existed in many LDCs of strongly growing stock markets, but a repressed and weak role for formal financial intermediaries generally, Singh (1994, 122) has identified what he calls a 'reverse pecking order.' In advanced countries such as the US and the UK the 'pecking order' pattern in finance was first to use retained profits as far as possible to meet investment needs; then either to go to the banks or issue long-term debt if external finance is required, and only to go to the equity markets as a last resort. Given the low level of development of LDC financial markets and the considerable market imperfections, considerable reliance on internal finance might be expected of large corporations in LDCs. In fact, Singh finds that large LDCs corporations follow an almost reverse pecking order to those in advanced countries, using the equity market as a first port of call.

The roots of financial innovation

European financial markets have been transformed since the 1950s and 1960s when New York was the market European borrowers turned to increasingly to satisfy their needs for new long-term bond issues. New York provided borrowers and investors alike with an extensive primary and secondary market, which offered a wider range of instruments and superior liquidity to that available in their domestic markets.

The Segré Report (an EC study undertaken in 1966) concluded that European capital markets discriminated in favour of domestic borrowers, especially national governments, and that institutional investors were excessively regulated in the range of securities they could invest in. There was little evidence of a Europe-wide capital market and few European companies were listed on stock markets elsewhere than in their country of domicile. The limited nature of most European financial markets forced companies to tap the extensive long-term borrowing opportunities that the US market offered (OECD 1967).

By the end of the 1950s there were some signs of change in the existing European financial order. London's financial markets were more lightly regulated than their counterparts in the rest of Europe (McRae and Cairncross 1985), and a number of highly innovative security houses began to participate in the formative development of the Eurodollar wholesale market. Swiss banks also became active participants through their growing trading activities in US dollars.

The development of the short-term Eurodollar market was closely followed by the growth of a Eurobond market. The British merchant bank Warburg's took a major role in this, when in 1963 it lead-managed the first Eurodollar bond issue for Autostrade, the Italian toll motorway operator.

The Euromarket developments helped to broaden the interests of European financial institutions and integrate their activities more closely as players in the broader and increasingly global Eurocurrency market. This market is no longer restricted to Europe, and it now covers any currency which is borrowed and lent outside the country which uses that currency. Similarly, the Eurobond market is now purely a generic term to cover any bond issue which mobilizes funds simultaneously from various parts of the world economy.

This reduction in European insularity, spurred on by the growth in the scale of international business, changes in technology and a loosening regularity framework, led to the spreading (especially in the last two decades) of a vast array of new financial instruments and services. A partial list of these innovations would include new interest-bearing deposit accounts, hybrid types of security with both debt and equity features, securities offering various choices for conversion into other securities and different hedging instruments such as swaps, financial futures and options. The result has been a more complex European financial market, but one in which it is easier for transactions to find instruments to suit their needs.

Deregulation has given Europe's financial markets the ability to grow, diversify and innovate. But innovation itself partly accounts for this new-found regulatory freedom.

Financial innovation is often seen as a by-product of regulation (Silver 1983). The argument is that most financial innovations try to circumvent government regulation. The Eurodollar market, for example, owed its creation to the restriction on the rate of interest that US commercial banks could offer on their time deposits (Miller 1986). This restriction (which did not apply to the dollar-denominated deposits of West European branches of US banks) and the rise in interest rates in the late 1960s induced US banks operating overseas to bid competitively for short-term dollar-denominated accounts. In fact, the list of similar regulation-induced innovations is extensive and includes the Eurobond market, zero coupon bonds, financial futures and options, and other derivatives based on them. Financial instruments or practices are innovated to lessen the financial constraints imposed on clients and the financial services sector itself. Historically, most governments have preferred to change the regulatory structure, closing off the avenue of circumvention. This, however, has created new opportunities for financial innovation. This adoptive sequence of action and response constitutes the so-called 'regulatory dialectic' (Kane 1983). However, since the late 1970s, as a result of increased deregulation, the 'regulatory dialectic' has lost much of its significance, at least in the developed world.

Deregulation has eroded demarcation lines between formally separated sectors of the financial system. Up to the mid-1980s some European countries had imposed restraints on the extent to which banks could engage in securities activity and the provision of non-banking financial products for prudential reasons and to prevent the concentration of economic power. Limitations on the scope of permissible business activities also arose in response to concerns about conflict of interests. For example, banks engaging in security trading activities could underwrite and distribute low quality stock or overlend to underwriting clients, in order to enhance customer relationships, thus impairing the safety of the underwriting institutions. The policy of blurring the demarcation lines between the various segments of financial services markets throughout Europe in the 1980s was the result of the perceived need to increase efficiency and favour the development of large indigenous institutions which could compete on equal footing with strong foreign competitors. In the light of these relatively new policy objectives, concerns about the concentration of power, soundness and conflict of interest lost support.

The liberalization of price restrictions has also been an integral part of the deregulatory process. Up to the early 1980s controls on interest rates had been widespread in almost all the European countries. Such controls were designed to reflect prudential considerations. Complete freedom in the determination of bank lending or deposit rates could lead to excessive interest rate competition among banks, undermining their stability (OECD 1986). On the lending side, controls on interest rates combined with direct lending controls and/or mandatory investment regulations were applied to channel the desired amount of funds at artificially low interest rates into specific sectors of economic activity and/or government paper and bonds. This was especially the case in France, and the South European countries, where more interventionist industrial policies were pursued.

Since the early 1980s, however, controls on interest rates, as well as direct lending controls and mandatory investment regulations, have been seen as a distortion to the free flow of funds. Lenders and non-priority borrowers who were adversely affected by regulations tended to turn to unregulated financial channels (OECD 1989). Banks could generate loans and sell them packaged as securities for trading outside the regulated markets. As a result of the substantial flow of funds from the regulated to unregulated markets, the interest rate control system was increasingly bypassed. Deregulatory measures designed to reduce the scope of controlled interest rates became inevitable.

The deregulation of interest rates coincided with the liberalization of fees and commissions in financial services. Such liberalization was most noticeable in the securities sector. By the mid-1980s, most European countries removed all regulations on commission charges, leaving their determination to market forces. European countries were using the EC competition rules for dismantling restrictive business practices on fees and commissions, which had often taken the form of cartel agreements.

The process towards deregulation contributed significantly to the introduction of new financial instruments to offer to investors. Changes in financial regulation also affected the demand for new instruments. Financial institutions were taking on new risks by lending in new ways, developing new products, and acting in new financial markets on new terms. They became more concerned to hedge their risk exposure by innovating hedging instruments, such as floating rate instruments, futures, options and swaps, or by trading in these instruments. In the process new derivative products have been created which can be offered to clients. Furthermore, deregulation brought new players into existing parts of the financial system and competition intensified, which in turn made innovation increasingly necessary for survival. As a result of this a new profession of 'financial engineers', creating new securities, products and packages was born.

The nature of the adjustment process taking place is often misrepresented. It is argued that exogenous government action took place to reduce the regulatory restraints on financial firms. Such a perspective fails to raise the issue of why national authorities reduced rather than rebuilt obstacles to entry and operation in the financial services industry. Technology is an important factor.

Since the late 1960s major advances in information and telecommunication systems have changed dramatically the way financial services are produced and provided. The increased computing and storage power of microcomputers has enabled financial institutions to design new and relatively complex derivative instruments such as swaps, futures and options. Highly sophisticated computerized techniques have also allowed financial institutions to monitor and control their risk exposures better resulting from the issuance of such complex instruments. Technological advances have improved telecommunication links allowing low-cost instantaneous funds transference to take place, increasing the speed and efficiency of the delivery of financial products. The financial services industry, based on the manipulation of information, was the ideal area to implement new information and communication technology.

Product and process innovation generated by technological change has rendered foreign exchange controls increasingly ineffective. Foreign currency could be bought in parallel markets with virtually no premium on the official rate. Legislation could have been made tougher and applied more rigorously, but at what price in terms of perverse effects and costs? The danger was that the drive to circumvent rules would become more attractive, loopholes would be sought out and found and regulation in general flouted. Regulatees could always be a step ahead of regulators in finding escape routes. The elimination of foreign exchange controls provided investors with increased opportunities to engage in arbitrage between markets and strengthened competition among financial centres, another important cause of deregulation. But it was technological change which was the spur to the whole process.

Product lines of traditionally heterogeneous institutions were rapidly focusing into a homogeneous blend due to technological change (Kaufman 1984). The fragmentation between banks and investment banks became less pronounced since banks could securitize their assets and liabilities and investment banks offer instruments similar to banks. The technical distinctions between banking and insurance products became less clear-cut with the advent of new instruments used by banks where the underlying business is based on actuarial concepts (e.g. futures, options and certain types of standing letters of credit). Life insurance products have increasingly become saving products containing only a small element of death-risk protection. Such developments made the controls on the separation of the various segments of the financial services industry increasingly ineffective.

In view of the growing inefficiencies of tight regulatory regimes on the scope of business, allocation of credit and the pricing and delivery of financial products, European governments were forced to review their controls and adopt a more liberal stance. In other words, deregulation became the *ex-post* reaction by the authorities to the new economic realities of the marketplace. The whole process of deregulation is essentially market-driven. It was not initially a deliberate policy choice by national authorities, but was forced on them by technological innovation. The wave of financial innovation generated by technological change led to an unprecedented circumvention of the government control over money and finance. Under such circumstances preserving controls implies their intensification, but the economic costs involved (especially because business may be driven offshore) made such a route unattractive compared to deregulation.

However, financial innovation has serious consequences for the soundness and stability of the financial system since it collectively encourages the absorption of a higher proportion of risky assets into portfolios, thus enhancing financial fragility (Carter 1989). As a result, since the late 1980s various countries have introduced additional controls to deal with actual and potential new market failures. Deregulation could not continue unlimited. Although in country after country structural price and allocative controls were eliminated or relaxed in the 1980s (mostly as a result of financial innovation), there has been a growing emphasis on prudential controls on capital, liquidity and risk exposure. A degree of reregulation has taken place, particularly to ensure adequate reserves of capital to support business activity (Hall 1993).

A particular recent area of concern for regulators has been the growth of derivative markets, which are largely new and hence hitherto unregulated. The complexity of some derivative trades has caused regulators to wonder whether the directors of financial institutions actually understand the trades taking place by their own traders, and hence the risks to which the institution is being exposed (Catterall 1994). Recent concerns about derivative market growth have been expressed by the IMF, the Bundesbank, the Bank of England, the Bank for International Settlements, the US Accounting Office, the US Congress, and most recently, following the 1995 Barings collapse, by the House of Commons. In the Barings case, senior management appear to have been unaware of the trading risks they had become exposed to in Asian markets by one of their traders.

So far international regulators and the financial services sector itself seem to be concentrating on internal company controls rather than overall supervision of the derivatives market to ensure all activities are approved and regulated. The Basle Committee, and the International Organization of Securities

Commissions issued guidelines in July 1994 on derivative use and development. Although these stress the importance of internal controls on risk reporting, they do not address the wider regulatory issues, which the demise of Barings highlighted. Even though the problems at Barings seem to have left the markets relatively unruffled, were there to be other bank failures as a result of disastrous dealing errors, the prospect of the contagious spread of systemic risk across markets and institutions remains a possibility.

The heterogeneity of financial markets and institutions
The globalization of financial services is the clichéd but to a large extent accurate description of the effects of the technologically based product and process innovation which has been an important theme in the evolution of developed financial markets since the 1960s (and more especially in the last fifteen years). It is easy to assume that all developed Western financial markets have been changing at a similar pace, but much of the general analysis which appears in discussions of what has occurred is based on the experiences of the most highly developed markets of the US and the UK. Especially because of progression towards the integration of European financial markets and financial services provision, there is a perception that financial services provision within the EU has become relatively homogeneous, except for differences in whether the banking sector is dominated by universal banks or more market-driven structures. Even in this latter respect there has undeniably been a movement towards convergence: according to Cottrell (1994) the UK's 'big bang' of 1986, which allowed a whole host of new foreign entrants to stockbroking in London, resulted in 'British clearing banks assuming the mantle of "universal banks"', in anticipation of the change.

Although convergence was undeniably taking place, European financial markets still remained highly heterogeneous in character. There had been enormous differences in the pace of development of the different national markets and the services which financial intermediaries provided, partly because the starting points from which development occurred were different, partly because deregulation proceeded at different paces in different places, and because national attitudes and historical experiences played a great role in influencing the demand for different kinds of financial service. As a result it is wrong to see the EU at present as consisting of a collection of highly integrated and uniform financial markets and institutions. Some examples illustrate this point.

Most obviously the banking institutions and financial markets of Greece are the least developed in the EU. They remain 'overconcentrated, overregulated, underdeveloped and uncompetitive' (Dixon 1993, 12). During the 1960s and the 1970s the financial system was highly regulated, with the commercial banking sector almost wholly state-owned, subject to interest rate controls and controls over deposits and lending activities, and as a consequence acting as the main conduit of deficit financing for the government. After the fall of the dictatorship in 1974, the situation did not change, and in fact state control of the banking system intensified as the state secured control of the Commercial Banking Group (Dritsas 1994). This group together with the National Bank of Greece and the Agricultural Bank of Greece controls over 80 per cent of the financial market. Although foreign banks began to enter Greece in the early 1970s, this movement has not proceeded very far and the private banking sector still remains small. Financial liberalization in Greece has been problematic due to the weakness of the drachma, in part because of the large public-sector deficits that have existed and a high inflation rate (annual average consumer price increases of 16.6 per cent, 1986–91). This has made the removal of foreign exchange controls difficult. Greece's hopes of attaining the Maastricht treaty convergence criteria for public-sector debt and inflation (despite some progress in this direction since 1992) remain a distant prospect.

Spain and Portugal have apparently more sophisticated financial institutions and markets than Greece. However, in practice the financial services sectors are still relatively underdeveloped and through much of their histories this apparent sophistication has been a 'mirage' (Tortella 1994a). Modern institutions appeared to exist, but again were heavily dominated by the public sector and provided a conduit for funding public-sector deficits. Since the ending of dictatorship in both countries there has been considerable financial liberalization and private-sector financial services development (often in association with other European banks), but the countries' financial markets and institutions still remain behind those in Northern Europe (Lygum et al. 1988 and 1989). In the case of Spain, the new liberalization after Franco was closely followed by a banking crisis which lasted from 1977 to 1985. This resulted from a delayed impact of the oil crisis on Spain. The crisis finally hit the country in 1975 (after the end of the dictatorship), having had its impact delayed by Franco's attempts to muffle the oil price shock and contain the rise in energy prices through the state monopoly of oil distribution. The crisis was most strongly felt in the tourist, real estate, construction and public works, and heavy industrial sectors – areas in which the nascent new private banking sector had heavily invested. Of 110 private banks operating in 1977, 60 were in some sort of trouble during the next eight years (Tortella 1994a; 1994b). Only a few of the banks disappeared, with the majority being taken over by a deposit insurance corporation jointly owned by the Bank of Spain and the private sector, and later resold. This was an inauspicious start for the modernization of the Spanish banking sector.

Another way to look at the development of financial markets and financial services generally is to consider how much of the national population is using the products that the sector offers. Although the prime focus here is retail customers, what emerges points to the highly different usages European populations make of financial intermediaries. This is also the key to the development of those intermediaries and the markets in which they operate, as savers are the surplus units on which intermediaries base their activities in financial markets.

In Greece especially, but also in Spain and Portugal, there is much less retail market penetration of banking activities than in Northern Europe. Although this situation is changing fairly rapidly, there is a history of distrust of banks which tend to be seen as agents of government and which could behave arbitrarily by imposing conditions on the use of and access to accounts, and in which confidentiality of a depositor's wealth from the fiscal authorities is far from guaranteed. Even in Northern Europe, although banks are much more widely used than in the South, there are marked differences in the market penetration that financial intermediaries have managed to achieve. A 1992 report by strategic consultants Datamonitor illustrates the wide differences in investment habits that are apparent across the EU. UK citizens keep more money in their bank accounts than in the other countries. The average UK saver holds £4 500 on deposit where in France the equivalent is £3 900, and Belgium and Holland £1 800. Just over eight in ten UK adults have bank accounts. This compares with over 90 per cent in Germany but only just over half in Italy. On average Britons hold 2.5 accounts each. France, with an average of two accounts, is nearest. In Greece, only about 2 per cent of the population hold a current bank account.

UK bank clients also held more plastic cards per head of population than any other member state. A third of UK adults had credit cards and 29 per cent had direct debit cards. This compared with 1 in 100 Germans with credit cards and 1 in 20 for direct debit cards. This situation could reflect the fact that UK banks have proceeded farther with retail process and product innovation than other banks by offering more automatic teller machines (ATMs) than is usual in other EU states.

The credit card differences could well explain why the UK has higher household debts (£5 853 per head of population) than anywhere else. The personal debt burden in the UK more than doubled between 1986 and 1990. Even so, the Germans (£5 452) and French (£5 400) also know the taste of living beyond their means. This reflects the fact that it has been much more usual in the UK to own a home than elsewhere in Europe, where renting is the norm. Also, in some countries it is the tradition to pay for a home largely out of savings with at most a short-term bank loan to help out. This cultural characteristic could make it difficult for a foreign credit institution expanding across EU borders to win a significant market share.

A critical source of capital market investment arises through long-term saving intermediaries channelling the funds of surplus units to equity and bond markets. Institutional investors dominate the developed stock markets of Europe. But the usages that national populations make often vary markedly. In the private pensions field the UK is way ahead, partly explaining the more sophisticated markets it has developed over time. Datamonitor calculated that in 1992, 23 per cent of Britons had personal pensions compared with 18 per cent in Belgium, 17 per cent in Germany, 7 per cent in the Netherlands, 4 per cent in Italy and 1 per cent in Spain. There are also vast differences in life assurance premiums paid. UK premiums per head in 1990 were 1 400 ECU, those of France 800, and only 100 ECU in Italy. Considerable cross-border opportunities exist for the expansion of marketing activities by large life insurance companies and pension providers, particularly as the European population ages.

France and Belgium have a slightly higher proportion of shareholders than Britain (23 per cent for both against 22 per cent). In Germany there is a deep-rooted aversion to share ownership, with bonds preferred and perceived as much safer.

Although the postwar historical record shows that with a suitably diversified portfolio much greater capital appreciation can be made on the Frankfurt stock market (easily the biggest of six German exchanges), Germans generally favour investment in government securities. By 1991 the value of Germans' investments in bond funds stood at DM 102 billion, a fivefold increase since the early 1980s. Equity unit trusts in contrast only just managed to double their value from DM 8 billion to DM 20 billion over the period.

Germans stay away from investment in shares because they do not like the volatility of stock markets. There are also painful memories of the hyperinflation of 1923, which wiped out the value of paper securities. Moreover, in Germany it is against the law for company managers to put the interests of the shareholder first.

Not only has the EU become the world's biggest banking market, it aims that its combined stock market will achieve this as well. At present the combined EU stock market is much smaller than the Japanese and US stock markets. In equity trading the continental European markets are in turn much smaller than that of London. At the end of 1990, London-listed domestic companies had a market capitalization of US$888 billion, which was larger than the two biggest markets in continental Europe put together (France, US$342 billion and Germany, US$343 billion). London accounts for more than nine out of ten cross-border share trades in Europe, and it regularly accounts for half the domestic equity turnover in German, French and Italian shares (Amlôt, 1992). London also has well developed futures and options markets matching those of the US in the range of contracts traded. So far there is little international interest in commodity trading elsewhere in Europe and the only financial futures market so far to have attracted attention is

Table 9.2 Continental European stock markets

Market	Proportion of Continental European capitalization 1990, %	Proportion of Continental European trading volume 1990, %
Germany	22.2	38.9
France	22.1	16.1
Switzerland	10.8	14.0
Italy	9.7	5.3
Netherlands	9.6	10.2
Rest of Europe*	25.6	15.5

Note: * Excluding UK, but including Austria, Belgium, Denmark, Finland, Ireland, Luxembourg, Norway, Spain and Sweden.

Source: Goldman Sachs

France's MATIF. Table 9.2 indicates the relative sizes of the continental stock markets.

London is uniquely placed in a time zone between New York and Tokyo and has long been the main centre for international equities trading in Europe. In terms of domestic turnover, the London stock exchange ranks fourth, below Tokyo (and Osaka) and New York. But if turnover in foreign shares is used to assess size, London's total is about one and a half times that of New York and ten times that of Tokyo. London has nearly one half of total global foreign equity turnover. At present, Paris, Frankfurt and Amsterdam are distant threats to London's pre-eminence.

It is apparent that the financial scene in the EU is far from actually having a 'single' market in financial services. Considerable heterogeneity exists in the nature, degree of sophistication and development of financial markets and financial services providers, and considerable regulatory controls still remain in some member states. The preconditions for further integration and development have been laid, but the services provided and the use of financial markets is far from uniform. But this heterogeneity is small in relation to that which exists in the developing world, where in many areas there remains an almost complete absence of any formal structure for financial intermediation. This extreme pole in the main relates to the poorest parts of Africa, where social, economic (especially drought and starvation) and political difficulties have militated against the emergence of financial markets (McCarthy 1990).

However, even where there appear to be relatively developed financial systems, what is observed is very often a 'mirage' (similar to the case of Spain at the end of the Franco period).

Nigeria is a case in point. Although it superficially had a relatively sophisticated system of bank and non-bank financial intermediaries based on the Anglo-Saxon model at the time it ceased to be a British colony in 1960, these institutions had little role in financing enterprise. The banking system, which was effectively under government control, provided little medium- or long-term capital for industrial development, and the stock exchange provided less than 2 per cent of private-sector investment. From May 1967 until January 1970, the banking system made a spectacular contribution towards financing the government's civil war effort. Thereafter, the banking system continued to be a conduit for funding government deficits and was subject to strong allocative controls. At times the banking system has been awash with cash, with a liquidity ratio as high as 96 per cent in 1970, even after a substantial growth in lending to government-favoured projects (Woolmer 1977, 277). The stock market was slow to develop, and even today after reforms to increase its efficiency and openness, and the start of a privatization programme, it still remains tiny by international comparison. In general financial repression has caused the development of financial markets to lag behind the development of the overall economy, with the bulk of finance for domestic enterprises mainly coming from retained profits, or from the government (or under government direction from the banking system) in the case of favoured projects, or in the case of multinational enterprise from external inflows.

It is clear that financial markets across the world are extremely heterogeneous in nature, and it is quite wrong to regard the deep, diverse, highly liquid and innovative markets of the major financial centres as characteristic of all areas of the West, let alone areas of the world with significantly lower levels of income and economic development generally. There is also the case of Eastern Europe, where the road to economic and financial reform is only at its earliest stages. The tasks facing the former command economies include separating the central bank from commercial banking (thus creating a two-tier rather than 'mono-banking' sector), privatizing the commercial banking sector, allowing the banks to compete for savers funds and use them in a way which yields the highest returns consistent with the security of deposits, establishing other mechanisms for long-term capital provision to enterprise (such as stock and bond markets), broadening the base of financial intermediation so that long-term savers are linked to the new capital markets (for example through pooled investment products such as unit trusts and mutual funds), and establishing a regulatory regime for the financial services sector which provides appropriate conduct of business rules and adequate prudential safeguards. Rybczynski argues that:

In view of the fact that per capita income in Central and Eastern European countries is relatively low it would appear desirable, in the light of historical experience in the West, that the restructured financial system should be initially centred on the banks and probably to a small extent on other depository institutions, and that capital markets, at least in the years ahead, would play a relatively modest role. (1992, 259).

However, this objective does not meet with universal acceptance by policymakers in the former command economies, where a prominent and active stock market is seen as an index of maturity, indicating progress towards integration with Western capitalism. The danger of this approach is that enterprises too small to access the stock market will be deprived of capital, and the surpluses of small savers which could be effectively mobilized for industrial use through more developed banks and non-bank financial intermediaries may remain relatively unexploited.

Similarly some LDCs may be placing undue emphasis on stock market development for reasons of prestige. Not only may this create a modern-day variant of the 'Macmillan gap' (Cmd. 3897 1931, 404), where only the larger enterprises are able to tap external capital sources, it may also set in train a market for corporate control. A scenario could arise where predatory conglomerates and institutional investors battled for acquisitions through mergers and takeovers – as indeed occurred in Western financial markets during the 1980s. Given the highly concentrated nature of much economic activity in the LDCs, this could reduce product market competition and lead to dynamic inefficiencies, and hinder the growth of smaller firms by increasing their financing difficulties and their ability to compete in increasingly oligopolistic markets (Singh 1994, 135).

Financial liberalization in Asia

Many Asian economies have been introducing measures of financial reform during the later 1980s, particularly the centres of high growth in East Asia, but also in India. Partly technological forces have influenced these countries in similar ways in which financial markets in the West have been influenced, but there are also elements of prestige involved and a desire to emulate the liberalizations of the West in order to participate in the globalization of financial activity. Western investors have also played a key role in encouraging financial liberalization, by seeking out new avenues for higher-return investment, as confidence has returned in the less developed world's economic stability.

An example of the liberalization measures which have occurred is provided by Taiwan's (Taipei China's) financial reform programme. Since the mid-1980s Taiwan has deregulated interest rates, allowed greater competition in the banking sector (including from foreign banks), allowed foreign insurance companies to operate in the country, opened the securities markets to foreign investors, allowed greater freedom for exchange rate movements and for spot trading in key currencies, and relaxed exchange controls on current and capital account transactions. However, significant though these measures are, it is also noteworthy that they have only been introduced after the country had achieved newly industrializing country status and had turned from trade deficits to trade surplus with a large build-up of foreign exchange reserves. Indeed had this not been achieved, it is questionable whether financial reform involving greater exchange rate freedom and freedom of capital flows would have been possible. Such reforms as well as encouraging capital inflows also present risks of capital flight, if basic conditions of macroeconomic stability are not attained. Price stability and control over budget deficits become critical issues if freer financial markets are a goal – a problem well appreciated in Europe by Greece.

The Taiwanese experience is shared by other parts of East Asia as well as numerous Latin American economies: rapid economic growth has occurred before the development of sophisticated financial markets has taken place, casting doubt on whether financial markets are crucial to the initial stages of the growth process. The standard theoretical assumption is that savings would be held back in repressed financial systems by interest rates below the rate of inflation and there would be an absence of intermediaries capable of channelling the limited savings into the most productive uses. However, such a view fails to recognize the motivations for saving. Historically saving in East Asia has been seen as a virtuous activity (as it was in Britain during the early phases of industrialization) and appears to have been driven much more by the ability to save as a result of rising growth and incomes than the inducement of positive real interest rates. Moreover, retained profits have played a highly important role in the development process (again a common feature with Britain's industrial revolution) and the whole saving–investment allocation problem may have looked worse than it was because of informal credit markets which were performing an important role in supplying external capital. (Here again there is a parallel with the industrial revolution, where, for example, solicitors were an important intermediary in channelling the savings of surplus units into productive uses – Checkland 1964, 203). Additionally some channels of credit may only exist because of restrictions on traditional banks and may not appear to fit Western notions of advanced intermediation. The Postal Savings Bank system in Japan is one example: it is highly effective at mobilizing the savings of farmers and small town dwellers for use in public investment programmes and investment in bank debentures (Prindl 1981, 27; McKenzie and Stutchbury 1992, 30).

The availability of savings

Until the 1980s, Japan remained classified by the OECD as a newly industrializing country. However, her experience contrasted significantly with that of many other similarly classified countries, especially in Latin America, due to her low inflation and high savings ratio. Her economic growth experience since the 1950s provides an example of a 'virtuous circle' whereby high levels of investment relative to GNP have resulted in strong productivity growth and export sales, leading to increasing profits and even greater levels of investment. A high investment ratio has been made possible by the effective mobilization by the financial services sector of a high level of personal savings (exceeding 20 per cent of disposable income during the 1960s), and substantial levels of corporate savings in the form of retained profits (Allen 1981, 203).

The high level of personal savings has been influenced by a low level of personal consumption and owner occupation, a relatively underdeveloped social security system encouraging prudential saving, the fact that many employees receive a substantial proportion of their salaries by way of biannual bonus, and a tax system which largely exempts interest on savings from taxation (Allen 1981, 99). Banks and other financial institutions have lent these savings at relatively low rates of interest to the business sector, often with government encouragement, and to which strong links often exist through a bank-dominated *zaibatsu* structure, or because of the existence of a *keiretsu* grouping – 'a closely knit, vertical hierarchy of undertakings centred on a large concern which organises and in part finances a population of associated firms and subcontractors' (Allen 1981, 126). In this setting Japanese firms have not usually gone to the equity or bond markets to finance expansion, but they have sought indirect sources of finance through the banking sector acting as an intermediary for mobilizing the high level of domestic savings (Suzuki 1987, 23). Through much of the period when Japan was gaining her immense economic power it is evident that she had a rather narrow and unsophisticated range of financial markets. The role of banks was all-important and was based on a harmony of interest which existed between industry, governmental institutions, the financial system and its customers on both sides of the market.

Japan is not alone in having a high savings ratio: many of East Asia's current newly industrializing countries have even higher saving ratios, ranging from around 21 per cent in the Philippines in 1992 to 26.7 per cent in Taiwan, 34.9 per cent in Korea and 37.7 per cent in Indonesia (Andersen 1993). All these economies have underdeveloped financial markets compared to the most sophisticated in the West, and in each (as well as Japan) the government has taken a firm hand in allocating capital resources. In the former East European command economies such a suppression of market forces has led to considerable inefficiencies and a far from optimal credit allocation – similar examples exist in Southern Europe and Latin America – yet the East Asian economies do exhibit incredible foresight in terms of industrial development and a knack of 'picking winners'. Andersen regards this as 'the best explanation of how Asian countries combine high growth with underdeveloped financial markets'. Unfortunately it is 'not easily exportable as a policy lesson for other countries' (Andersen 1993, 85).

Inflation and public-sector deficits

The dangers of excessive creation of money for personal savings and financial markets have been evident since the German hyperinflation of 1923. Personal and corporate savings are destroyed and investment in paper securities discouraged as inflation erodes their real value. The process of financial intermediation is disrupted, dislocating industrial development (Lewis 1949).

It is noteworthy that between 1970 and 1992 inflation in Asia averaged less than 10 per cent per annum, whereas consumer prices in Latin America and Africa rose at annual rates of 85 per cent and 15 per cent respectively. Asia achieved a real growth rate of 7.5 per cent per annum over the period, but Latin America and Africa achieved much lower real growth of 4.2 per cent and 3.7 per cent respectively. High levels of inflation have frequently been the result of government-funded development programmes (for which international funding has often been forthcoming), but there is little ability to pick winners and an incredible expansion of state bureaucracy and institutionalized corruption often appears to have been the result (Bandow and Vasquez 1994, 154).

The recent history of Latin America, quite different to that of Japan and East Asia, provides plentiful modern examples of the damaging effects of the hyperinflationary process. Excessive monetary growth and ensuing inflation have been the result of the inability of the political system to check excessive expenditure, or what is in effect insufficient savings. This excess spending has been located in public-sector schemes either to improve the infrastructure or to directly stimulate export sectors. For a time governments were able to finance the bulk of the public sector debt through international financial markets, but ultimately greater reliance had to be placed on the limited resources of the domestic financial service sector as international markets became increasingly nervous about excessive levels of borrowing. The result was ever-increasing levels of nominal interest rates in an attempt to produce real returns for savers and the 'crowding out' of private capital expenditure.

Since the late 1970s many Latin American countries have seen the folly of their ways and sharply checked monetary expansion. Chile in the late 1970s, Bolivia in the mid-1980s, Mexico in the late 1980s, and Argentina, El Salvador, Peru and others in the early 1990s have all had stringent monetary stabilization programmes (often in the form of IMF-sponsored structural adjustment programmes). Of the largest countries, Brazil and Venezuela have both found the problems of high inflation difficult to address, with a 733.5 per cent and 68.8 per cent consumer price increase respectively in the year to the end of January 1995. Colombia has managed to follow a less spectacular gradual disinflation from moderately high levels of price increases. But a dramatic success was Chile's experience in 1975–81, when inflation fell from 400 per cent to 30 per cent, enabling domestic and international financial markets to return to their role as a conduit between savers and industry and much reducing the danger of capital flight (Fontaine 1994).

The experience of Latin America lends considerable support to the view that monetary control is best exercised by an independent central bank with the specific objective of preventing inflation. Low inflation would benefit capital market development by giving savers confidence in the paper assets they acquire and by reducing other distortions to the credit allocation process. Research (Cukierman 1992) suggests that in most cases economies that have an independent central bank tend to show less inflation (Japan being the notable exception where low inflation coexists with a central bank that is very much an arm of government). The relative success of independent central banks in Germany, Switzerland and the US has increased support for this approach throughout much of the world and in particular in Chile, Argentina, Colombia, Mexico and Venezuela, which have all created independent central banks since 1989. However as Posen (1993) shows, this may not be much use unless political circumstances are favourable. New Zealand, where inflation fell below the 2 per cent target in 1994, has introduced the novel experiment of linking the governor of the Bank of New Zealand's tenure and remuneration to his success in pursuing the inflation objective. On the other hand, East Asia does not appear to need this kind of reform; it has achieved the macroeconomic stability necessary to liberalize financial markets and capital flows with central banks under the direct control of government.

The 1990s and beyond
In terms of global capital flows into equity markets, the period 1990–94 has been markedly different to the previous decade. Investors in the advanced countries have shown a much greater appetite for risk, and cross-border transactions have had a much greater impact in determining share prices, a factor which keeps the costs of equity capital to companies low. Attention of investors has refocused from the highly liquid stock markets of the advanced nations towards the emerging markets. Tables 9.3, 9.4 and 9.5 illustrate this new global trend. Table 9.3 shows the aggregate position for all markets. Table 9.4 shows the aggregate of all primary issues made to global investors,

Table 9.3   Net cross-border equity flows to world markets, 1986–93 (US$bn)

	1986	1987	1988	1989	1990	1991	1992	1993
North America	19.8	20.3	–3.7	13.8	–15.9	9.6	–3.9	32.3
US	19.1	16.5	–1.4	11.4	–14.6	11.0	–4.1	24.3
Canada	0.7	3.8	–2.3	2.4	–1.3	–1.4	0.3	7.9
Europe	33.6	29.7	23.0	47.7	15.9	24.2	25.5	68.5
UK	7.8	19.5	9.7	11.2	5.4	5.8	10.1	19.6
Japan	–15.8	–42.8	5.8	7.0	–13.3	46.8	8.9	20.4
Emerging markets	3.3	5.9	3.5	10.1	13.2	15.8	21.2	62.4
Pacific Rim	3.4	6.0	2.5	3.4	3.9	4.7	10.9	40.1
Latin America	0.2	0.4	0.7	7.0	9.9	11.2	9.6	20.0
Other	–0.3	–0.6	0.3	–0.3	–0.6	–0.1	0.7	2.2
Rest of world	1.0	3.4	9.2	8.1	3.3	4.2	2.0	12.8
Total	42.0	16.4	32.9	86.6	3.2	100.6	58.7	196.3

Source: Baring Securities.

Table 9.4   Primary issuance in the international equity market, 1986–94 (US$bn)

	1986	1987	1988	1989	1990	1991	1992	1993	1994 to end Q3
Developed markets	11.47	19.94	8.57	13.89	12.62	17.79	18.10	25.55	33.16
US	1.90	2.58	1.50	1.65	2.74	6.16	8.69	9.71	7.26
Japan	0.00	0.21	0.19	0.95	0.91	0.00	0.05	0.00	0.24
UK	1.70	6.81	2.44	2.17	3.58	4.44	3.27	1.39	0.64
Continental Europe	7.06	7.37	2.89	6.49	3.98	4.19	4.28	11.12	23.06
Rest of world	0.81	3.16	1.55	2.83	1.43	3.00	1.86	3.33	1.96
Emerging markets	0.09	0.42	0.51	0.17	1.64	6.03	7.28	11.08	12.37
Latin America	0.00	0.00	0.00	0.00	0.11	4.23	3.93	5.97	3.72
Far East	0.09	0.37	0.51	0.14	1.35	1.02	2.55	4.38	4.26
Other	0.00	0.05	0.00	0.03	0.18	0.78	0.80	0.73	4.39
Total	11.56	20.36	9.08	14.06	14.26	23.82	25.38	36.63	45.53

Source: Euromoney Bondware.

Table 9.5   Net cross-border equity flows to emerging markets, 1986–95 (US$bn)

	Asia	Latin America	Rest of world
1986	3.43	0.20	−0.29
1987	6.03	0.43	−0.58
1988	2.45	0.72	0.30
1989	3.36	6.98	−0.27
1990	3.89	9.89	0.62
1991	4.73	11.15	−0.10
1992	10.95	9.64	1.86
1993	34.50	20.00	2.00
1994E	15.00	15.00	10.00
1995E	6.00	12.00	7.00

Note: Figures for 1994 and 1995 are estimated.

Source: Baring Securities.

and Table 9.5 shows net flows to emerging markets (i.e. total equity cross-border purchases less total cross-border equity sales).

So far Thailand, Hong Kong, South Korea, India, Mexico, Brazil and Argentina have been particular targets of investors. According to Baring Securities, there have been two distinct phases of emerging market investment in the 1990s. First investment was concentrated on the larger regional markets of Latin America and Southeast Asia. The main determinant appears to have been the issue of new securities, although a favourable climate for investors was created by deregulation, privatization and IMF-sponsored structural adjustment programmes which, particularly in Latin America, created greater investor confidence in continuing levels of lower inflation. However, throughout 1994, the focus of foreign investors was much more on the remote and less liquid emerging markets. 'For example, over US$ 500m flowed into Russian stocks during the first six months of the year, and India, Pakistan, South Africa, have proved especially popular, not to mention Oman, Jamaica, Morocco and Zimbabwe' (Baring Securities 1994).

Baring Securities expects these trends to continue and by the year 2010 they forecast that the emerging stock markets (including South Africa, Singapore and Hong Kong) will comprise between 40 and 45 per cent of overall world stock market capitalization compared to 15 per cent at the end of August 1994. As far as UK private-sector investors are concerned, Barings believe this growth will lead to a situation comparable to 1913, when UK

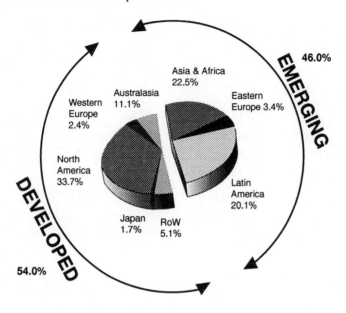

Source: *Baring Securities, Crossborder Analysis.*

Figure 9.1   *Breakdown of UK private-sector portfolio investments (1913 – percentage composition)*

investors held 46 per cent of their investments in emerging markets and 54 per cent in the developed world. Barings predict that 11.6 per cent of UK private-sector investment will be in Latin America in 2010 (compared to 20.1 per cent in 1913), 27.4 per cent in Asia and Africa (compared to 22.5 per cent in 1913), and 4.7 per cent for emerging Europe (3.4 per cent in 1913). Figure 9.1 shows the pattern of UK investment in 1913.

Barings express optimism about these developments, believing the opportunities which they believe exist for equity investors in terms of returns will 'provide the funds that developing countries need to industrialise.' The ageing population and rising savings ratio in the rich industrial countries will cause economic power and capital to increasingly switch from North to South and from West to East.

Although this is a highly speculative analysis, it also is a highly optimistic one in the light of the history of international capital flows. Capital flows can be fickle and reversible over short periods of time in response to changing perceptions of risk and return. Given the free movement of capital with which deregulated financial markets are associated, there seems no reason to believe that economic growth in the less developed world can be guaranteed a flow of finance from the richer nations. During the 1980s, many LDCs, of which Mexico is the most striking example, experienced capital flight and a reversal of previous inflows, as they were hit by shocks such as volatile oil prices, falling commodity prices, large rises in dollar interest rates, and associated government deficit problems. International capital in the deregulated world that now exists is highly mobile, and may be attracted by superior returns elsewhere, particularly if the European economy grows stronger.

Consider for example the situation of Germany in the second half of the 1920s. Recovery was advancing rapidly in 1924, on the basis of inflows of capital particularly from the US, but also from elsewhere. However, this situation was reversed by the rise in capital appreciation offered by the New York stock market in the second quarter of 1928. This cut off long-term lending by the US, particularly to Germany, but also to other areas of Europe, and to the world periphery, represented by countries such as Argentina, Australia, Chile and Latin America generally (Kindleberger 1973; 1985). The onset of world depression was heavily influenced by the highly unstable international capital flows of the late 1920s. The ending of the externally financed German recovery was a key factor in this depression. Similar out-flows could hit the LDCs in a world where capital controls have been re-moved, creating exchange rate instability and as a result provoking further destabilizing capital flows.

Because of the danger of the reversal of capital flows – evident on many occasions since 1927 although with less dramatic international effects – the Barings analysis seems highly optimistic. It seems to assume that interna-tional economic growth is a steady and harmonious process, unpunctuated by changes in economic fundamentals and random shocks. This seems an opti-mistic 'golden scenario', which may also explain Barings' traditional enthu-siasm for investing in emerging markets. This was not only a factor in the bank's own downfall in 1995, but it was also a factor in the Baring Crisis of 1890, when the bank ran short of liquidity after sub-underwriting South American bond issues (Orbell 1985; Ziegler 1988). Then it became the first bank to be rescued by the Bank of England. In 1995 it has become the first major bank not to be rescued in this way, perhaps reflecting a new 'hands-off' approach by the UK government to the control of the financial system. (It is interesting to note here that Sir Francis Baring, one of the bank's founders in 1762, was one of the earliest advocates of the idea that the Bank of England should act as 'lender of last resort' – Baring 1797).

The Barings' optimism regarding international capital flows providing LDCs with the funds to develop also ignores another theme of this chapter. Whereas rising share prices in emerging markets do provide opportunities for the largest companies in LDCs to obtain low-cost finance with relative ease, they do little to help smaller businesses (often sole traders, partnerships and cooperatives) to expand. Especially in the poorest parts of the world, these enterprises are critical in the development process and retained profits and informal credit markets remain their only sources of capital supply.

Barings' demise also focuses attention on the issue of the regulation of the new derivative markets, which have grown approximately tenfold in size from around US$2.5 trillion in 1987 to US$25 trillion in 1994 (*The Economist* 1995, 21). This is an area where strong arguments exist for greater regulatory control, especially if more than one bank were to collapse over a short period of time, sparking off a systemic crisis affecting the developed and developing world (Folkerts-Landau and Steinherr 1994).

Financial deregulation has created a world in which there is a danger of increased financial flows having destabilizing effects. Deregulation implies an absence of controls over cross-border capital movements (both in and out). Investors will seek the highest returns consistent with their own assessment of an acceptable level of risk. The ageing population in the developed world has entrusted immense accumulated wealth to institutional investors such as pension funds, fund management groups and life assurance companies, to provide their clients with income and capital for a comfortable retirement. These institutional investors in turn have a duty to secure the best returns for their clients consistent with the safety of capital invested. Stable exchange rates have an important role in restricting capital flight and encouraging inward investment. Much therefore depends in countries seeking private sector funds to finance economic expansion on governmental abilities to create and maintain conditions of macroeconomic stability which encourage capital inflows. The interaction between politics and economics is of course highly relevant in this respect (Posen 1993).

In the process of financial liberalization, in which so much of the world is already seeking to be a player, what is being seen on a global scale is the unrestricted mobilization of capital, similar to that which has occurred within the UK as the industrial revolution gathered pace and funds were transferred by the then rudimentary process of intermediation from surplus to deficit areas.

In the 1980s and the 1990s the mobilization process involves a much greater range of financial instruments, financial institutions and financial markets, but it has essentially the same role of moving funds from surplus to deficit areas, but on this occasion on a global scale across national boundaries (not just within them).

Such mobilization is probably not a necessary condition of rapid growth during the early stages of the take-off of developing countries, where the capital requirements of individual enterprises are likely to be relatively small – nor was it a necessary condition during the first industrial revolution. However, at a later stage a diversifying and maturing economy will have a need for greater capital resources, with different types of financing required for different types of project, and it is then that capital allocation becomes too complex a process for limited and undeveloped financial institutions and markets to undertake. Then financial market development becomes critical, and it is difficult for this to take place unless government has the ability and political will to create conditions of macroeconomic stability in the form of low inflation and prospects for stable growth, which give savers and investors prospects of real returns. This lesson applies to all countries – developed and developing – and to all points of the compass – north, south, east and west.

References

Allen, G.C. (1981), *The Japanese Economy*, London: Weidenfeld & Nicolson.

Amlôt, R. (1992), *Dawn Traders' Guide to World Markets*, London: Boxtree.

Amsden, A. and Euh, Y. (1990), 'Republic of Korea's Financial Reform: What are the Lessons?', United Nations Conference on Trade and Development, Discussion Paper, No. 30, April.

Andersen, P.S. (1993), 'Economic Growth and Financial Markets: The Experience of Four Asian Countries' in R. O'Brien (ed.), *Finance and the International Economy: 7*, Oxford: Oxford University Press.

Bandow, D. and Vasquez, I. (eds) (1994), *Perpetuating Poverty: The World Bank, the IMF, and the Developing World*, Washington, DC: Cato Institute.

Baring, Sir F. (1797), *Observations on the Bank of England*, London.

Baring Securities (1994), *Crossborder Analysis*, London: Baring Securities Ltd, October.

Carter, M. (1989), 'Financial Innovation and Financial Fragility', *Journal of Economic Issues*, 3, September.

Catterall, R.E. (1994), 'The Extent and Impact of Deregulation on the European Financial Services Industry', paper presented at the ESRC/NIESR Conference on The Evolution of Rules for a Single European Market, University of Exeter, September.

Checkland, S.G. (1964), *The Rise of Industrial Society in England*, London: Longmans, Green & Co.

Cmd. 3897 (1931), *Committee on Finance and Industry Report*, London: HMSO, June.

Cottrell, P.L. (1994), 'The historical development of modern banking within the United Kingdom' in M. Pohl and S. Freitag (eds), *Handbook on the History of the European Banks*, Aldershot: Edward Elgar in association with the European Association for Banking History E.V.

Cukierman, A. (1992), *Central Bank Strategy, Credibility and Independence: Theory and Evidence*, Cambridge, Mass.: MIT Press.

Dixon, R. (1993), *Banking in Europe: The Single Market*, rev. edn, London: Routledge.

Dritsas, M. (1994), 'The structure of the Greek commercial banking system, 1840–1980' in M. Pohl and S. Freitag (eds), *Handbook on the History of the European Banks*, Aldershot: Edward Elgar in association with the European Association for Banking History E.V.

Economist, The (1995), 'The Collapse of Barings: a Fallen Star', 334 (7904), 4 March.

Euh, Y. and Barker, J. (1990), *The Korean Banking System and Foreign Influence*, London: Routledge.

Folkerts-Landau, D. and Steinherr, A. (1994), 'The Wild Beast of Derivatives: To Be Chained Up, Fenced In Or Tamed?' in R. O'Brien (ed.), *Finance and the International Economy: 8*, Oxford: Oxford University Press

Fontaine, J.A. (1994), 'Applying Monetarism: What Have We Learned?', paper presented at the 12th Annual Monetary Conference of the CATO Institute, Mexico City, May.

Geisst, C.R. (1993), *A Guide to Financial Institutions*, 2nd edn, Basingstoke: Macmillan.

Goldsmith, R.W. (1969), *Financial Structure and Development*, New Haven, Conn.: Yale University Press.

Goldsmith, R.W. (1985), *Comparative National Balance Sheets: A Study of Twenty Countries, 1688–1978*, Chicago: University of Chicago Press.

Hall, M.J.B. (1993), *Banking Regulation and Supervision: A Comparative Study of the UK, USA and Japan*, Aldershot: Edward Elgar.

Kane, E. (1983), 'Policy Implications of Structural Changes in Financial Markets', *American Economic Review*, 4, May

Kaufman, G. (1984), 'The Role of Traditional Mortgage Lenders', *Conference on Housing Finance*. London, March 30.

Kim, T. (1993), *International Money and Banking*, London: Routledge.

Kindleberger, C.P. (1973), *The World in Depression 1929–1939*, London: Allen Lane.

Kindleberger, C.P. (1985), *A Financial History of Western Europe*, London: Allen & Unwin.

Lewis, W.A. (1949), *Economic Survey 1919–1939*, London: Allen & Unwin.

Lygum, B., Ottolengi, D. and Steinherr, A. (1988), 'The Portuguese Financial System', *European Investment Bank Papers*, 7, December.

Lygum, B., Perée, E. and Steinherr, A. (1989), 'The Spanish Financial System', *European Investment Bank Papers*, 12, December.

MacKinnon, R.I. (1973), *Money and Capital in Economic Development*. Washington, DC: Brookings Institution.

McCarthy, S. (1990), 'Development stalled: the crisis in Africa: a personal view', *European Investment Bank Papers*, 14, December.

McKenzie, C. and Stutchbury, M. (1992), *Japanese Financial Markets and the Role of the Yen*, Sydney NSW: Allen & Unwin.

McRae, H. and Cairncross, F. (1985), *Capital City: London as a Financial Centre*, London: Methuen.

Miller, M. (1986), 'Financial Innovation', *Journal of Financial and Quantitative Analysis*, 4, December.

OECD (1967), *Capital Markets Study: General Report*, Paris: OECD.

OECD (1986), *Capital Markets, Special Report*, Paris: OECD.

OECD (1989), *Prudential Supervision in Banking*, Paris: OECD.

Orbell, J. (1985), *Baring Brothers & Co., Ltd. A History to 1939*, London.

Pagano, M. (1993), 'Financial Markets and Economic Growth: An Overview', *European Economic Review*, 37.

Pomfret, R. (1992), *Diverse Paths of Economic Development*, Hemel Hempstead: Harvester Wheatsheaf.

Posen, A.S, (1993), 'Why Central Bank Independence Does Not Cause Low Inflation: There is no Institutional Fix for Politics' in R. O'Brien (ed.), *Finance and the International Economy: 7*, Oxford: Oxford University Press.

Prindl, A.R. (1981), *Japanese Finance: A Guide to Banking in Japan*, Chichester: John Wiley.

Rybczynski, T.M. (1992), 'The role of finance in the restructuring of eastern Europe' in A. Steinherr (ed.), *The New European Financial Market Place*, Harlow: Longman Group.

Scott, W.L. (1991), *Contemporary Financial Markets and Services*, St Paul, Minn.: West Publishing.

Silver, W. (1983), 'The Process of Financial Innovation', *American Economic Review*, 4, May.

Singh, A.J. (1994), 'How do Large Corporations in Developing Countries Finance their Growth?' in R. O'Brien (ed.), *Finance and the International Economy: 8*, Oxford: Oxford University Press.

Suzuki, Y. (ed.) (1987), *The Japanese Financial System*, Oxford: Clarendon Press.

Tortella, G. (1994a), 'Modern Financial Institutions in Twentieth-Century Spain and Portugal: a Report on Recent Research', in D. Feldman, U. Olssen, M.D. Bordo and Y. Cassis, (eds), *The Evolution of Modern Financial Institutions in the Twentieth Century*, Proceedings of the Eleventh International Economic History Congress, Session B12. Milan, September.

Tortella, G. (1994b), 'Spanish banking history, 1782 to the present' in M. Pohl and S. Freitag (eds), *Handbook on the History of European Banks*, Aldershot: Edward Elgar in association with the European Association for Banking History E.V.

Tucker, A.L., Madura, J. and Chiang, T.C. (1991), *International Financial Markets*, St Paul, Minn.: West Publishing.

Valdez, S. (1993), *An Introduction to Western Financial Markets*, London: Macmillan.

Woolmer, K.J. (1977), 'The Financial System and Economic Development in Nigeria 1950–1971', in W.T. Newlyn (ed.), *The Financing of Economic Development*, Oxford: Clarendon Press.

Ziegler, P. (1988), *The Sixth Great Power. Barings 1762–1929*, London.

Index